The SPIRIT OF HINDUISM

THE SPIRIT OF HINDUISM

A CHRISTIAN PERSPECTIVE ON HINDU THOUGHT

David G. Burnett

MONARCH
Tunbridge Wells

First published 1992

Unless otherwise indicated, biblical quotations are from the
New International Version.

ISBN 1 85424 194 X

British Library Cataloguing-in-Publication Data.
A catalogue record for this book is available
from the British Library.

Production and Printing in England for
MONARCH PUBLICATIONS
Owl Lodge, Langton Road, Speldhurst, Tunbridge Wells,
Kent TN3 0NP by
Nuprint Ltd, Station Road, Harpenden, Herts AL5 4SE

CONTENTS

CHAPTER 1

East Meets West

I T WAS A WARM sultry day in London and the fine weather
had enticed crowds out onto the streets in search of
bargains in the shops. A casual glance along Oxford Street
left one with the impression that people from every quarter of
the globe were pressed together in the same small geographical location. Dark-robed ladies from the Middle East followed their husbands from one shop to another. Japanese
students congregated in little groups as they looked for English language schools. American tourists in their bright clothes
carefully studied their street maps of London. African visitors
wrapped up in warm clothing in contempt at the weak English
sunshine eagerly sought for the best bargains to take home.

Suddenly, through the general noise of London traffic
came the beat of a drum. As the sound grew louder, I could
hear the chanting of human voices. Then, from out of the
crowds came a little group of devotees of the Lord Krishna.
'Hare Krishna, Hare Krishna...' they chanted as they walked
along the busy street.

In the 1970s, people stopped in amazement to look at this
strange sight. In the 1990s, people took hardly any notice.
Without a glance, people simply walked around and past the
eagerly chanting group. The devotees of Krishna have now
become a familiar part of the life of this busy street. They
looked almost out-of-date, like mementos from the 60s that
had become stranded on the shores of time.

Now even the major London stores offer ethnic fashions

and Asian clothes. Eastern shapes and symbols are common in jewellers' windows and fashionable stores. Students attempt to make a little money by handing out leaflets advertising the latest course on personality development, yoga, martial arts, rebirthing, or mind-expanding programmes.

Oxford Street illustrates the changes that have come to the West in the last few years. The strong confident culture of the Euro-American people that had spread around the world has gradually been infused by ideas and practices from the East. The initial surprise at the exotic sights and sounds of the Orient has been lost, and they have become accepted as part of a way of life that is becoming increasingly multicultural.

There are two questions that I have posed myself in this chapter. The first: Why should the average white Anglo-Saxon take the time to study the religious beliefs of the people of the Indian subcontinent? Christians especially may distance themselves from such an examination, considering this to be the task for missionaries and teachers. Second: How may one go about studying something as complex as Hindu beliefs?

THE QUESTION OF 'WHY?'

There have been three ancient centres of cultural development in human history. One was in the Middle East, stretching from Egypt along the fertile river shores of the Tigris and Euphrates to the Persian Gulf. The Westerner has become familiar with its history through the stories of the Old Testament. The second, and less known in the West, was that of the Chinese people dwelling alongside the banks of the River Yangtze. The third cultural basin was that of the Indian subcontinent. All three have interacted with each other during the past centuries, but geographical distances and difficulty of travel kept a distinct degree of separation that allowed each to develop in their own ways.

East and West met occasionally, and such encounters left each with a sense of perplexity concerning the other. The story is told that shortly after Alexander the Great invaded India in about 330 BC, he unexpectedly came upon a company of naked sages. These ascetics were settled on the outskirts of the town of Taxila, where they practised yogic austerities.

These practices astounded the Greeks and caused Alexander to put to them many questions that were considered insoluble. Alexander was so impressed by their subtle replies that he richly rewarded them. The Greek scholars accompanying Alexander's army complained that trying to understand Indian philosophy was like 'making water flow through mud'. However, so impressed was Alexander that he took one of the greatest Indian sages to be his guru in replacement of his boyhood tutor Aristotle.[1] Aristotle would have been amazed at the behaviour of his pupil. Aristotle despised all 'barbarians', and would have been shocked at this first encounter between East and West.

It was in the first century BC that sailors realised the effect of the monsoon winds. In certain months of the year, instead of making the long coastal voyage round Arabia and Baluchistan, they could spread their sails to be blown across the open seas to India. Later in the year, the winds reversed direction, and they would be blown safely back to the mouth of the Red Sea. In this way, trade developed between Rome and south India. This may have been the route the apostle Thomas used to reach India, but here history blends with myth. What is known is that from the first or second century AD, there existed a Christian church in south India that credited its foundation to St Thomas. Although the Christian community has been subject to many social pressures over the centuries, it remains a small but vigorous society in India.

Further invasions were to come to India from the northwest, the most significant of which was that of the Muslims in the seventh century. For almost 1,000 years, Islam was to act as both a bridge and a barrier between Europe and India. The discovery of the sea routes to India in the sixteenth century again brought the Europeans into contact with the people of India. By the nineteenth century, the mutual isolation of East and West had virtually ended.

Throughout the nineteenth century, European scholars were fascinated by the different spiritual orientation they found in the Indian civilisation. They discovered ideas that were as sophisticated as their own, and yet radically different in character. Here were spiritual ideas that could point back to no one founder and had no one system of theology. Rather, there was a myriad of religious ideas and practices. In an attempt to understand, the European scholars recognised the beliefs of the superior Brahmin caste and designated them by the term 'Hinduism'. The word itself comes from the Persian for 'the people across the Indus River'. Significantly, it is the only world religion (apart from Judaism) that is named after a people rather than a founder or doctrine.

There are various reasons why Anglo-Saxons, with their Christian heritage, should study Hinduism. First, in Europe and North America there are many Hindu communities who are an important part of our contemporary society. Another reason for studying Hinduism is the presence of many neo-Hindu missionary groups, such as the Hare Krishna movement. Yet another reason is to understand how Hindu ideas and practices are mixing with many areas of Western culture to produce something that is different and new.

Hindus in dispersal

Hindu communities are now found throughout the world—in the West Indies, Canada, the USA, Singapore, New Zealand, Fiji, and East Africa, as well as throughout Europe. This is in itself of interest because, as we have seen, the term 'Hindu' indicates the people of the land of India. This geographical definition is now clearly inadequate. Sociologists have preferred to use the term 'ethnicity'. This is not, as some have understood it, a euphemism for 'race' or 'colour'. It may best be regarded as an alliance based on informal interests that operate through a shared way of life. Ethnicity is therefore a matter of shared culture and history. However, its meaning only has significance when two or more groups interact and compete with each other.

In my home town of Bradford, in the north of England, I well remember as a child noticing the growing number of Asians coming to the city. Bradford has been host to thousands of migrants for almost 200 years. Before World War II, most were from Ireland, but soon after the war they started arriving from Poland and many other East European countries. By the 1960s, it was from the so-called New Commonwealth countries of India, Pakistan, and the West Indies that they came. They were invited to work the unsocial hours in the woollen mills of the city. The 1961 census gave totals of 3,457 Pakistanis, 1,512 Indians, and 984 West Indians.[2] By 1966, the total of New Commonwealth immigrants in Bradford had risen to 13,410.

The Hindu Cultural Society of Bradford was founded in 1968 by representatives of several Hindu families resident in the city. It was not until 1974 that adequate premises were acquired for the religious activities of the association. The temple was dedicated to the deities Radha and Krishna on 3 August 1974.[3] From this time, several other temples have been established in Bradford and among the many other Hindu communities in Britain.

In 1980, the Hindu Cultural Society redefined their aims and activities more fully. They recognised the two-way traffic that was occurring between the Hindu and Anglo-Saxon communities, and made the following affirmation:

> We do not intend to remain isolated from the total community composed of different religious groups and classes, sects and ways of life. In today's multi-ethnic and multiracial society we wish to reach out to those groups which like to know more about our faith, culture and way of life.[4]

A new generation of Hindus has grown up in Bradford, with no personal experience of the land of India. On one hand, they are aware that they are members of an ancient and often undervalued civilisation. On the other hand, they are members of Western society in which English is the spoken language. As British Hindus, they live in the tension between two cultures. What has happened in the city of Bradford has been duplicated in London, Leicester, Loughborough, and many other towns in Britain. It has also happened in the major cities in North America and continental Europe. Hindu communities have become an important part of the economic and social reality of multicultural Western society and cannot be ignored.

Neo-Hindu missionaries

In 1893, Vivekananda became one of the first Hindu missionaries to the West. He travelled first to the United States, and
then on to Britain, France, Switzerland, and Germany. He
spoke about a particular school of Indian philosophy known
as 'Vedanta', which will be discussed in Chapter 14. This he
called 'the essentials of Hinduism', and for this reason
Vedanta has become one of the Western perceptions of Hinduism. Vivekananda found an appreciative audience among
the intellectuals who had become intrigued by the accounts of
colonial explorers and officials. His presence was marked by
the establishment of the Vedanta Society. It consisted of
Western people who, in the main, made a conscious decision
to leave Christianity, even though allegiance had been merely
by nominal profession.

Vivekananda has been followed by many other teachers
and gurus. Pop musicians of the 1960s looked to India for new
inspiration, and invited Indian teachers to the West to pro-
claim their particular teaching. Each came proclaiming their
own philosophy and the form of Hinduism that they considered to be the answer to the problems of the West.

A two-page advertisement in *Time* magazine of 12 March
1990 featured His Holiness the Maharishi Mahesh Yogi. The
advertisement read:

> Maharishi offers every government alliance with nature's
> government through Maharishi's Vedic Science and
> Technology to create heaven on earth! Access to the
> unified field and natural law to raise every area of life to
> perfection.

It invited governments to correspond with him to achieve this
goal.[5]

New Age movement

In the same year that Vivekananda travelled West—1893—
Annie Besant travelled eastwards from Britain to India to
discover new spiritual realities. Annie Besant spoke of 'the
husk of an outworn creed' that she was leaving behind for
something more genuine. In Hinduism, she believed that she

could find something more spiritual and beautiful. She was a major influence in the foundation of the Theosophical Society, which was later to provide a stimulus to the rise of the so-called New Age movement.

The Eastern influence is not merely one of different clothes, or sounds, or behaviour. It has brought ideas and beliefs that are radically different from those that have been accepted in Europe and North America for centuries. These Eastern ideas have gradually been adopted as part of a new emerging Western culture. The situation may be likened to an iceberg. The tip of the iceberg is only the visual expression of the greater mass hidden in the waters. Groups such as the Hare Krishna movement are only the visual expression of a slow change in attitude within the wider Western society. These ideas are now going beyond the small number of committed followers into the wider society.

In reaction to the ideas of secular materialism, a new awareness of spirituality is emerging. The quest is not religious, but spiritual. Ancient Indian and Chinese philosophies are being drawn into Western thought and practice. New writers speculate with a mixture of ancient myths and assumptions in an attempt to make them relevant to people at the end of the twentieth century.

A desperate search is under way for new answers to the problems of Western society. People are turning to ideas that come from before modern history, and those that are beyond the pale of Western society. Like a magpie in search of new items for its store, many in the Western world are looking in foreign and exotic places. One assumption is characteristic to all, which is that Western culture has somehow failed to provide all that it had promised. In its place is the hope that beliefs from other cultures may provide that which Western society has lost in its drive for material gain.

In 1991, over one quarter of British people said that they believed in reincarnation. Twenty-five per cent said that they believed in astrology at one level or another. Fifteen per cent of the population regularly meditate—a larger percentage than of those who regularly attend church. All over Britain, spiritual retreat centres are being established, and they are attracting greater numbers every year. The Findhorn Community in Scotland had a print run in March 1991 of 25,000 programmes, produced twice yearly, and posted to 20,000 persons.[6]

Alternative healing centres are becoming a common part of the Western way of life. Nearly every town and village in North America and Europe has practitioners advocating their natural healing methods. Reflexology, crystal healing, colour therapy are all part of the growing alternative tradition. Christian ministers are now commonly asked their views concerning whether a Christian should have acupuncture or practise yoga.

This new movement has become a growing business as more and more people are willing to buy New Age products. Crystals are sold in many shades and colours. Meditation stools are produced for those unable to make their limbs conform to the lotus position. Chakra candles comprise seven rainbow-coloured layers, each with its own unique fragrance. Cotton T-shirts declare one's friendship with planet earth. Fantasy pictures merge with beautiful scenes of nature in the mail order catalogues and shop displays. New board games claim to help one to receive new insight into one's life.

Perhaps it is with the books and magazines that one can see the greatest growth. In 1990, some 800 titles on New Age matters exploded into the British shops. Today, every major bookshop has a section on 'New Age', with books on an ever growing variety of alternative spiritual practices.

During the 1992 British election, many were startled to read extensive advertisements in most of the national newspapers setting out the manifesto of the Natural Law Party. This new party follows the teachings of Maharishi Mahesh Yogi, founder of Transcendental Meditation. The people of Great Britain were invited to bring their national constitution into alliance with the constitution of the universe, which was Maharishi's gift to the world in 1991.[7]

Although the New Age movement is relatively new to Europe, this is not so in the West Coast of the United States. Here the New Age is not so new. It has become part of the way of life of many people in San Francisco. A recent survey showed that while only 44 per cent believed in a Christian God, an equal number believed in an inner spirituality. American opinion polls have observed that 42 per cent of Americans have sought to contact the dead, 25 per cent believe in reincarnation, and 67 per cent of adults read astrology, 37 per cent of whom believe it is actually scientific.

On the West Coast, the movement is no longer a marginalised section of society. More formal New Age institutions are coming into being. For example, there is a New Age radio station. The movement that has been characterised by personal religious creativity is now taking on some of the characteristics of organised religion. The Radiant Light Ministry is attracting a growing number to its meetings, that have many characteristics of an ordinary church. As well as an opportunity for personal meditation, there is singing, and benedictions and sermons are given.

New philosophies

William Bloom sees the New Age phenomenon as 'the visible tip of the iceberg of a mass movement in which humanity is reasserting its right to explore spirituality in total freedom. The constraints of religious and intellectual ideology are falling away.'[8]

For Bloom, the New Age consists of recognising an invisible and inner dimension to all life. The task before us as individuals and groups is the exploration of the inner reality. He identifies four major fields within the movement. The first is 'new paradigm/new science', from which emerges a radically new assessment of reality. The second theme is that of ecology. Human beings are perceived as part of the total cosmos, and through this interdependence they must accept responsibility for the state of planet earth. Third is the 'new psychology' that advocates a release of the unconscious. In this way, the transpersonal becomes expressed, so enabling stressed Western individuals to become integrated human beings. This belief is based upon ideas that the psychologist Abraham Maslow called 'self-actualisation'. Finally, Bloom identifies the theme of 'spiritual dynamics'. This is a product of honouring all esoteric, mystical and religious wisdom traditions, including Gnostic Christianity, Jewish Qabalah, Sufism, Zen Buddhism, Hinduism, and the traditional religions of all societies. Included also is the shamanism of the North

American Indians, and Wicca and Druidism of Celtic Europe.⁹

Bloom's first category has been popularised as the 'new physics'. This theme shows how Eastern beliefs and practices are not restricted to the areas of the current fashion or religion. They have penetrated into almost all areas of contemporary life. In 1979, *Newsweek* reported that 'a new school of theoretical physicists, many of them based at the University of California's Lawrence Berkeley Laboratory, is using mystical modes of thought in an effort to create a unified philosophy of how the universe works.'¹⁰

From the time of Newton, physics has tried to maintain a strictly empirical approach. This has demanded a dispassionate observer and the belief in an objective reality waiting to be discovered and analysed. Since the time of the ancient Greeks, European science has tried to understand matter by dividing it into ever smaller parts in an attempt to discover the fundamental building block, the atom. Modern science has shown that the atom is not some irreducible element of the particular material, but consists of subatomic entities, such as electrons and protons, that display the properties of both waves and particles.

The German physicist Max Planck suggested that light is discontinuous and consists of small energy units that he called quanta. Einstein took the development a stage further by showing an association between light and matter.

Quantum physics has shown that it is not possible to examine atomic particles objectively. In 1927, Werner Heisenberg presented his famous uncertainty principle and sparked off a continuing debate. In simple terms, Heisenberg stated that the observer alters the observed electron by the mere act of observation. He was not implying that consciousness has any direct effect upon the outcome, but was referring to the problem of observing atomic particles.

The outcome has been that many people have questioned the very nature of reality. If the world about them which appears so real is only a matter of waves and probability, how much can they trust their own perceptions? Is the world as real as it initially appears?

It is at this point that Eastern philosophy impinges on the

discussion. Writers have turned to the mystic philosophies of both China and India. Comparisons are made between quantum mechanics, modern psychology, and Eastern mysticism. Gary Zukav has used the Chinese ideogram 'Wu Li', meaning organic energy, to discuss the idea of the quanta, and therefore entitled his book *The Dancing Wu Li Masters*.[11]

From Indian philosophy, the concept of *maya* has provided an important idea for those seeking to draft the new physics. *Maya* suggests an illusory nature of the physical world. The appearance that it is physical and objective is the greatest illusion.

New physics makes the radical assertion that the concept of the 'observer' is replaced by that of the 'participant'. Our perceptions of space and time exist only to the extent that we conceive them.

Books on the new physics are read with interest by university students in a desire to reach beyond the questions left unanswered by Planck and Einstein. The publisher of Michael Talbot's book *Mysticism and the New Physics* writes:

> According to the author, we are experiencing the first pangs of a radical change in our view of reality. Slowly and painfully we are realizing the obvious—our concepts are based upon a most intriguing *maya*. Our constructs need amending. The very epistemological foundations of our environment and ourselves must shift as our prejudices are attacked.[12]

Eastern mysticism is interacting with Western thought to produce a synthesis of ideas and practice. By a process of 'mix-and-match', theories and customs are being brought together into a profusion of new ideas. To our first question of why study Hindu spirituality, the answer is that without doubt there is a need for those who are the product of the Western civilisation to be aware of the ancient civilisation of India. In a multicultural world, this is no longer an option, but a necessity.

THE QUESTION OF 'HOW?'

Turning now to the second question, we must ask ourselves: How should we undergo a study of Hinduism? This is not an easy question to answer. Hinduism is more than a series of religious tenets, more even than a way of life—it is a civilisation. Where does one start, how does one proceed, and what is to be selected? The search for broad perspectives has often led to misleading generalisations and rash characterisations as to the nature of Hinduism. One may even feel disappointed at the way that Western scholars have reduced something so deep and rich to make it the subject of objective study and analysis. Any study of something as complex as Hinduism must be undertaken with a spirit of humility.

Various metaphors have been used to understand Hinduism. Spears proposed the illustration of a sponge.

> Hinduism has been likened to a vast sponge, which absorbs all that enters it without ceasing to be itself. The simile is not quite exact, because Hinduism has shown a remarkable power of assimilating as well as absorbing; the water becomes part of the sponge. Like a sponge it has no clear outline on its borders and no apparent core at its centre.[13]

The Western love for clear definition and neat pigeon-holes is left unsatisfied as it approaches the religions of India. Although the nature of Hinduism is not clear, it soon becomes obvious as to what it is not. The fact that Spear used this particular metaphor leaves one with the idea of Hinduism being a mysterious and amorphous entity.

Another widely used metaphor of Hinduism that is even more exotic to the Westerner is that of a jungle. Sir Charles Eliot writes:

> As in the jungle every particle of soil seems to put forth its spirit in vegetable life and plants grown on plants, creepers and parasites on their most stalwart brethren, so in Indian art, commerce, warfare and crime, every human interest and aspiration seek for a manifestation in religion, and since men and women of all classes and

occupations, all stages of education and civilization, have contributed to Hinduism, much of it seems low, foolish and even immoral. The jungle is not a park or garden. Whatever can grow in it, does grow. The Brahmans are not gardeners but forest officers.

The analogy of the Brahmins as forest officers is an apt one. The Brahmins do not try to bring order to the jungle, for they inherit its disorder, but they seem to introduce a degree of rationality.

The apparent disorder in Hinduism does not mean that the beliefs are unknowable. It possesses a character that is unique to the soil of India. There is a luxuriance of intellectual thought and practical ritual that contrasts and complements at the same time. No wonder Western scholars have been fascinated by the civilisation of India. To the European, India has always been described in terms of the exotic and considered as the 'other'. We will return to the significance of this observation near the end of our study.

One way to study the spiritual ideas and practices of India is to look at their growth through history. Just as one would watch the growth of a plant, one can see the emergence of new shoots, leaves, and even flowers. Branches twist and grow around one another in a confusion of maturation. While some growth bursts forth into beautiful bloom that delights the eye, other branches fall to the ground and die. The spiritual development of the people of the Indian continent manifests each and all of these. No one book can claim to achieve a full understanding of Indian spiritual thought, and each writer has his own particular perspective. Just because the task is difficult, this does not mean that it should not be attempted.

To begin to understand the influences of Hindu thought upon Western society one must first turn to the distant past.

Notes

[1] H. Zimmer, *Philosophies of India* (London, 1951), p 507.

[2] C. Richardson, *A Geography of Bradford* (University of Bradford: Bradford, 1976), p 168.

[3] David G. Bowen, 'The Hindu Community in Bradford', in D.G. Bowen, *Hinduism in England* (Bradford College: Bradford, 1981), pp 33–60.

[4] *Ibid*, p 48.

[5] Peter Brierley, *The New Age Is Coming!* (MARC: London, 1991), p 9.

[6] Michael York, 'The New Age Movement in Great Britain'; paper presented at the Fifth Annual International Conference on New Religions, 1991.

[7] *The Independent* (16 March 1992): pp 16–17.

[8] William Bloom, *The New Age* (Rider: London, 1991), pp xv–xvi.

[9] David Burnett, *Dawning of the Pagan Moon* (MARC: Eastbourne, 1991).

[10] K. Woodward and G. Lubenow, 'Physics and Mysticism', *Newsweek* (23 July 1979): p 85.

[11] Gary Zukav, *The Dancing Wu Li Masters* (Rider/Hutchinson: London, 1979).

[12] Michael Talbot, *Mysticism and the New Physics* (Routledge & Kegan Paul: London, 1987).

[13] P. Spear, quoted in Ronald Inden, *Imagining India* (Basil Blackwell: Oxford, 1990), p 57.

CHAPTER 2

Images from the Past

T O UNDERSTAND THE present, one needs to look at the past. To comprehend the religion which is commonly called Hinduism, one must dig in the soil of India. Only as we begin to understand the history of a people do we learn to appreciate the growth and development of their spiritual ideas. There, beneath the Himalayas, over 4,000 years ago, rose a civilisation that would shape the ideas of future generations in India.

In 1921, Sir John Marshall and his colleagues commenced excavating at the enormous earth-covered mounds rising along the eastern bank of the River Ravi in the Punjab. They were relatively unaware of the remains of the ancient civilisation they were going to discover in the brown soil. Others had previously noticed the vast quantities of bricks in the area and the strange indecipherable seals found near the mounds. Little did scholars realise that these excavations were going to transform our understanding of ancient India and the religion known as Hinduism.

THE FIRST URBAN SOCIETY

The first site was at a place called Harappa. The name comes from the word 'Hara', a name later associated with the god Siva. Radiocarbon dating has verified that from 2300 to 1750 BC, Harappa was a great city no less than three and a half miles in circumference.[1] The massive walls were 40 feet thick at the base, and protected a city which could have numbered at least 35,000 persons.

The city was laid out roughly on a north-south axis, with a great fortified citadel mound to the west and a larger lower city to the east. The streets of the lower city was laid out in a grid pattern with the main street being straight and as much as 30 feet wide.[2] The houses were entered from the side lanes, and consequently blank walls were presented to the main roads. The most common building material was burnt brick, and timber was used to construct the flat roofs. The houses were often two storeys or more, and though they varied in size, they were all based on the same general plan. Around a square courtyard were built several rooms. The houses had bathrooms provided with drains which took the water to sewers under the main streets and then to soak-pits. Not until the Romans, some 1,500 years later, were any people to construct a better sewage system.

Large granaries were also constructed, with ventilation ducts to allow the free circulation of air through the thick-walled buildings. These were built on platforms to protect them from floods, and were more than adequate for a population of 35,000. The main crops appear to have been wheat, barley, and peas. Rice was not one of the crops. This seems first to have been cultivated by the Harappans' contemporaries to the east in the Ganges valley. Cattle, goats, sheep, dogs, and chickens were domesticated. The bullock was probably the usual beast of burden. Cotton was, to the best of our knowledge, first used by the Harappan people.

Between the granaries and the walled citadel have been discovered smaller and simpler two-roomed dwellings. Even at this time there may have been a class distinction between the wealthy, and the workmen or slaves. Harappa provided a comfortable, if a somewhat unimaginative way of life for its people.

The city of Harappa was not alone. The city of Mohenjo-daro lay near the bank of the Indus, and was at least as large as Harappa. Its inhabitants had a similar way of life. These two large cities formed the hub of a network of smaller towns and villages throughout the Indus valley. Excavations have revealed more than seventy sites of varying size extending along the Indus to the sea (see Figure 2.1). This was a civilisation which may be compared with the two similar river cultures of Egypt and Mesopotamia. The three river basins of the Nile, Euphrates, and Indus provided good agricultural land that was not covered by dense vegetation and therefore provided the means for easy agriculture. Even so, the local differences allowed each area to develop its own distinct character.

Discoveries of the Harappan civilisation reveal a wide variety of crafts and technology. Copper and bronze were hammered to make knives, spears, arrow heads, and fine vessels. Gold, silver, and lead were all owned and used. Remains of pottery show the use of some kind of wheel for its production prior to firing. On the whole, the Harappans were not an artistic people, and their products were plain. A feature which has intrigued scholars is that although they were a Bronze-Age people with strong tools, their weapons were poor.[3] Does this indicate that they were a peace-loving people?

How did this fascinating civilisation emerge? There is some indication of trade with the regions of modern Iran and Afghanistan, and possibly as far as ancient Summar, but the evidence is unclear. It would certainly seem possible that people and ideas from outside acted as a stimulus to the emergence of the Harappan civilisation. However, recent archaeological studies have led most scholars to consider the Harappan civilisation to be an indigenous development in the region. As Allchin concludes, 'Its actual emergence must be seen primarily as a dynamic socio-economic process taking place on Indian soil, and not as something implanted from outside.'[4] Whatever its origin, the Harappan society was one of the great civilisations of the ancient world.

SPIRITUAL EXPRESSION
The archaeological excavations provide a considerable body of information to allow speculation concerning the religious beliefs of the Harappan people.

Buildings
At first, excavators were surprised at a lack of anything resembling a palace, obelisks, or temple. Some have argued that the

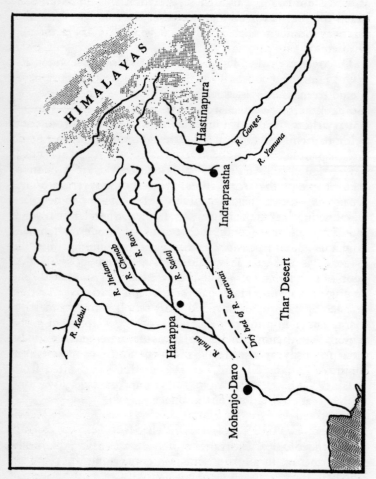

Figure 2.1. Geographical area of the Indus valley civilisation

citadel areas were primarily for ceremonial use, as also may have been the large tanks found in certain areas. The great bath at Mohenjo-daro measured 39 x 23 feet, and was enclosed by verandas. Because ablutions were well catered for in private houses, it has been suggested that these tanks may have been for ritual bathing. It could be that these were used in a way similar to the temple tanks found in India today.[5] Oval and square pits have also been discovered which clearly were used for fires. This has led some scholars to speculate that these were fire altars, but others have dismissed them as being merely rubbish pits.

No royal tombs have yet been identified, but at Harappa a graveyard containing sixty skeletons has been partly exposed to the south of the citadel. Most of these were arranged in an extended position, with the head pointing towards the north.[6] This burial custom contrasts with the practice of cremation common to both later Aryan culture and to modern India.

Perhaps one of the most notable artistic achievements of the Harappans was the engraving of seals, many hundreds of which have been discovered. The seals are square, with sides from 2 to 3 centimetres, and with a perforated boss at the back for handling and suspension. There has been much discussion as to what the seals were used for. It has been suggested that they were used in commerce. In this case, the image on the seal was equivalent to the mark of a guild, and was therefore a sign of ownership. Others think that the seals had some form of magical significance. The former reason need not exclude the latter; the seals could have provided a protective taboo on commercial items.

The goddess

The popular art of the Harappans was creating terracotta figurines. The majority of these are standing females, usually naked or with very short skirts, but wearing elaborate head-dresses and laden heavily with jewellery. From the time of Marshall, most scholars have considered these to be icons of the mother goddess, seen today in the cults of the village goddess or *gramadevatas*. These figurines have been found in such numbers that they must have been kept in almost every home.[7] Generally, they were crudely fashioned, suggesting that the goddess was not favoured by the upper classes, who engaged the services of the best craftsmen. The images of the goddess may therefore have been produced by less skilled craftsmen to meet popular demand.

In support of the identification of the mother goddess, Marshall cited the evidence from the many small seals. One oblong seal depicts a nude female upside down with her legs apart and a plant or tree growing from her vulva. The intention of depicting this scene would seem to be that of showing the production of vegetation from the womb of mother earth.

Trees, notably the pipal, are another common representation on the seals. One seal depicts a scene with the figure of a horned goddess or priestess in a pipal tree, worshipped by a figure also with horns, and a row of seven pigtailed women in attendance. The parallel to shamanistic practices where the priest(ess) stands in a tree has not gone without comment.

The horned god

Standing male figures, some with beards and horns, have also been discovered, together with a terracotta mask of what has been regarded as a horned deity. One of the most renowned seals is that known as the 'Proto-Siva Seal' (see Figure 2.2).[8] The seal depicts a figure seated on a platform with the legs drawn up close to the body and the two heels touching. This position would be quite impossible to most Europeans without much practice, but is one well known to Indian yogi. This yoga posture is believed to be emblematic of divinity.[9] The figure is considered by some scholars to be naked except for a necklace and what seems to be a head-dress consisting of a pair of horns with branches and leaves between them. The face has a fierce bovine look, and to the right and left are protuberances, which were believed by Sir John Marshall to be two other faces on either side.

Marshall considered the figure to be ithyphallic (with an erect penis), and so suggesting that he may have been a god of fertility. For these reasons, scholars have presumed the deity to be a prototype of the god Siva. Some scholars prefer to say that 'this may be a fertility god whose power is as strong as that of wild animals, or whose domain of power includes them.'[10] Sullivan even questions whether the suggested erect

Figure 2.2. The 'proto-siva' seal

phallus is anything more than a tie or tassel hanging from a waistband.[11]

Many cone-shaped objects were also discovered by Marshall, who regarded them as formal representations of the phallus. As we shall see later, the phallus, or *linga*, was to become a common symbol of Siva in later Hinduism. However, it is impossible to say how many of these conical stones were actually *lingas*. The earliest known Siva-*lingas* are dated from the first century BC, many centuries after the end of Harappan civilisation.

Another piece of evidence for the association of the figure with Siva is the way in which many of the seals show the person surrounded by animals such as elephants, tigers, buffaloes, and deer. Although Siva, as the lord of beasts, is associated with animals, in later Hinduism these are always domestic animals and not wild ones. A common image found on the seals is that of a bull, usually drawn with only one horn. This is not a unicorn; it is more likely the artist was trying to portray a normal bull whose second horn was concealed by the first. In later Hinduism, the bull is regarded as the mount upon which Siva rides. Other figures are composites of animals, such as that of a bull with the head of an elephant. The figure half-tiger, half-woman, has been regarded as a prototype of Siva's consort Durga.

Evidence to support the view that many of these animals were kept in captivity is the manger depicted in front of some of them. Animals are today associated with the various gods of Indian mythology, each deity having his or her own particular animal as a vehicle upon which to ride.

There is always a great danger of reading associations into the archaeological discoveries of Harappa. As Sullivan writes:

> Considering the available evidence, then, it would appear that Marshall's interpretation of the religion of the Indus civilization is not the only one possible and, indeed, not even the most plausible. Given the few archaeological facts we have, the most that can be said with any certainty is that there appears to have been a cult centred around the figure of a mother goddess. If

there was any distinct male deity, it is impossible to say just what his nature and his role were.[12]

It is, however, likely that many symbols of later Indian religions draw for their inspiration on the past images of Harappa. The mother goddess continues throughout the long history of the peoples of the subcontinent, mainly in the images of the village goddess. As we shall see, the same theme emerges with the worship of the great female deities of later Hinduism, and the teaching of Tantra that we will consider in Chapter 16.

THE HARAPPA PEOPLE

Questions abound as to who were these people who built such a civilisation. It is clear that they were not an Aryan people. Skeletal remains suggest that the Harappans were a mixture of two elements. The first, a Mediterranean type, found all over the ancient Middle East, and characterised by long heads and narrow noses. The second element was the Proto-Australoid, with flat noses and thick lips similar to the hill tribes of modern India.

Writers have been led to conclude:

> It might be suggested that the Harappa people consisted of a Proto-Australoid element, which at one time may have covered the whole of India, overlaid by a Mediterranean one, which entered India at a very early period, bringing with it the elements of civilization. Later, under the pressure of further invasions, this Mediterranean element spread throughout the sub-continent, and again mixing with the indigenous people, formed the Dravidians.[13]

This view cannot be advanced with complete confidence as archaeological evidence is little, but it appears reasonable.

Language provides us with another element in the discussion. There are three main linguistic groups in India—Munda, Dravidian, and Indo-Aryan. Attempts have been made to associate the languages with the social types just mentioned, but some care must be taken. This assumption would argue that Munda languages represent those of the earliest inhabitants of India, the Proto-Australoid. The Dravidian languages and the Indo-Aryan relate to the Dravidians and Aryans respectively. The Dravidian and minority Munda languages are found mostly in the south of India, which agrees with the general premise of this theory.

Many of the seals carry inscriptions, but there is too little lettering to allow any clear analysis. Originally, it was considered that the script was associated with the Middle Eastern picture-grams, but this now seems unlikely. Many scholars have tried to link it to the Dravidian languages, as a primitive form of the south Indian language, Tamil. One convincing piece of evidence for this association is the phenomenon of Brahui, a Dravidian language, in the remote northwest of Pakistan. It appears as a relic in a sea of Indo-Aryan languages. Even so, recent evidence has only added to the complexity of the situation, and the mystery of the Harappa people.

Some time around 1750 BC the Harappan civilisation began to disintegrate. The causes of its end are not clear. Certainly, there was a breakdown of social order, as indicated by the groups of sprawling skeletons found in Mohenjo-daro. Mansions were converted into tenements, the street plans were no longer maintained, and hoards of jewellery were left buried in the soil. When the downfall of the city came, most of the citizens appear to have fled, leaving a few stragglers to be overtaken by the incoming Aryan groups.

One likely suggestion is that the River Indus, which flows through a relatively arid area of the Punjab, made one of its periodic changes of course. This meant that water was no longer available for agriculture or as a means of transportation. The cities could therefore no longer sustain such large populations. The civilisation entered a dark age during which it became an easy prey for invaders.

The view propagated by Sir Mortimer Wheeler that the cities of the Indus valley were totally destroyed by the Aryan invasion from the northwest now appears unlikely. What is more likely is that during the decline of Harappa society, a series of regional cultures emerged in the Indian subcontinent that shared in some of the general Harappan culture. The

Aryan people probably came in a series of small migrations, and began to interact with the local people. From this process was to develop the complex religious phenomenon that is now called Hinduism.

Many hundreds of thousands of bricks from Harappa were plundered more than a century ago to provide ballast for 100 miles of railway track on the Lahore to Multan railway.[14] This extensive use of Harappan bricks has made it impossible to identify many of the buildings within the city walls. Just as the bricks of one civilisation have been reworked by a later civilisation, so the religious ideas of ancient Harappa have provided many of the notions for the modern expressions of the spirituality of India.

There is, perhaps, no other country where the prehistoric elements are so markedly discernible. India has carried her Stone Age along with her into the era of atomic power and satellite television. This capacity to transform the archaic myths and rituals into the living present is what has fascinated many Western people.

The earth mother of the ancient Harappa people has caught the imagination of many, and has been a stimulus to recent Western interest in goddess spirituality. Harappa has been pointed to as an example of a universal ancient goddess cult that was lost by Western society.

> The advent of a new phase of spirituality is upon us in the shape of the Goddess. Many people are discovering her for the first time, yet for humanity in general this is not something new but the resurgence of a once familiar deity. The questions arise: where has the Goddess been? why has her archetype been missing for so long from our culture?[15]

However, as David Kinsley has shown, it is too easy to speculate on the mute evidence of the Indus valley.[16] Perhaps only when the Harappan script has been deciphered will we be able to discover the significance of the figurines.

Notes

[1] G.L. Possehl, *Harappan Civilization: A Contemporary Perspective* (Aris & Phillips Ltd: Warminster, 1982).

[2] Sir Mortimer Wheeler, *Civilizations of the Indus Valley and Beyond* (Thames & Hudson: London, 1966), pp 22–23.

[3] D.D. Kosambi, *The Culture and Civilization of Ancient India in Historical Outline* (Vikas Publishing House: Delhi, 1972).

[4] F.R. Allchin, 'The Legacy of the Indus Civilization', in Possehl, *op cit*, p 326.

[5] Kosambi, *op cit*, p 68.

[6] Wheeler, *op cit*, pp 34–36.

[7] A.L. Basham, *The Wonder That Was India* (Sidgwick & Jackson: London, 1967), p 21.

[8] Seal no 420 from Mohenjo-daro.

[9] Doris Srinivasan, 'Unhinging Siva from the Indus Civilization', *J. Royal Asiatic Society*, vol 1 (1984): pp 77–87.

[10] *Ibid*, p 82.

[11] Herbert P. Sullivan, 'A Re-examination of the Religion of the Indus Civilization', *History of Religions*, vol 4, no 1 (1964): p 119.

[12] *Ibid*, p 125.

[13] Basham, *op cit*, p 25.

[14] Stanley Wolpert, *A New History of India* (Oxford University Press: Oxford, 1982), p 14.

[15] Caitlin Matthews, *The Elements of the Goddess* (Element Books: Shaftesbury, Dorset), p 3.

[16] David Kinsley, *Hindu Goddesses* (University of California Press: Berkeley, 1988), pp 212–220.

CHAPTER 3

Aryan Expansion

THE ARYANS HAVE often been portrayed as wild, bold, nomadic warriors. Riding their horses, they swept into India from the northwest. This image owes much to the romanticism of nineteenth-century Germany. The word *arya* has come from Sanskrit into most of the languages of India. Now, the word means 'freeborn', or 'of noble character', and generally refers to members of the three higher castes. Originally, the word referred to a particular ethnic group who moved into the subcontinent from the region of the Iranian plateau. It seems that the coming of the Aryans coincided with the end of the Harappan civilisation.

THE ARYAN PEOPLE

In 1786, Sir William Jones first observed that the Sanskrit languages of India and Persia were closely related to the languages of Greece, Rome, the Celts, and Germans. Later philologists began to find many words with common roots for father, mother, sister, daughter, son, father-in-law, cow, horse, dog, yoke, door, copper, and so on. Pronouns such as me, thou, he were similar, as were verbs such as to be, eat, sew. The word 'Aryan' itself survives in the Persian word 'Iran', and even 'Eire' is a cognate. In contrast, no fundamental resemblance can be traced between any language of this group and others in the world, such as Chinese, Arabic, or the Bantu languages. From these facts, philologists have come to the conclusion that the ancestors of most of the modern

European languages, Persian, and Sanskrit, are all descended from the same source. The term 'Aryan', or 'Indo-Aryan', is therefore used for this family of languages.

Max Muller was one of the scholars who took the association beyond that of language to that of race. In 1861, he asserted:

> When the first ancestors of the Indians, the Persians, the Greeks, the Romans, the Slavs, the Celts, and the Germans were living together within the same enclosures, nay, under the same roof...the ancestors of the Indians and Persians started for the South, and the leaders of the Greeks, Romans, Celts, Teutonic, and Slavonic colonies marched towards the shores of Europe.[1]

Even by the end of the nineteenth century, criticism was being directed at this association. However, it was the Nazi regime which gave to the term 'Aryan' a more sinister twist with a racial association.

Today, most scholars would agree with D.D. Kosambi:

> It is difficult to believe that blond Scandinavians and dark Bengalis belong to the same race, however loosely defined the term 'race' may be.... Aryan was to be taken as a linguistic term, with no reference to ethnic unity.[2]

The Aryans who entered India were a nomadic pastoral people herding cattle. It appears most likely that they migrated from central Asia, where they had domesticated the horse. These chestnut horses were harnessed to light chariots with spoked wheels which gave them speed and mobility in war, and enabled them to disrupt the agricultural people of the Indus valley. The importance of the horse and chariot was reflected as a common metaphor in their hymns and stories.

Now, it is generally believed that the Aryan occupation of India was not a single concerted action as had previously been thought, but one covering centuries and involving many migrating groups. The first wave probably arrived in the Indus valley about 2000 BC. Apart from some grey-black pottery similar to that found in Iran, there is little archaeological evidence until about 1000 BC. However, it is possible to piece together some picture of the era from the Aryans' religious 'Books of Knowledge'—the *Vedas*. These were preserved by the priests of each tribe by careful memorisation. The earliest of the *Vedas*, the *Rg Veda*, was compiled between 1500 and 1000 BC. It consists of 1,017 Sanskrit poems, and is the world's oldest surviving Indo-European oral literature. The period of Indian history from 1500 to 1000 BC is commonly called the Vedic Age (see Figure 5.1).

VEDIC HISTORY AND CULTURE

Before reviewing the historical material of the *Vedas*, it is important to understand that they are not historical books as is the Old Testament, but religious chants and hymns. As Kosambi has commented:

> The historical value of the *Vedas* is rather small in comparison with that of the Old Testament of the Bible, which was always presented as history by people who retained contact with their particular land. The archaeology of Palestine, much more advanced and more scientifically conducted than in India, provides ample confirmation of many Biblical events. The Aryans, on the other hand, were always on the move.[3]

The geographical information which may be gleaned from the *Rg Veda* agrees with details of the area of the Punjab. The *Rg Veda* mentions the names of rivers and mountains which are associated with the area. Seven major rivers are mentioned which flow from the north, and to the south is the sea. The word 'Punjab' means 'seven rivers'. When the hymns were composed, the focus of Aryan culture seems to have been in the region between the River Jamna and Satlaj. At this period, the Sarasvati was a major river which obstructed the eastward migration of the Aryans, but then the river dried up, allowing them to migrate further. Today, the river is an insignificant stream which becomes lost in the Thar desert of Rajastan.

The *Rg Veda* says nothing of fixed Aryan settlements, let alone brick-built cities. Technology amounted mostly to the construction of chariots, tools, and weapons of war. There is a complete absence of reference to writing in the *Rg Vedas*, which suggests that the Aryans were illiterate. The Vedic hymns were passed on by word of mouth; only much later were they written down.

The Aryans were essentially a war-like people whose culture seems to show a likeness to that of the Vikings, as described in the text *Beowulf*. Like the Vikings, they developed their own forms of fine art and story-telling. The Aryan tribes were ruled by warrior chiefs with the title *raja*, a word related to the Latin *rex*. The government of the tribe was the responsibility of a council, who provided a check upon the authority of the *raja*. The tribal assembly was the centre of the men's social life, and the 'men's house' was the scene of their favourite activity—gambling. The early Aryan warriors were incurable gamblers, and the later texts show them to have had a reckless disregard for home and family. This is seen in the *Mahabharata* when King Yudhisthira gambles away not only his kingdom, but his brothers, himself, and even his wife. It is not surprising that the 'Gambler's Lament' is one of the few secular poems which survived into the Vedic texts.[4]

The basic unit of Aryan society was the family, and a group of families formed a clan or village. The family was patriarchal and sons were important. Despite the male dominance, a woman, as wife and mother, enjoyed a position of respect.[5] Marriage was usually monogamous, and there is no reference to either divorce or the remarriage of a widow in the *Rg Veda*.

The Aryan warriors were the social élite, and appear to have had few of the taboos of later Indian people. They liked drinking the inebriating *soma* and *sura*. *Soma* was drunk at the religious sacrifices, whereas *sura* was purely for secular occasions, but both were evidently very potent. They loved music, and played the flute, harp, cymbals, and drums.

Very important was the chief priest (*purohita*) who, by his sacrifices, ensured the prosperity of the tribe and victory in war. Often the *purohita* appears as a tribal shaman, performing magical rituals and uttering spells to give victory. In the early Vedic period, as in ancient Greece and Rome, any senior male of the family or clan could fulfil the duty of priest. Later, the specific Brahmin families were to emerge.

As the Aryans moved westwards, they came in conflict with people they called the 'Dasas'. The term 'Dasa' has been the focus of much discussion. In the *Rg Veda*, the word is applied to hostile non-Aryan people who may represent the survivors of the Harappan civilisation. The Dasas were a people who were noticeably different from the Aryans. They are described as 'black-skinned' (literally *krishna*), and flat-nosed. The modern Dravidians found in the south of India do have dark skin, but are not necessarily flat-nosed.[6] It would therefore appear that the advancing Aryans gradually pushed the Dravidian peoples further to the south of the subcontinent.

The Dasas were dismissed by the Aryans as being without religious rites. In *Rg Veda* X:22:8 the *rishi*—a sage, or teacher—says, 'We live in the midst of the Dasyu tribes who do not perform sacrifices, nor believe anything. They have their own rites, and are not entitled to be called "men".' On the other hand, the texts show us that the Dasas were not primitive people, but had fortresses of stone, and were wealthy, with powerful kings. The Aryans called upon their god Indra to aid them in the destruction of the towns and buildings of the Dasas.

Although many of the Dasas were destroyed, others became slaves. In classical Sanskrit the word *dasa* regularly means a slave, and in the *Rg Veda* the feminine form *dasi* is used of a slave-girl. Some of the Dasa chiefs agreed terms with the Aryans, adopted their way of life and patronised the Brahmins. Intermarriage between the Aryans and the indigenous people occurred, with the mixing of language and tradition.

When the Aryans entered India, there appears to have been already the beginnings of class division within their society, with priests, rulers, and tribespeople. In the earliest hymns we read of *ksatra*, the nobility, and the *vis*, the ordinary tribesmen. Basham writes:

> As they settled among the darker aboriginals the Aryans seem to have laid greater stress than before on purity of blood, and class divisions hardened, to exclude those Dasas who had found a place on the fringe of Aryan

society, and those Aryans who had intermarried with the Dasas and adopted their ways. Both these groups sank in the social scale. At the same time the priests, whose sacrificial lore was becoming more and more complicated, and who therefore required greater skill and training, were arrogating higher privileges to themselves. By the end of the Rg Vedic period society was divided into four great classes, and this fourfold division was given religious sanction and looked on as fundamental.[7]

EASTWARD MIGRATION

The battle of Dasharajna (literally, 'ten kings') was the major historical event of this period. A confederacy of ten kings challenged King Sudas (literally, 'good king') of the Bharata clan. The cause of the battle was that the ten kings tried to divert the waters of the River Parushni. This is a stretch of the modern River Ravi, which has changed its course on several occasions. The diversion of the waters of the Indus is still a cause of animosity between India and Pakistan today.

The quarrel here was not between Aryan and non-Aryan, but between various confederations of Aryan clans concerning water for their herds. Later tradition even makes the Bharatas, a branch of the opposing Purus, the most powerful tribe of the confederacy. The incident illustrates the division of the Aryans which occurred between those who remained west of the Indus, and those who moved east. History tells us no more of the Purus or Bharatas, but of a new clan, the Kurus. It is likely that the two clans merged as a result of the conquest.

As the Aryans gradually pushed further down the Gangetic valley, their culture adapted itself to the changing environment. The people had little difficulty initially penetrating the valley because the area was thinly forested. However, within fifty miles of the river itself the forest was dense, causing the migrants great difficulties because they used the slash-and-burn method of agriculture. The Aryan settlements therefore extended eastwards along the Himalayan foothills. Cities emerged, such as Hastinapura in Kuru-land, Indraprastha (Delhi), and Kasi (Benaras) on the Ganga (see Figure 3.1).

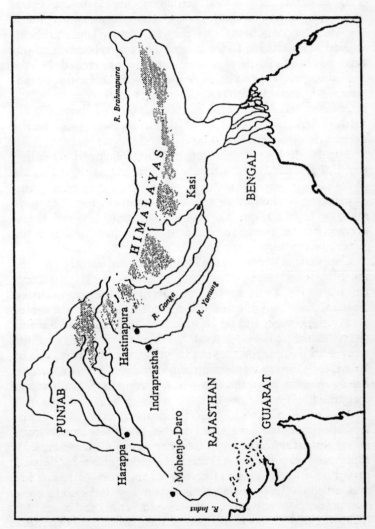

Figure 3.1. North India at the time of the eastward
migration of the Aryans

The city of Hastinapura provided the setting of much of the story of the great *Mahabharata* text. Archaeological study has dated the earliest levels of the city as being from between 1000 and 700 BC. The original settlement at Hastinapura was accomplished by the Kuru clan, but as a result of a dynastic dispute a second branch of the clan, called the Pandavas, cleared and settled in Indraprastha. The two related kingdoms finally fought a battle of mutual annihilation, recorded in the *Mahabharata*, which probably took place not far from modern Delhi. According to tradition, the battle took place in 3102 BC, but archaeological evidence gives a date of about 850 BC. Little exists of the city as it seems to have been finally destroyed by a disastrous flood.

This battle is magnified into mythical proportions within the *Mahabharata* epic, with the dispute involving the whole of India. The war was looked upon by following generations as marking the end of an age. The persons of the story have taken on mythical qualities, as we shall see in Chapter 7. The literary importance of the incident was as great as that of the Trojan war in Greek history.

Copper was known in the Punjab and was adequate for the local situation, but iron tools were needed to clear the dense forest regions. The discovery of iron ore in the area occurred after 1000 BC, and allowed the Aryans to settle in the fertile area of the Ganges and set up kingdoms in Kosala and Banaras (Kasi) in the mid-Ganges valley.[8] It is in this area that the story of the *Ramayana* takes place. Despite the great fame of Rama, early literature gives little information. Rama may have been a minor king in the area whose story was elaborated and magnified by generations of story-tellers. The *Ramayana* may be read as an allegory of the Aryan domination of the non-Aryan people. The jungle around the Aryan settlements must have brought repeated raids upon the Aryan settlements, with rape, murder, and kidnap threatening those who went beyond their homesteads. This can be seen in the story of Rama. He was exiled to the forest with his beautiful wife Sita. Here she was kidnapped by Ravana, who carried her off to Lanka.

The historical reconstruction of this period has been made in the *Puranas*, a group of texts composed in the first half of the first millennium AD (see Figure 5.1). They provide a mythical list of kings for nearly 3,000 years from the time of the flood which devastated Hastinapura.

One interesting account of the expansion of the Aryans is written in the *Brahmanas*. This tells the story of the fire god, Agni, who moved eastwards, burning up the earth, until he came to the River Sadanira (now called Gandak), where he stopped. No Aryan would cross the river because the purifying fire god had not burned the ground. Agni instructed chief Mathava to carry him over the water to the other bank. Agni was thus able to resume his purification of the land, and the eastward migration continued. The story probably illustrates the use of slash-and-burn agriculture by the Aryans.[9]

As the Aryans expanded far into India, their old home in the Punjab was forgotten. Later Vedic literature mentions it rarely, and usually with contempt. The culture of the later Vedic period was materially much advanced to that of the *Rg Veda*. The Aryan clans now had consolidated into little kingdoms, and had set up permanent capitals. Royal power was symbolised by the more elaborate rituals that we shall discuss in the next chapter.

Throughout the period, more and more land was cleared and agriculture extended. The use of iron tools and rice cultivation increased the prosperity of the people. By 600 BC, trade between the various city states had become an important economic activity. Specialised trades and crafts appeared, including basket-making, rope-making, weaving, dying, carpentry, pottery, and metalworking.

SOCIAL DEVELOPMENTS

During this shadowy period of the Aryan expansion, great religious developments also occurred. First, the stratification of society became firmly fixed. The initial distinction between the Aryan and non-Aryan people on the basis of colour (*varna*) became the *varna* order of caste hierarchy. The social classes of the Aryan people—priest, warrior, commoner—assumed the position of the three 'twice-born' castes of Brahmin, Kshatriya, and Vaishya. The Dasa and mixed Aryan became the 'once-born' Shudra peasant caste. The indigenous peoples caused to flee into the forest and hills were to become the Untouchables. We shall return to consider the social repercussions of the caste system in Chapter 7.

As the migrants realised their minority status in the area, an increasing fear of loss of identity and purity probably developed. The *Mahabharata* may be interpreted as an attempt to re-establish the Aryan identity. This fear probably led to a further development within the social structure of the varnas, with the mechanism for integrating the occupational groups as the *jati*, or subcastes. The *jati* became endogamous kinship groups that perpetuated hereditary specialist occupations.

Second, the elaboration of ritual increased the status of the Brahmin priests. Much of the Brahmanic literature is devoted to instructions for the meticulous performance of the sacrifices. The term 'Veda' designates the sacred knowledge that the Aryans brought with them into India and developed during the following centuries in the subcontinent. The Vedic texts themselves are collections of hymns, prayers, and ritual formulae written in verse. They are held to have emanated from the ultimate reality (Brahman), and to have been 'breathed' in the form of words received by their human writers. There are four distinct collections.

1. *Rg Veda*—a series of hymns recited at the sacrifices.
2. *Yajur Veda*—sacrificial formulae abounding with mantras borrowed from the *Rg Veda*.
3. *Sama Veda*—the melodies for chanting the hymns.
4. *Atharva Veda*—magical formulae.

The fourth *Veda*, the *Atharva Veda*, is different in character from the other three that particularly relate to the sacrificial rituals which will be discussed further in the following chapter. The *Atharva Veda* is a collection of spells, charms, and magic. Its contents may be regarded as falling in the overlap between religion and magic. The text provides the basis for Vedic medicine, in which most diseases are attributed to demons.[10]

In addition to the four *Vedas* are the *Brahmanas*, which are the Brahmanic explanations of the four collections of Vedic texts. The substance of these is an exposition of the doctrine of sacrifice. The priests were skilled in composing hymns for use at the sacrifices, and they memorised these hymns for use in the rituals.

The third social change which occurred with the Aryan expansion was the interaction between Aryan and non-Aryan. This resulted in a two-way process of acculturation and assimilation. This syncretistic process continued over the centuries and resulted in many regional variations. Before turning to the repercussions of this interaction, we need to examine the fascinating religious beliefs and practices of the Aryans during the Vedic period.

Notes:

1 N. Kumar Dutt, *The Aryanisation of India* (Firma Mukhopadhyay: Calcutta, 1970), pp 1–2.

2 D.D. Kosambi, *The Culture and Civilization of Ancient India in Historical Outline* (Vikas Publishing House: Delhi, 1972), p 73.

3 *Ibid*, p 78.

4 Wendy Doniger O'Flaherty, *The Rig Veda* (Penguin: Harmondsworth, 1981), pp 239–242.

5 Katherine K. Young, 'Hinduism', in Arvind Sharma (ed), *Women in World Religions* (State University Press: New York, 1987), pp 60–72.

6 Dutt, *op cit*, p 70.

7 A.L. Basham, *The Wonder That Was India* (Sidgwick & Jackson: London, 1988), p 35.

8 Kosambi, *op cit*, p 84.

9 Basham, *op cit*, p 40.

10 Margaret Stutley, *Ancient Indian Magic and Folklore* (Routledge & Kegan Paul: London, 1980).

CHAPTER 4

Vedic Religion

THE TERM *VEDA* denotes the sacred knowledge that the Aryans brought with them into India and developed during the following centuries in the subcontinent.

VEDIC MYTHOLOGY

The *Rg Veda* itself consists of a collection of 1,028 hymns of praise to a group of largely male deities who seem to personify various powers of nature, such as the sun, fire, sky, and rain. The *Rg Veda* contains little by way of mythology in the classical Greek sense of the word, but the hymns are full of symbolism. From the content of the hymns it is possible to gather various mythical themes. These themes sometimes weave together with each other, and at times even seem to be in contradiction. The outcome is that Vedic mythology has an ambiguity that has intrigued many through the ages.

To apply any classification to such a complex system of myths lays one open to the charge of oversimplification. However, we will here seek to place the main myths under two classes: myths of the gods, and myths of the cosmos.

Myths of the gods

Some of the most elaborate myths are those relating to the various gods, called *devas*. This word is cognative with the Latin *deus*, from which the English word 'divine' is derived. Like the early Greeks and Germanic peoples, the Aryans of India were patriarchal, and consequently most of their deities were conceived of as male. The chief attribute of the Vedic gods was their power over the lives of human beings. The four most important were Varuna, Indra, Agni, and Soma.

Indra is the most popular god of the *Rg Veda*, with 250 hymns addressed to him. These frequently mention his heroic deeds and his great strength, especially under the influence of soma. Indra is perceived as a rowdy amoral deity, fond of feasting and drinking. Like Zeus and Thor, he was associated with storms, and it is he who releases the waters from the clouds. In his hand he carries a thunder bolt.

A popular hymn tells of how Indra slayed the dragon Vrtra, an act that caused the releasing of the waters which Vrtra had held back. In *Rg Veda* 1:32, Vrtra may be imagined as a serpent without arms or legs. The battle is waged not only with weapons, but also with magic. At one point Indra uses magic to make himself as thin as a horse's hair, and Vrtra uses magic to create fog and lightning.

> Let me now sing the heroic deeds of Indra, the first that the thunderbolt-wielder performed. He killed the dragon and pierced an opening for the waters; he split open the bellies of mountains.... Over him as he lay there like a broken reed the swelling waters flowed for man. Those waters that Vrtra had enclosed with his power—the dragon now lay at their feet (RgV 1:32).[1]

Indra is victorious and the dragon slain! The word *vrtra* actually comes from the root meaning 'obstacle' or 'barrier' rather than 'demon'. Most scholars therefore relate this myth to the freeing of the rivers from dams that held back the waters. As Kosambi writes:

> Flood-irrigation by special dams, sometimes temporary, had been the Indus practice, as noted. This would have made the land too swampy for Aryan cattle herds, while the blocked rivers made grazing over long reaches impossible. With the dams vanished there was the possibility of an enduring Aryan occupation of the Indus cities, the annual rainfall being low.[2]

More remote than Indra is the figure of Varuna, who is frequently regarded as once having been the superior deity in the pantheon. Varuna was not a boisterous warrior like Indra, but a mighty king ruling from his great palace in the heavens. Varuna, like several other gods, is credited with the act of creation—he 'placed the sun in the sky', and 'stretched out the middle realm of space' (RgV 5:85). Varuna later became regarded as the administrator of the cosmic law (*Rta*), which regulates all activities in this world. Consequently, the function of Varuna was to ensure that no transgression of the law occurred, and that the worshipper was protected.

Varuna was pure and holy, and the mere performance of sacrifice would not ensure his favour because he abhorred sin.

> Not only did Varuna punish the sins of the individual but, like the Yahweh of the Old Testament, he visited the sins of his ancestors upon him, and his ubiquity ensured that there was no escape of the sinner.[3]

He caught up sinners in his snares so that they became ill and descended to the 'house of clay', apparently a place similar to Sheol in the Jewish concept of the after-life. Some of the hymns to Varuna remind one of the penitential psalms of the Old Testament. In classical Hinduism, some of the aspects of Varuna's character were transferred to the gods Visnu and Siva, who subsequently became the focus of devotion; the worship of Varuna has now ceased.

Agni, as the god of fire, has an important place within the *Rg Veda*. His name is related to the Latin word *ignis* from which the English word 'ignite' is derived. With some 200 hymns addressed to him, he is the second most frequently mentioned deity. Agni was personified and deified, especially as the sacrificial fire. He was conceived of as present as a guest in every household on the domestic hearth.

> He is the fire on the altar, and so is instrumental in conveying the sacrifice to heaven and, by extension, in bringing the gods down to the sacrifice.[4]

The very first hymn of the *Rg Veda* invites Agni down to

the sacrifice (1:1). It is therefore not surprising that Agni has an important ritual role. Agni is the god who, as fire, consumes the sacrifice and, as priest, presents it to the gods above. He is the mediator between humans and gods.

> I pray to Agni, the household priest who is the god of the sacrifice, the one who chants and invokes and brings most treasure (RgV 1:1).

Many societies have stories concerning the coming of fire and so, likewise, do the Vedic Aryans. The mystery of his birth, as well as his rebirth, is often told in the many hymns that mention him. In some hymns his 'birth' on earth is produced by the two fire-sticks, the upper being the male and the lower the female. By analogy he is, on the macrocosmic scale, the son of heaven and earth. In other hymns Agni hides in the waters and is lured out by Indra (RgV 10:124). He is represented like the sun, hiding behind the clouds from whence he may also descend in the form of lightning.

Closely linked with Agni is Soma. Whereas Agni is fire, Soma is the plant that is sacrificed. These two play an important part in the Vedic sacrifices, as we shall see later. One hundred and twenty hymns are devoted to Soma, and one of the most popular stories is the theft of Soma from the heavens by Indra mounted on an eagle (RgV 4:26–27).

Hymns speak of the pressing of Soma to extract the sacred juices that are filtered into a vat containing milk and water (RgV 9:74; 10:94). The process is likened to rain falling through the sieve of the sky to fertilise the earth (RgV 9:37:3). All this is expressed in the pressing and filtering of the *soma* plant to produce an intoxicating drink conferring immortality on gods and humans. The effects of *soma* were believed by Western scholars to give vivid hallucinations, similar to those produced by the drug hashish. *Soma* is now generally associated with the plant Ephedra, which grows in many parts of central Asia and India and provides a stimulant.[5] The story of how Soma invigorated Indra in his fight with Vrta is often recalled in the *Vedas*. He is called King Soma, doubtless because of his ritual importance.

Less important *devas* include Yama, lord of death. He was

the first human to die, and so became lord of the dead. Rudra and Vishnu are two deities that have little place within the *Rg Veda*, but they are of significance for the role that they were to play later in Hinduism. Rudra was a remote god, dwelling in the mountains, and generally the object of fear. He was an archer god, whose arrows brought disease, and in this he resembles the Greek god Apollo. In later Hinduism, many of the characteristics of Rudra are associated with Siva. The most prominent myth concerning Vishnu in the *Vedas* is that of his three strides (RgV 1:154). The three steps establish the cosmological system as understood in the *Vedas*.

In addition to the *devas* were many lesser gods and spirits. The *maruts* were storm deities that rode with Indra in their chariots, singing martial songs. *Rbhus*, meaning 'faithful workmen' or craftsmen, were spirits somewhat like gnomes who worked with metal in the depths of the earth. The *Vedas* spoke also of the lovely Apsarases, similar to the nymphs of Greek mythology, who might become the mistresses of gods and men.

Myths of the cosmos

The essential cosmology of the *Rg Veda* recognises thirty-three gods connected with a three-storeyed cosmos: heaven, earth, and the waters of the air. The *Rg Veda* contains several theories of creation that entwine with each other in the older parts of the text, in books 2 to 9. It is only in the last book that more distinct notions of creation emerge. Several important creation myths can be identified.

The first theme is that of a creator pictured as an artisan, a sculptor (10:81:2), a carpenter (10:81:4), an arranger (10:190), or a weaver (10:130). This creator is perceived as working with some material and fashioning it into its present form, but there is no inference of any concept of creation from out of nothing as found in the Judeo-Christian tradition.

> The sacrifice that is spread out with threads on all sides drawn tight with a hundred and one divine acts, is woven by these fathers as they come near: 'Weave forward, weave backward,' they say as they sit by the loom that is stretched tight (RgV 10:130:1).

A second theme relates to myths based upon pregnancy and birth from the original waters. Just as a person is created by his parents, who naturally exist before him, so the dawn gives birth to the sun.

> In the beginning the Golden Embryo arose. Once he was born, he was the one lord of creation. He held in place the earth and this sky (RgV 10:121).

This golden embryo, we are told in the last stanza of the hymn, is Prajapati, the 'lord of creatures'.

Third, there are myths of creation out of a unity-totality.

> There was neither non-existence nor existence; there was neither the realm of space nor the sky that is beyond. What stirred? Where? In whose protection? Was there water, bottomlessly deep? (RgV 10:129).

This cosmology has caused much debate over the centuries and is generally regarded as a high point in Vedic speculation. The hymn is, however, meant to puzzle and challenge rather than to provide answers.

A fourth theme is that of ordering out of chaos, rather than creation out of nothing. The Vrtra myth is such an example, with Vrtra symbolising chaos. By killing him, Indra separated land from water, the upper regions from the lower, and so caused the sun to rise in an act of creation repeated every day.[6]

Finally, the creation by sacrifice is one of the most important themes, and this is also found linked with other mythical themes. The most famous hymn is that of the cosmic man, Purusa, who was dismembered by the gods to create the cosmos (RgV 10:90). The myth of dismemberment is a common theme among the Indo-Aryan peoples. The dismemberment of the Norse giant Ymir makes a striking parallel.

The myth serves as the model for all creation.

> The Man has a thousand heads, a thousand eyes, a thousand feet. He pervaded the earth on all sides and extended beyond it as far as ten fingers....
> When they divided the Man, into how many parts did

they apportion him? What do they call his mouth, his two arms and thighs and feet?

His mouth became the Brahmin; his arms were made into the Warriors, his thighs the People, and from his feet the Servants were born.

The moon was born from his mind; from his eye the sun was born. Indra and Agni came from his mouth, and from his vital breath the Wind was born....[7]

It can be seen that the hymn provides a mythical explanation of the four *varnas* (castes). The Brahmins speak the word of the sacred hymns and come from the mouth; the Ksatriya are the warriors and come from the strength of the arms; the Vaisya do the manual work and so come from the thighs; the Shudras come from the feet.

The hymn tells that it is the gods who sacrifice the Purusa, but this leads to a paradox. Where did the gods come from to perform the sacrifice?

The importance of sacrifice for creation underlies the necessity of sacrifice for the continuation of existence. Without sacrifice the universe will disintegrate. The role of the priests therefore becomes essential. This hymn is recited in one of the rites following the birth of a son, in the ceremonies for the foundation of a temple, and in the purification rites of renewal.[8]

The Hymn of the Primeval Man marks the transition to a new stage of Indian religion. Sacrifice had always been among the most important elements of the Aryan cult, but now its significance increased a hundredfold.[9]

VEDIC RITUALS

As we have stated, the hymns of the *Rg Veda* are essentially for ritual purposes. The *Brahmanas* that were composed after the *Vedas* provide a commentary for these hymns, where the expositors provided a sacrificial system for use by the Brahmin priests. Sacrifice becomes of major importance within Vedic religion. As Louis Renou writes, 'The Vedic sacrifice is presented as a kind of drama, with its actors, its dialogue, its portions set to music, its interludes and its climaxes.'[10] The chief purpose of the sacrifices was to please the gods in order to gain boons from them.

The *Brahmanas* identified three classes of sacrifice: animal, *soma* and vegetable, and other oblations. The Vedic cult had no sanctuaries, and the rites were performed either in the homes of the sacrificers or on a nearby grassy area. The rites were either domestic (private) or solemn (public). The former were performed by the master of the house, and the latter by the Brahmin priests. The *Rg Veda* is, however, more concerned with the great public sacrifices paid for by the wealthy kings.

Domestic rites

Among the private rites were the keeping of the domestic fire and the agricultural festivals. The most important were the rites of passage: birth, consecration, marriage, and death. These ceremonies were all comparatively simple, involving non-flesh oblations and offerings. The *Rg Veda* throws little light on birth rituals, but those for marriage and death were basically the same as in later Hinduism. Marriage was an indissoluble relationship established by rituals centring on the domestic hearth. The funeral rites of the rich included cremation. Mythically, Yama is perceived as the first mortal to reach the other world and so is the path-maker for all who follow him. This story is celebrated in *Rg Veda* 10:14, which is a common hymn used in funeral rites.

It is, however, the public rituals that are most significant for our discussion. From the wide variety of such rites we will here take the most important.

Agnihotra

The 'oblation to the fire', Agnihotra, is the simplest of the public rites, and in a sense the most important. Every Brahmin and Vaishya family must offer this sacrifice morning and evening throughout their life. It takes place just before the rising of the sun, and the appearance of the first star. The sacrifice is an oblation of milk to Agni, followed by libations of water to several other deities.

The *soma* sacrifice: Agnishtoma

From the time of the *Rg Veda*, the *soma* sacrifice has been the most popular. The ritual is performed in the spring. The climax of the ceremony consists of the pressing of the *soma*.

As we have already suggested, the original plant may have been a variety of hemp. However, in later centuries this may have been replaced by other more local botanical species. The plant is pounded with a stone while it lies on a skin. The yellow juice extracted is then filtered through sheep's wool to produce a clear liquid. The squeezing takes place in the morning, at noon, and in the evening. In this form the liquid is offered to Indra and Vayu. The liquid is mixed with water and milk to sweeten it. At the midday squeezing there is a distribution of gifts. The ritual usually takes only one day, but it can take as many as twelve, or even a year.[11]

The mythical significance of the ritual is clear to the priest.

> The priest who crushed the *soma* stalks knew that this ritual meant the killing of King Soma in order to set free his victorious, invigorating and life-promoting power.[12]

The mixing of the *soma* with water is often seen to symbolise Soma as a bull fertilising the waters that are his cows.

Agnicayana

The most famous of the Vedic rituals is the Agnicayana—the piling (of bricks for the altar) of fire. This ritual takes 12 days in total and consists in the construction of an altar from 10,800 bricks, piled up in 5 layers in the form of a bird. A small image of a man and a living tortoise are buried in the lowest layer of bricks.

The building of the altar symbolises the creation of the universe, with the three levels of creation represented by the lower, middle, and upper rows of bricks. These are separated by two other rows signifying the distinction of the levels of creation. The construction of the altar is likened to the formation of Prajapati and the cosmic sacrifice. The form of the bird is a symbol of the sacrificer's mystical ascent to heaven. After the chanting of various hymns of the *Vedas* by groups of priests, ablutions and offerings of *soma* are made. The whole altar is then ignited.

This rare ritual has survived mostly in the extreme south of India. In 1975 and 1990, it was performed in Kerala in the full light of Western scholarship. A horse was part of the ritual, but it was not sacrificed as probably occurred in the Vedic period. It will be remembered that the horse was an important element of the Aryan way of life, and became the central offering in the great 'horse sacrifice', the Asvamedha.

Asvamedha

The Asvamedha could be performed only by a victorious king, but the results of the sacrifice benefited the entire kingdom. The preliminary part of the ritual took a whole year, but the final ritual, which occurred in February or March, lasted only three days. A stallion was left at liberty with 100 other horses for the whole year. The horse was guarded by 400 young warriors who kept it from approaching the mares. The ritual proper lasted four days. On the final day the horse was suffocated. Four queens with their attendants walked around the body. The senior wife lay down beside the body and, under the cover of a cloak, simulated sexual union, thus channelling its energies for the prosperity of the kingdom. When the queen arose, the body of the horse and other sacrifices were cut up.

The horse was a supreme symbol for the victorious Aryan peoples in their conquests, and occurs in many of their hymns (RgV 1:162; 1:163; 10:56). This ritual included many cosmological elements. The horse was identified with the cosmos, equivalent to Purusa. Its sacrifice symbolised the act of creation and was intended to regenerate the entire cosmos. In so doing, it established the social classes and the royal power.

DEVELOPMENTS IN VEDIC RELIGION

The Vedic rituals clearly originated from the myths of the *Rg Veda*, but developments can be seen within the Vedic rituals. It is these changes which were to have important repercussions in the future development of Indian religious thought, as we will see in following chapters. First, the institution of sacrifice was greatly elaborated by the speculations of the Brahminic priests. The *Brahmanas* contain detailed instructions concerning the performance of the Vedic rituals, in many cases with little reference to the context of the original myth. As Dasgupta writes:

> During the particular ritual observances the different verses were often torn out of their contexts and were combined with others which apparently had little or no relation with them and no conceivable bearing on the performance during which they were chanted or uttered. They were simply the means for the performance of the sacrifices.[13]

Second, as the world was produced by sacrifice according to Vedic mythology, so there had to be a continual performance of sacrifice to maintain it. The emphasis therefore shifted from the rituals as an enactment of the myths, and they became of primary significance in themselves. Religion generally includes the sense of a relationship with some divinity to whom the person submits, but by the time of the *Brahmanas* the importance was the ritual, not the gods.

> For the Vedic people, the sacrifices were more powerful than the gods. The gods could be pleased or displeased; if the sacrifices were duly performed the prayers were bound to be fulfilled.[14]

The gods themselves were dependent on the rituals, and the sacrifices were dependent on the priests who alone could perform them correctly.

Third, the emphasis upon the sacrifices, therefore, was associated with the increase in the power and prestige of the priests. So great became the power of the priests that they were regarded as gods upon earth and feared more than the gods of heaven.

> Truly there are two sorts of gods, for the deities indeed are gods and the Brahmins who have studied and teach religion are human gods; sacrifice to them is of two

sorts: oblations for the sacrifice to the deities and the gifts to the priests that are human gods (Sat Br 2:2:2:6).

Fourth, the emphasis upon correct ritual meant that the Vedic religion became imbued with ideas of sympathetic magic to cope with the practicalities of living in this world. The later texts include love charms, formulae for protection against evil spirits, and even the hymn to the ruined gambler (RgV 10:34). Even though the personalities of the Vedic gods of the *Rg Veda* ceased to be of importance and become lost in a maze of ritual, the myths still provided many themes for later writers.

Throughout the history of India, the *Vedas* have kept their place as the most sacred texts of the Brahmins. In the last few years, the *Vedas* have become the focus for a new growing fundamentalist movement in India. In contrast to the usual tolerant face of Hinduism, there has emerged a militant form of Hinduism expressing itself politically with the Bharatiya Janata Party (BJP), under the leadership of Atal Bihari Vajpayee.

The ideological position of Hindu fundamentalism is based upon four dogmas. The first is that the *Vedas* alone are true, and all other scriptures are perversions of the truth. The *Vedas* alone can claim supreme authority, and so the call is 'Back to the *Vedas*'. Second, Hinduism alone has the answers to the world's problems. It alone has true spirituality, which must be defended and propagated. Third, India alone is the land of perfect spirituality and so is the foremost nation on earth. Finally, a true Indian is a Hindu, and a Hindu alone is a true Indian.

The politicisation of Hinduism is an important byproduct of Hindu fundamentalism. It presents a hostile form of nationalism that threatens the political stability of the Indian state. The fundamentalists' answer to the vexing problems of modern India is to return to the teachings and lifestyle of the *Vedas*. This would require the Hinduisation of all non-Hindu Indians in the country. Beyond this, the fundamentalists have the vision to spread their teachings to the whole world.

In times of social stress, many societies look back to what they regard as a golden age, but in reality the age was merely an illusion of history. The religion of the *Vedas*, with its rituals and sacrifices, failed to satisfy the needs of all the different social groups that inhabited the land of India. Many individuals rejected the dogmatism of the Vedic rituals and sought for deeper spiritual experiences within a monistic philosophy.

Notes:

[1] Wendy Doniger O'Flaherty, *The Rig Veda* (Penguin: Harmondsworth, 1981), pp 148–151.

[2] D.D. Kosambi, *The Culture and Civilization of Ancient India in Historical Outline* (Vikas Publishing House: Delhi, 1972), p 80.

[3] A.L. Basham, *The Wonder That Was India* (Sidgwick & Jackson: London, 1988), p 237.

[4] J.I. Brockington, *The Sacred Thread* (Edinburgh University Press, 1989), p 14.

[5] Harry Falk, 'Soma I and II', *Bulletin of the School of Oriental and African Studies*, vol LII (1989): pp 77–90.

[6] Brockington, *op cit*, p 11.

[7] O'Flaherty, *op cit*, pp 30–31.

[8] Mircea Eliade, *A History of Religious Ideas*, vol 1 (University of Chicago Press: Chicago, 1978), p 225.

[9] A.L. Basham, 'Hinduism', in R.C. Zaehner, *Encyclopedia of Living Faiths* (Hutchinson: London, 1988), p 219.

[10] L. Renou, *Vedic India* (Susil Gupta Ltd: Calcutta, 1957), p 101.

[11] Eliade, *op cit*, p 217.

[12] Brockington, *op cit*, p 17.

[13] S.N. Dasgupta, *Hindu Mysticism* (Atlantic Paperbacks: New York, 1959), p 14.

[14] *Ibid*, p 6.

CHAPTER 5

Philosophers of the Forest

What is the cause? Brahman? Whence are we born?
Whereby do we live? And on what are we established?
Overruled by whom, in pains and pleasures,
Do we live out various conditions, O ye theologians?[1]

T HIS IS THE CRY that came from a scholar of ancient India, but its echo has continued down throughout human history. It is a cry of one who seeks meaning from a world that seems to give no answer. Perhaps this is the reason for the relevance of the ancient writings of the philosophers of India to many in Western society today.

THE SAGES OF ANCIENT INDIA

Who were these people that raised questions concerning the very meaning of life? Their questions and the answers they gave have intrigued Western scholars from the nineteenth century onwards, when the *Upanishads* were translated into the languages of Europe. As we have seen, Vedic religion was essentially ritualist in its content, and this gave importance of place to the role of the Brahmin priestly caste. Modern scholars consider the doctrines of the *Upanishads* to be in some way a reaction to the excessive ritualism of the earlier Vedic texts.

Various explanations have been proposed for this response to Vedic religion. One of the earliest suggestions was the environmental theory that was popular among Indologists of the nineteenth century. Bloomfield (1855-1928), for example, insisted that when the Aryans first arrived in the Punjab they were 'a sturdy, life-loving people'. As the Aryans pressed eastwards along the Ganges valley, the tropical climate induced a more melancholic character. This attitude led to the development of a world-denying mystical philosophy. There are few today who would hold to this view.

A second theory that has been proposed is based upon racial contact. As the Aryans mixed with the non-Aryan peoples of the Ganges valley, there was an interchange of ideas and beliefs. The 'Proto-Siva Seal', described in Chapter 2, is often given as evidence of this. Most scholars recognise that such a cross-fertilisation of ideas must have occurred, but this might not have been the whole story.

A third theory is that the mystical traditions were a reaction of the warrior caste to the sterility of the sacrificial cult. Vivian Worthington writes:

> The Brahmins jealously guarded their knowledge contained in the four *Vedas*. Knowledge is power, as they well knew, so while the knowledge was their monopoly they alone had power over the rest of the community.[2]

This could have been part of the reason, as seen in the fact that both Buddha and Mahavira (the founder of Jainism) were from the non-priestly Ksatriya caste. Even so, other exponents of the mystic philosophy were not Ksatriyas, and some were even Brahmin priests. Generally, the *Upanishads* do not oppose the Vedic sacrificial cult, and speak respectfully of the Brahmins. By the sixth century BC, asceticism appears to have become an acceptable alternative to mainstream Indian religion.

Yet another theory is that as the Aryans settled in the Ganges valley, great social changes occurred that produced a loss of identity among many Aryans. In the sixth century BC, new towns were being built, coins were introduced as a means of currency, and writing was probably developed at this time. It was a period of change and social tension. As Basham writes:

The feeling of group solidarity which the tribe gave was removed, and men stood face to face with the world, with no refuge in their kinsmen.... Despite the great growth of material civilization at the time, the hearts of many men were failing them for fear of what should come to pass upon earth. It is chiefly to this deep feeling of insecurity that we must attribute the growth of pessimism and asceticism in the middle centuries of the first millennium BC.[3]

Whatever the full explanation of this new movement of philosophical speculation, it resulted from men, and some women, who left their families and the securities of the Aryan settlements to live in the forests. Even in the later hymns of the *Rg Veda*, one reads of the long-haired ascetics (*munis*, silent ones) who drink a drug in the company of gods. The ascetics experienced the sensation of flying outside their own bodies, and riding the wind as if it is a horse.

> Long-hair holds fire, holds the drug, holds sky and earth.
> Long-hair reveals everything, so that everyone can see the sun.
> Long-hair declares the light.
>
> These ascetics, swathed in wind (naked), put dirty rags on.
> When gods enter them, they ride with the rush of the wind (RgV 10:136).[4]

By the time of the *Upanishads*, asceticism had become an accepted alternative to the orthodox sacrifices of the priests. Some ascetics were solitary practitioners dwelling in the depths of the forest. Others dwelt on the outskirts of towns, where they would indulge in self-torture, such as lying on a bed of thorns, hanging head downward from branches of trees, or holding their arms motionless above their heads until they atrophied.

Most of the new philosophical development came from those who practised the more moderate practices, and gained a gathering of disciples. The concern was with the achievement of knowledge—*Pramana*—which, translated, means 'reliable knowledge'. The Brahmins claimed power because of their birth and training, but the ascetics sought new sources of power through meditation and altered states of consciousness.

The ascetics transformed the concept of offering sacrifices into one in which the person himself became the sacrifice. The magical potency formerly ascribed to the sacrifices was now attributed to asceticism, considered to liberate a unique magic power generally known as *tapas*. The ascetic power of *tapas* was often considered to be heat. In later Hindu thought, *tapas* is especially relevant to the god Siva, who creates through the power of his asceticism.

As the ascetic practised his mystical exercises, it was believed his psychic faculties developed. The ascetic obtained insights which no words could express. He understood the deepest of mysteries concerning life and death, the nature of the universe and the nature of himself. Indian mysticism developed methods and techniques far beyond those of any other people. It was as a result of these ascetic practices that the philosophy of the *Upanishads* emerged.

THE *UPANISHADS*

The *Upanishads* are the first recorded attempt at systematic philosophy within the subcontinent. The word *Upanishad* comes from the two roots: *upa* meaning 'near', and *shad* meaning 'to sit'. The word therefore means 'sitting down near', as a disciple would sit at the feet of a guru who imparted esoteric teaching.

The *Upanishads* are not easy reading, but they ask important questions. Where did we come from? Why are we here? By what power do we exist? What is the cause of everything?

There are ten principal *Upanishad* texts, but this number is often increased to thirteen by some authorities. These texts are dated around 600 BC, just before the rise of Buddhism (see Figure 5.1). Many of the *Upanishads* are set as a conversation, and some record set debates in which individuals competed for a prize. One of the most outstanding is the debating contest organised by King Janaka, who offered a prize of 1,000 cows, each with 10 pieces of gold on its horns.[5]

The following outline is an attempt to present something of

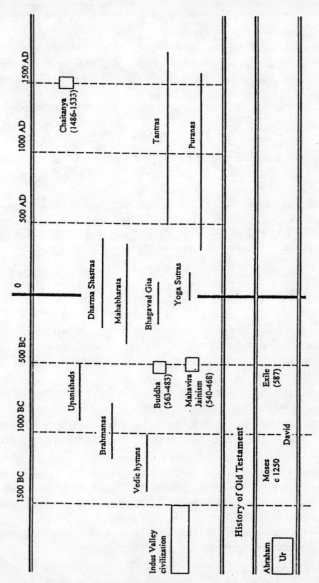

Figure 5.1. Time chart showing approximate dating of main Hindu texts

the character of the *Upanishads* before we consider the philosophical issues they present.

The **Brihadaranyaka Upanishad** is the oldest and longest (*Brihard* means 'great'). Its title means 'teaching of the forest', and it is set in six parts. These consist of an enquiry into the nature of ultimate reality called Brahman.

The **Chandogya Upanishad** contains the story of Svetaketu, a boy who is sent away by his father to be educated. He returns at the age of twenty-four, proud of his learning and with a high opinion of himself. His father, seeing this, begins to instruct him in deeper wisdom about the nature of reality and his own nature.

The text of the **Katha Upanishad** begins with the story of the boy Nachiketas who is granted three wishes by Yama, the god of death. The first two concern the family of the boy, and are immediately granted. The boy's third wish concerns the knowledge of what happens after death. Yama pleads with Nachiketas to ask something else, but the boy insists. Thus follows the discussion with death that is the heart of this *Upanishad*.

The **Prasana Upanishad** consists of six questions asked of a teacher by his students. They relate to the nature of the universe, the supreme being, and the meditative sound OM (pronounced AUM).

Taittiriya Upanishad is given its title from the name of the teacher who tries to help his student realise the nature of Brahman. After many attempts, the student sets himself to pray for a long time, during which he finally realises Brahman as joy.

The **Isa Upanishad** is the shortest of all the *Upanishads*. The title comes from the first word of the text, *Isa*, which means 'lord', and is one of the names used for deity. It deals with human relationship with the cosmos.

The **Mandukya Upanishad**, like previous ones, is named after the teacher. Its main teaching concerns the four states of consciousness: waking life, dream, deep sleep, *samadhi* (state of pure consciousness of oneness with ultimate reality).

The title of the **Kena Upanishad** means 'by whom', or, in other words, 'at whose command'. It contains some direct questions concerning the nature of reality behind outward appearances.

Mundaka means 'razor', and is applied in the ***Mundaka Upanishad*** as a simile for wisdom which cuts the knot of ignorance. The higher knowledge of Brahman is distinguished from that of the ordinary world.

The *Svetasvatara Upanishad* deals with the subject of the soul as it relates to the universe. The universe is a wheel, and revolving on it are all living things, bound to the cycle of birth, death, and rebirth.

Whereas the Vedic religion focused upon the action of ritual, the teaching of the *Upanishads* centred upon insight and wisdom.

PHILOSOPHY OF THE *UPANISHADS*

The teaching of the *Upanishads* forms the themes of a world-view that is radically different from those familiar to Western society. It is because of this that Western students have found the teaching of the *Upanishads* difficult to conceive, but so fascinating. The speculative thought of the *Upanishads* provides much of the basis of future Indian philosophy.

Brahman

The earliest use of the term 'Brahman' in the *Rg Veda* appears to be in the sense of a magical word or prayer that fills space and time. In this sense it is the ultimate reality from which the whole universe, including the gods themselves, have emerged. The inscrutability of Brahman is indicated in the *Kena Upanishad* by the ignorance of the gods themselves. Brahman appears to the gods, but they did not understand who it was.

Agni, the god of fire, was first sent to find out the identity of the being. Agni was challenged to burn a straw, but failed. He returned to the other gods baffled. The god of wind, Vayu, was then sent on the same mission. He boasted of his power to blow away anything, and was challenged to blow away the straw. He failed, and was also baffled. Indra was the next emissary, and to him appeared a beautiful woman who is an allegory of wisdom. Wisdom dispelled Indra's ignorance.

The great knowledge that the *Upanishads* claim to impart is not the mere recognition of the existence of Brahman, but the continual consciousness of ultimate reality.

> Sir, tell me the mystic doctrine (*upanishad*)!
> The mystic doctrine has been declared to you. Verily, we have told you the mystic doctrine of Brahman.
> Austerity (*tapas*), restraint (*dama*), and work (*karman*) are the foundation of it. The *Vedas* are all its limbs. Truth is its abode.
> He, verily, who knows it [ie, the mystic doctrine], thus, striking off evil, becomes established in the most excellent, endless, heavenly world—yea, he becomes established! (Kena U).[6]

Throughout the history of Indian thought, from the period of the *Upanishads* until the present day, there has been a controversy as to whether Brahman is 'without characteristics' (*nirguna*) or 'with characteristics' (*saguna*). The early sages seem to have preferred the former, but they could not avoid personifying the impersonal world spirit. Later sages do learn to conceive of a truly impersonal Brahman and a fully developed monism.

In monotheism, God is considered as the effectual cause of creation. He is distinct from the creation that he made from nothing. In contrast, the Upanishadic sages perceived of no sharp cleavage between God and the universe, but one universal reality that embraced all phenomena as its parts.

Atman

Brahman is not merely external to the individual, but Brahman *is* the human soul—*atman*. The Sanskrit word *atman* derives from a root word meaning 'to breathe', and is related to the German *atmen* for 'breathe', and the Greek *atmos* for 'vapour'. In English, the word has often been translated as 'self', but this tends to imply a too individualistic meaning to the word. The soul is the inner self of a human being, but it is not essentially individual. When a person realises this fully, he is free from the cycle of transmigration. His soul becomes one with Brahman.

The philosophers used many images and illustrations in an

attempt to express this teaching. In the *Chandogya Upanishad* is the famous story of Svetaketu and his father. During their conversation, the father uses sixteen illustrations which picture the *atman* in various ways. Sometimes *atman* is described as a tiny manikin in the heart, or a fluid in the veins, or even the immeasurable.

> 'Bring hither a fig from there.'
> 'Here it is, sir.'
> 'Divide it.'
> 'It is divided, sir.'
> 'What do you see there?'
> 'These rather fine seeds, sir.'
> 'Of these, please, divide one.'
> 'It is divided, sir.'
> 'What do you see there?'
> 'Nothing at all, sir.'
> Then, he said to him: 'Verily, my dear, that finest essence which you do not perceive—verily, my dear, from that finest essence this great Nyagrodha [sacred fig] tree thus arises.
> 'Believe me, my dear son,' said he, 'that which is the finest essence—this whole world has that as its soul. This is reality. That is Atman (Soul). That art thou, Svetaketu.'[7]

The identification between Brahman and *atman* is one of the greatest developments of the Upanishad period. It has profound implications that the *Upanishads* only begin to explore. Brahman is the one eternal undifferentiated essence which takes on an expression I experience as 'self'.

> Though it fills the whole of space, by a mysterious verity which defies logic but is proved by experience it dwells in the core of the human heart.[8]

This is what Svetaketu did not know even though he had been away from home studying for twelve years and had read all the *Vedas*.

As the great refrain of the *Chandogya Upanishad* says:

That which is the finest essence—this whole world has that as its soul. That is reality. That is Atman (Soul). That art thou, Svetaketu (ChU 6:15:3).

To illustrate what is meant by 'That art thou', a series of illustrations is given in the *Upanishad*. Those of the bees and the rivers give an understanding of the nature of the doctrine. Bees collect nectar from different trees and the whole is reduced to the one honey in the hive. Just as the nectar in the many flowers may be perceived as separate, and all become one, so human individuality will transcend to a higher reality. The rivers also flow into the sea, losing themselves and merging in the greater whole, the individual being lost in the whole.

Maya

If reality is one all-encompassing monistic entity, the next question must relate to its nature. It must possess as many qualities as there are in the universe that it constitutes.

Verily, this whole world is Brahman.... He who consists of mind, whose body is life (*prana*), whose form is light, whose conception is truth, whose soul (*atman*) is space, containing all works, containing all desires, containing all odours, containing all tastes, encompassing this whole world, the unspeakable, the unconcerned—this Soul of mine within the heart is smaller than a grain of rice, or a barley-corn, or a mustard-seed, or a grain of millet, or the kernel of a grain of millet; this Soul of mine within the heart is greater than the earth, greater than the atmosphere, greater than the sky, greater than these worlds (ChU 3:14).[9]

A distinction thus occurs between that which is sensually perceived and that which cannot be brought into consciousness, but can only be thought. This carries with it the idea that there is much of reality which is not within the sphere of the senses. In places the *Upanishads* speak of 'two forms of Brahman'.

There are, assuredly, two forms of Brahman; Time and the Timeless. That which is prior to the sun is the Timeless without parts. But that which begins with the sun is Time, which has parts (Maitri 6:15).

These two forms of Brahman, one with sense qualities, and the other a superphenomenal unity, are both accepted as real, though in different ways. They make up the subject matter of the two forms of knowledge that may be known. The lower knowledge is that studied by science, while the higher knowledge is that of the mystic.

Reality is one! Therefore diversity is only an appearance. This is the springboard to the theory of cosmic illusion—*maya*. All human cognition is illusion. This does not mean that the universe is only illusion, but that it gives us a distorted view of reality by making what is intrinsically one appear as many.

This whole world the illusion-maker projects out of this (Brahman).
And in it by illusion the other is confined.
Now, one should know that Nature is illusion,
And that the Mighty Lord is the illusion-maker (Svet 4:9–10).

How, then, is the real Brahman to be known? The higher Brahman is not accessible to sensory knowledge, nor by thought. We are therefore in a great paradox. On the one hand is an illusory universe, and on the other an unknowable reality. The answer to the dilemma is not found outside of self, but within it. Self is the unity for which the ascetic had been looking.

Thus that world-ground, that unity of being which was being searched for realistically outside of the self, and which, as it was being approached, seemed to recede back into the illusory and into the unknowable, is none other than the self, which had eluded cognition for the reason that, as the subject of consciousness it could not become the object.[10]

THE SPREAD OF MONISTIC IDEAS

The sixth century BC saw the appearance of many ascetic movements in India. Although there seem to have been considerable differences between them, many adopted the radically new worldview expressed in the *Upanishads*. Gradually, the concept of *karma* and transmigration became generally accepted by the people. Monistic ideas merged with the polytheism of Vedic religion. Ideas of creation, whether they were by a personal god or an impersonal absolute, were rejected in preference to a model of a universe that went through unending cycles of advance and decline. The new religious movements came with a message of how their followers might achieve release from the bondage of birth, death, and rebirth. Of these new sects, two were to become of historical significance—Jainism and Buddhism. Buddhism especially, was influential in spreading many of these new ideas through China to Korea and Japan, and into many of the countries of southeast Asia.

In India, in later centuries, major schools of philosophy developed around the ideas inherent within the *Upanishads*. The most important was that proposed by Sankara in the eighth century AD. We shall return to his Vedanta philosophy in Chapter 14. The school of Vedanta imparted a new vigour to the speculations of the philosophers of the forest that would give it an appeal a thousand years later.

The writings of the *Upanishads* did not reach Europe until 1771, when the French scholar Anquetil Duperron translated a Persian edition into French. In 1801, the *Upanishads* were also translated into Latin. These two translations obliterated the barrier caused by the Sanskrit language and made the material available to Western scholars. The Latin rendering was widely circulated and influenced scholars, especially in Germany. It introduced a new dimension into the whole discussion of philosophy.

The dominating philosophy of the nineteenth century was that of secular materialism. This theory regards matter, and with it time and space, as having absolute existence. This results in the Cartesian dualism in which matter is considered as distinct from the mind that comprehends it.

The philosopher Arthur Schopenhauer (1788-1860) was

influenced by the teaching of the *Upanishads* in his criticism of materialism as a philosophy. He argued that the fundamental absurdity of materialism lies in the fact that it starts from the 'objective' and takes it as the ultimate, irrespective of the need for a 'subjective'. Schopenhauer was dogmatic on the point that there is no object without a subject, and this renders all materialism as impossible.[11] However, Schopenhauer's ideas were to remain at the periphery of scientific thought in the nineteenth century.

Another person much influenced by the ideas of the *Upanishads* was the radical Madame Helena Blavatsky (1831-1891), who founded the 'Theosophical Society' in 1873. In her book, *Secret Doctrines*, Blavatsky proposed three fundamental propositions. First, there is an eternal, boundless principle that transcends the power of human conception. Second, the universality of the law of periodicity, or ebb and flow that is common to all aspects of life. The third principle is the fundamental identity of all souls with the universal oversoul.

Madame Blavatsky referred repeatedly in her book to the accumulated wisdom of the ancient seers of India. She held the view that the universe and everything in it is illusion—*maya*. This universe appears to be real only to the conscious beings who are as unreal as it is itself. Her idea of *maya* is not exactly the same as that of the Indian philosopher Sankara (see Chapter 14). To Sankara, the universe is *maya* in the sense that it gives us a distorted view of reality by making what is intrinsically one appear as many. To Blavatsky, it is *maya* because it is in flux. Although Blavatsky was influenced by the *Upanishads*, she interpreted their teaching in her own way.

Despite the fact that her life ended in scandal, with accusations of fraud, her influence was to continue into the twentieth century. Blavatsky's successor was Alice Bailey, who coined the phrase 'New Age', a phrase which recurs throughout her writings.[12] Her approach has encouraged many other Westerners to explore the philosophies of the *Upanishads*.

The monistic ideas of the philosophers of the forests of ancient India have come to many in the New Age movement as an intellectual revolution. Monism has provided a radically different way of understanding reality. It has come to challenge the very foundations of Western secular materialism.

Notes:

[1] R.E. Hume, *The Thirteen Principal Upanishads* (Oxford University Press: Delhi, 1990), p 394.

[2] Vivian Worthington, *A History of Yoga* (Arkana: London, 1982), p 13.

[3] A.L. Basham, *The Wonder That Was India* (Sidgwick & Jackson: London, 1988), pp 246–247.

[4] Wendy Doniger O'Flaherty, *The Rig Veda* (Penguin: Harmondsworth, 1981), p 137.

[5] Hume, *op cit*, p 107.

[6] Hume, *op cit*, pp 339–340.

[7] Hume, *op cit*, pp 247-248.

[8] Basham, *op cit*, p 251.

[9] Hume, *op cit*, pp 209–210.

[10] Hume, *op cit*, p 43.

[11] P.C. Mukhopadhyay, *Journey of the Upanishads to the West* (Firma KLM: Calcutta, 1987), pp 112–113.

[12] Russell Chandler, *Understanding the New Age* (Word Books: Milton Keynes, 1989), p 47.

CHAPTER 6

Karma and Reincarnation

'IF A MAN DIE will he live again?' It was Job who is first recorded as asking this innocent-looking question. Depending upon which answer is given, one is led into surprisingly different repercussions. Until recent years, the materialistic West would have been unanimous in giving the answer 'No', though Christians may have expressed their hope in a resurrection. The East would answer in the affirmative, expressing a fundamental belief in the reincarnation of the soul. However, a recent opinion poll has revealed that 27 per cent of British adults now believe in reincarnation.

The great assumption made by the Upanishadic sages was that the soul is immortal and eternal. Its connection with the world of matter is therefore only transient, and part of an endless cycle of existence known as *samsara*. The word *karma* comes from the root *kr*, meaning a deed or action, but it has subsequently come to have a broader meaning, referring both to actions and their consequences. The law of *karma* has come to be the fundamental assumption of nearly all Indian systems of moral philosophy.

THE ORIGIN OF THE IDEA OF *KARMA*

The source of the doctrine of *karma* lies hidden in the history of the peoples of the Indian subcontinent. Although the theory of rebirths does not appear in the *Vedas*, there is evidence that the people of this period believed that their ritual actions had consequences for those who had died. Several theories have been proposed as to how the doctrine may have emerged from the concepts found in the *Vedas*.

As Zaehner writes:

> In the *Rig-Veda* the soul of the dead is carried aloft by the fire-god, Agni, who consumes the material body at cremation, to the heavenly world where it disports itself with the gods in perfect, carefree bliss.[1]

The *Vedas* also give hints of a hell, described as a place of 'blind darkness'. In the *Brahmanas*, the notion of a judgement after death appears for the first time. The deeds of the dead are weighed in the balance. The dead are then rewarded or punished in accordance with the appropriateness of their actions.

In the *Vedas*, the term *karma* is used for a religious rite. It was believed that every sacrifice produces its appropriate results or 'fruit'. Thus, a ritual performed correctly produces the results for which it was instituted, but one performed incorrectly will bring about catastrophe. *Karma* means not only the sacrificial act, but also the act in general. *Karma* therefore comes to mean acts which have consequences whether good or bad.

A theory proposed by Radhakrishna traces *karma* to the concept of an eternal law, or *Rta*. *Rta* is the order pattern seen in nature with the movement of the planets and the agricultural cycle, but it also relates to the pattern of human conduct and sacrificial acts. The gods were charged with guarding and maintaining this sacred harmony which, as the moral order, provides for humans and gods alike the standards of right conduct. Although this concept changed to mean simply the correct performance of sacrificial ritual, it supplied the foundation for the development of the law of *karma*.

It has also been suggested that the *karma* doctrine is not of Aryan derivation at all, but was incorporated from the religion of the indigenous peoples. Obeyesekere agrees that the concept of rebirth was part of the religion of the tribes of the Ganges region. However, their idea of rebirth lacked what he calls 'ethicisation'—the imposition of religious assessment of moral actions.[2] With the development of ethical asceticism there was a mutual interaction with the tribal, non-ethical rebirth eschatology into the *karma* eschatology.

Discussion continues as to whether the doctrine was an Aryan import or borrowed in whole or in part from the indigenous people. However, as Aryan culture pressed further down the Ganges, it seems to have developed a more complex eschatology.

The first form of the doctrine of transmigration is given in the *Brhadaranyaka Upanishad*.

> The souls of those who have lived lives of sacrifice, charity and austerity, after certain obscure peregrinations, pass to the World of the Fathers, the paradise of Yama; thence, after a period of bliss, they go to the moon; from the moon they go to empty space, whence they pass to the air, and descend to earth in the rain. There they 'become food...and are offered again in the altar of fire which is man, to be born again in the fire of woman', while the unrighteous are reincarnated as worms, birds or insects.[3]

The *Brhadaranyaka Upanishad* is dated by most Western scholars at about 650 BC, which is a century before Pythagoras in Greece (born about 570 BC). Philosophers in both civilisations devised similar doctrines of transmigration. Greece, unlike India, never saw a general acceptance of the theory, and it remained no more than the interest of a small minority.

In India, the doctrine of *karma* initially appears to have been a closely guarded secret in the earliest period of the *Upanishads*. In the *Brihadaranyaka Upanishad*, the sage Yajnavalkya is asked by a friend what survives when the body is destroyed. He replies:

> 'Artabhaga, my dear, take my hand. We two only will know of this. This is not for us two (to speak of) in public.' The two went away and deliberated. What they said was *karma* (action). What they praised was *karma*. Verily, one becomes good by good actions, bad by bad actions. Thereupon Jaratkarava Artabhaga held his peace (BU 3:2:13).[4]

One of the most important discourses given by Yajnavalkya was made to King Janaka, in which he is said to have introduced the doctrine for the first time in public. In the discourse he introduces the similes of the caterpillar and the goldsmith.

> Now as caterpillar, when it has come to the end of a blade of grass, in taking the next step draws itself together towards it, just so this soul in taking the next step strikes down this body, dispels its ignorance, and draws itself together (for making the transition).
>
> As a goldsmith, taking a piece of gold, reduces it to another newer and more beautiful form, just so this soul, striking down this body and dispelling its ignorance, makes for itself another newer and more beautiful form like that either of the fathers, or of the Gandharvas, or of the gods, or of Prajapati, or of Brahma, or of other beings (4:4:3–4).[5]

Many of the sages, both the teachers and the wanderers, appear to have rapidly accepted the doctrine of transmigration. It was probably through them that the concept reached the wider public, and became universally accepted in the subcontinent.

THE MEANING OF *KARMA*

The meaning of *karma* continued to evolve from the ideas found in the *Upanishads* to become a complex and subtle concept at the heart of Hindu thought. To fully appreciate the theory we will have to see how it developed in later Hindu literature, and especially in the teaching of the *Bhagavad Gita*.

First, the law of *karma* presupposes that all wilful actions have consequences. It is sometimes loosely perceived as people being accountable for all their actions. In other words, what we sow, we must reap. In later Hinduism, as in the *Bhagavad Gita*, the formulation of the law becomes more astute. It relates specifically to actions that are performed with the aim of achieving some result, or which arise from desires that bring about the karmic effect. Actions which are performed in a disinterested way, and stem from no desire, have no karmic effects although they may have effects *per se*.

The *Bhagavad Gita* teaches that a person must perform his appointed duty (*dharma*) in a spirit of detachment.

> (But) work alone is your proper business, never the fruits: let not your motive be the fruit of works nor your attachment to (mere) worklessness (BhG 2:47).

This means that the law of *karma*, in the *Bhagavad Gita*, differs from the causal account of human actions. In the case of causality, an action has consequences simply because the action has been performed, irrespective of the attitude of the doer. *Karma* supposes an ideal of life which it is the first duty of a person to pursue. Although we cannot escape the law of *karma*, any more than we can escape the law of gravity, by careful judgement and forethought we can utilise *karma* to future advantage.

Second, actions performed in accordance with *dharma* have good consequences, while actions not in accordance with *dharma* have bad consequences. This assumes a sense of moral uniformity in the cosmic order because the same quality of the action is produced in the effect. There is, however, a debate in Indian philosophy as to whether the effect is already contained within, and emerges from, the cause, or whether the cause can bring about a quality that it does not contain.

However, this feature of the law accounts for the allied law of retribution, which requires that the guilty should suffer for their evil actions. As the law of *karma* cannot be violated, people will inevitably suffer for the evil which they have done, or be rewarded for their good deeds. The moral quality of any action is passed on in such a way as to affect the doer of the action at a subsequent time. According to the law of *karma*, a person's present circumstances are the result of past actions.

Deussen refers to the case of a blind person whom he met during his Indian tour.

> Not knowing that he had been blind from birth, I sympathised with him and asked by what unfortunate accident the loss of sight had come upon him. Immediately

and without showing any sign of bitterness, the answer was ready to his lips, 'By some crime committed in a former birth.'[6]

The law of *karma* grants equality to all beings. Even the caste system was determined by *karma*. As Surama Dasgupta writes:

> All life is equal; from the plant life to the highest, it is guided by the principles of rebirth and *karma*. By good or bad actions every individual could attain superior or inferior caste and status in life.[7]

In contrast, the Judeo-Christian penal theory makes a connection between evil deeds and punishment through the conscious intervention of an agent of punishment—God. According to this theory, not all our pain and suffering is deserved, but may come upon an individual as a result of the sinful behaviour of other people. For example, a baby may be killed through the reckless driving of a drunk person, but this is not perceived as resulting from any fault of the child. Evil and suffering results from the continued disobedience of humanity as a whole to their Creator.

Third, the manifestation of consequences are not necessarily immediate or in this life, but in some future life. In contrast, the theory of causation applies to two events that are conjoined by an immediate temporal relationship. This is absent in the law of *karma*, which states that the effects may be manifested at some time in the distant future. Reichenbach suggests that it is possible to distinguish two kinds of effects: *phalas* and *samskara* (not to be confused with *samsara*).[8]

Phalas includes all the immediate effects, visible and invisible, which actions produce. They are the results of any action. *Samskara*, on the other hand, is the invisible dispositions produced in the agent as a result of the action. *Samskara* is frequently likened to seeds which, though produced at a particular time, lie dormant until the appropriate conditions for germination occur. The law of causation speaks to the production of *phalas*, and the law of *karma* to the production of *samskara*.

This distinction made by Reichenbach is helpful in explaining some of the points mentioned above. For example, all actions have *phalas*, but only actions produced out of desire recoil on the doer of the action as *samskara*. In other words, actions performed out of greed tend to produce a greedy disposition, and actions performed out of love produce a loving disposition. It is reasonable to assume that actions produced from complete equanimity produce no disposition at all. Thus, the intentions that the person has in performing an action are preserved as a corresponding disposition to perform such actions.

According to the various schools of Indian philosophy, *karma* determines three things in future lives: caste (*jati*), length of life, and life experiences. Hindus see *karma* as a way of explaining the caste system. A person is born into a particular caste as the result of past lives and therefore it is his, or her, own fault. Western advocates of the *karma* doctrine have tried to separate *karma* from caste, but this is to take the doctrine out of its historical and social context.

Although the distinction between *phalas* and *samskara* is useful, one must be careful not to draw too sharp a distinction. The law of *karma* cannot be restricted to *samskara*. The very strength of the law of *karma* is that it links the pain and pleasure that we experience with cosmic conditions, and these conditions in turn are linked with the nature of actions performed.

Fourth, the consequences of karmic actions are accumulated in the sense that the tendencies get stronger and bear fruit. This may be illustrated as a pool of dispositions which has been filled by the previous actions of the person. A person may add to the pool by performing actions, either right or wrong, which are in character with the pool. The pool may also be drained by actualising the karmic residues already present, or by performing actions to counteract the karmic residues. Further, to be liberated, all good or bad *karma* must be exhausted—the pool emptied.

In general, the events that we experience have no unique connection with any particular, prior action, but with the pool as a whole. There are cases where particular misfortunes are linked with specific past actions. One such example is the explanation given by the Buddha for why a man called Moggallana was killed by a highwayman. It was said that in a previous life he was goaded by his wife to get rid of his blind parents. He did this by imitating the cry of a highwayman and slew them to achieve domestic harmony.[9] In these cases, the karmic residues must maintain a separate existence, to become the causal effect at some later date.

Although the 'karma pool' theory explains the misfortunes that come to us as a result of our own dispositions, it fails to explain those evils that are done to us which have nothing to do with our own disposition. For example, suppose my house is burned down by a forest fire ignited by lightning. What is the causal link between my previous actions and the karmic pool they created, and the lightning and the forest fire? It seems odd to say that I have a disposition to have my house burned down by a forest fire.

To resolve this, some groups, such as the Vaisesikas, speak of an invisible moral force (*adrsta*) that bears the merit or demerit of karmic actions. This moral force attaches to, and can be accumulated by, the *atman*. It is capable of having effects on the physical world outside the individual's body with which it is associated. In the example of the forest fire, *adrsta* would be causally efficacious in causing the forest fire. However, as *adrsta* is invisible, it is not subject to any empirical verification.

Fifth, the doctrine of *karma* developed historically alongside the allied doctrine of reincarnation. The law of *karma* presupposes that the human person can undergo a series of transmigrations, and is often compared to an ever-rolling wheel. In this way, the rewards or punishments of past deeds are manifest.

This view comes from passages such as that of the *Bhagavad Gita* where transmigration is referred to as changing a set of clothes.

> As a man casts off his worn-out clothes and takes on other new ones, so does the embodied (self) cast off its worn-out bodies and enters other new ones (BhG 2:22).

The concept of *samsara* raises some important questions.

What is the fundamental nature of the self? The major schools of Hindu philosophy differ widely in their understanding of this point. However, all assume the persistence of self as essentially consciousness or subject to conscious experiences. The self is essentially simple and unchanging, but in its empirical existence it is complex and undergoes many changes. The self is eternal and omnipresent, though it is limited by its association with successive bodies as it transmigrates.

How does the immaterial self acquire not only a new body, but one that is karmically proper? In the *Upanishads*, the working of *karma* in acquiring a body seems random. Once the transmigrating entity is joined with the plant as 'guest', rebirth is determined by which animals or humans consume that plant. To avoid a dependency on chance, some karmic residue must be assumed as stored in the transmigrating entity, which must cause some effects in the physical world. For example, certain animals and individuals are attracted to eat certain plants containing specific transmigrating entities.[10] This unsatisfactory conclusion has been the subject of considerable Hindu philosophical debate, resulting in various speculations.

This current existence is governed by the law of *karma*. To avoid the misery of an endless cycle of existence, there must be a means by which the law is transcended. This can only occur when we have exhausted our accumulated *karma*, and thus are free from desires, cravings, and passions. This, in turn, means that the ideal karmic state occurs when the sum total of one's karmic residues is zero.

How may this zero karmic state be achieved? It is generally assumed that this is achieved when acquired merit compensates for acquired demerit until one achieve zero *karma* state. The problem then becomes one of how to maintain this balanced zero *karma* state. According to the *Bhagavad Gita*, a person could do their *dharma* for duty's sake with no desires or feelings. Some schools of Buddhism suggest that one may transfer accumulated merit to others who are in need. Both alternatives lead to various problems, but primarily they stress an introspection that becomes self-defeating.

THE CASE FOR *KARMA*

As we have already seen, the law of *karma* is a basic assumption of all Indian systems of moral philosophy. By its very character it is beyond scientific analysis, and so it is only reasonable to ask by what arguments it has been advanced.

1. Inborn reactions

The process of transmigration is interpreted differently by the various schools of thought, but all agree that the *atman* does not migrate in a state of complete 'nudity'. Although the subtle body of transmigration is deprived of sense organs, there are a few basic features which are remembered. For example, from the time immediately after birth, humans have the instinct of sucking at the breast. This is not something that is learned in this present life, but that which the child had experienced in a previous life. Similarly, it can be argued that the fear of death is not something that has been experienced in this life, but the person remembers the death he has suffered in previous lives.

Western science has shown that such instinctive behaviour is inherent in all animals. Examples include the nest-building of birds, the hatching of eggs, as well as the sucking of mammals. Instinct is considered to be a genetically inherent part of every species. The lack of any factual information concerning the previous existence of a person has meant that science has generally discounted the concept of transmigration.

Some Hindu sects have developed techniques for recapturing past memories, but it is difficult to see how these may be proven in a manner satisfactory for objective analysis.

2. Difference of temperament and intelligence

This argument is based on the observation that children born of the same parents and brought up in the same atmosphere have different inclinations, intelligence, and even looks. Some people are quiet and solitary, while others are outgoing and friendly. The law of *karma* explains these different tendencies as due to different experiences in past lives.

These differences, however, can just as equally be explained in terms of the genetic laws of inheritance. Further, no child is brought up in exactly the same environment. A male child will be treated differently from a female one, and a first child differently from the second, third, or fourth. Although there may be differences within the members of a family, there may also be striking similarities which the argument neglects.

3. The unequal distribution of happiness and misfortune

We are all aware that some people are born rich, and some poor. Some people seem to acquire success and fortune with seemingly little effort, while others struggle and fail. Some are well fed every day of their lives, but others are hungry and suffer many sicknesses. This inequality has puzzled people throughout history. When the disciples saw the blind beggar they asked Jesus, 'Rabbi, who sinned, this man or his parents, that he was born blind?' (Jn 9:2).

The law of *karma* provides an answer to the mystery of suffering that has perplexed all people. It says that we are destined to happiness or sorrow by our own actions in the past, and nothing else. If this is the case, one would expect that the great men of the past would be born to even greater lives in the future. The world should therefore have many wise and moral people. In practice, one does not find a Buddha or Christ has been repeated in history. Supporters of the theory of *karma* may say that such persons pass away to another existence, but this will require another assumption which is equally difficult to prove.

In response to the disciples' question concerning the blind beggar, Jesus rejected their speculative theory (Jn 9:1–7). He considered it to be his duty and privilege, and theirs, to care for the blind man. Jesus healed him, and welcomed him into a personal relationship.

4. *Karma* theory encourages people to good actions in this life

This moral argument for the law of *karma* is based on the belief that one's present actions affect one's future state. Thus, by fulfilling one's *dharma* in this life, one can look forward to a better life in the future. People should be content with what they have because they, and they alone, are responsible for it.

By doing good they can look forward to better lives in the future.

Critics would argue that such an assumption is essentially selfish, and leads to a lack of concern for those who are suffering or disadvantaged in this life. The motive for the giving of charity never goes beyond detached benevolence. Only actions performed in a disinterested manner have no karmic effect, apart from their intrinsic effects. The command is to do your *dharma* with a holy indifference.

This leads to a question that has been much debated by Indian scholars as to what to do if you think your *dharma* is wrong. Suppose that by doing your *dharma* you hurt others. This is the key issue in the text of the *Bhagavad Gita* (see Chapter 10). Arjuna refuses to fight against his cousins, the Kauravas. Krishna's advice is the model for *dharma*: Do your duty. The person should concern himself with the deed, and not with either the moral issue or the results. A fire burns; the flame cannot be concerned about whether it cooks food or destroys lives.

If the law of *karma* is held to be irrevocable, there is no room for individual acts of mercy and forgiveness. Each cause would have its appropriate effect according to its deserts. Even God cannot intervene in human affairs to offer grace and forgiveness. What value is there then to religious observances, and especially petitionary prayer?

5. *Karma* gives respect for all life

If all animals and insects have that spiritual entity that we may call 'soul', then one must treat all life forms with ultimate respect. Not only will this demand an ecologically responsible behaviour, but will require that one avoids killing any animal or insect. This insistence upon total non-violence is taken further in Jainism than in other Indian religions. Jaina monks usually carry a feather duster to brush ants from their path to save them from being trampled underfoot. They will wear a veil to prevent minute living things in the air being inhaled and killed.

Shirley MacLaine takes the argument in a different direction when she says she finds comfort in thinking that a 'soul' may sometimes be born as male and at other times as female.

She considers that *karma* implies an equality of the sexes. In practice, the very opposite is true. *Karma*, as we have seen, is the philosophical explanation for the social inequalities within the caste system.

6. The problem of evil and the omnipotent God

A question which is often asked of Christianity is that if God is all-powerful and all-good, how can he allow evil in the world? He is either not totally good or not totally omnipotent. The law of *karma* removes any such problem for the Hindu devotee. God does not have to be the judge, nor may God even have an existence. You reap whatever you sow. The problem is essentially one for theistic religions.

A Christian would argue that a deity who is not concerned with the actions of his creation must be morally indifferent and emotionally distant. Such a god cannot therefore be a god of love. Judgement and love are joined together in the Christian concept of God, and this provides an answer to the willingness to allow evil to continue in his creation. One day judgement will come, and evil will be destroyed.

7. The value of yogic practice

The greatest truth of *karma* lies in the realm of the self, which we are building up by our thoughts, emotions and actions. Each of us constitutes a world by himself and is seldom conscious of the mystery he is carrying within. We move on like automaton, without being conscious of it, and respond with animal impulses to the happenings outside, without reflecting on them. But we can be alert and create ourselves anew and spin out an ideal and destiny for ourselves. This the supreme truth of the theory of *karma*.[11]

This argument may also be criticised as being focused upon selfish attainments. In reply, exponents would stress the widespread positive influence of yogic practice on societies and the world as a whole. While practitioners of yoga would consider that there is adequate proof, outsiders still remain very sceptical.

CONCLUSIONS

The difficulty of 'proving' the theory of *karma* and rebirths cannot be denied. *Karma* is an inherent intuition of Indian philosophy and, as with all such postulates, is beyond objective verification. As with all worldview themes, there must be the element of commitment that goes beyond simple logical analysis. *Karma* may appear untenable to scholars studying it from a secular perspective, but to those accepting the basic dogma, it provides a fundamental theme of Hindu philosophy. The importance placed upon this one tenet depends on how meaningful and relevant the whole Hindu worldview is considered to be. A person is therefore left with the question: Is the Hindu worldview more relevant than either the secular worldview or the theistic worldview of Christianity?

Notes:

[1] R.C. Zaehner, *Hinduism* (Oxford University Press: Oxford, 1966), p 57.

[2] Gananath Obeyesekere, 'The Rebirth Eschatology and Its Transformations: A Contribution to the Sociology of Early Buddhism', in O'Flaherty, *Karma and Rebirth in Classical Indian Tradition* (University of California Press: Berkeley, 1980), p 137.

[3] A.L. Basham, *The Wonder That Was India* (Sidgwick & Jackson: London, 1988), p 242.

[4] R.E. Hume, *The Thirteen Principal Upanishads* (Oxford University Press: Delhi, 1990), p 110.

[5] *Ibid*, p 140.

[6] M. Hiriyana, *Outlines of Indian Philosophy* (George Allen & Unwin: London, 1932), p 32.

[7] S. Dasgupta, *Development of Moral Philosophy in India* (Oriental Longmans: Bombay, 1961), p 211.

[8] B.R. Reichenbach, *The Law of Karma* (MacMillan: Minneapolis, 1990).

[9] *Ibid*, p 20.

[10] Wendy Doniger O'Flaherty, 'Karma and Rebirth in the Vedas and

Purana', in O'Flaherty, *Karma and Rebirth in Classical Indian Traditions* (University of California Press: Berkeley, 1980), pp 3–37.

[11] Dasgupta, *op cit*, p 224.

CHAPTER 7

A Way of Life

THE GENERAL HUM of the streets and towns of India suddenly drops. People gather in great numbers around the various televisions in the towns and villages. Everyone is eagerly awaiting the next instalment of the programme that has caught the attention of the people of India more than *Dallas* or *Dynasty* has done in the West. The story has been produced in ninety-four instalments of forty-minute programmes. This television marathon portrayed something of the immensity of the great Hindu literary epic called the *Mahabharata*.

Over the centuries, the *Mahabharata* has played an important role in the lives of the people of India. It has not only influenced the literature and art of India, but has moulded the very character and culture of the people. The characters of the story are household names and the incidents told represent an encyclopedia of social and moral lessons.

As the Indian scholar, Dr V.S. Sukthankar has written:

Whether we realize it or not, it remains a fact that we in India still stand under the spell of the *Mahabharata*. There is many a different strand that is woven in the thread of our civilization, reaching back into hoary antiquity. Amidst the deepest of them there is more than one that is drawn originally from the ancient Bharatavarsa and Sanskrit literature. And well in the

centre of this vast pile of Sanskrit literature stands this
monumental book of divine inspiration....[1]

As we have seen in previous chapters, the expansion of the
Vedic Aryans in the period between the eighth to fourth
centuries BC produced great social and political change. The
old social values were under threat and people were seeking to
establish a new way of life. The concept of *dharma* (duty)
spread through the Aryan communities in an attempt to bring
order into the newly forming society. The stories of the epics
provided a means of communicating a framework of values
and behaviour for a new way of life. The epics were recited at
public ceremonies, such as sacrifices. Story-tellers and writers
deliberately included regional customs in the local application
of the stories. The establishment of *dharma*, with an emphasis
on duty and truth, was a major aim of the authors of the
Mahabharata.

The *Mahabharata* can rightly claim to be the world's
largest epic. It is four times as large as its sister epic, the
Ramayana, eight times the joint length of the *Iliad* and the
Odyssey, and three and a half times the length of the Bible.
Traditionally, it is supposed to consist of 100,000 couplets, or
200,000 lines. There are, however, various editions of different length and emphases. The northern version, for example, contains 82,136 couplets, the southern 95,585, and the so-
called critical edition 73,900.[2]

The origin of the work is still a matter of controversy.
Traditionally, it is ascribed to Vyasa, who is presented both as
author and a character in the action. However, it is considered
impossible for a single author to have composed such a gigan-
tic work single-handed. In addition, the style varies consider-
ably, with contradictions and additions. It is therefore
generally considered that the *Mahabharata* developed over a
long period before reaching its present form.

The text has frequent references to Yavanas (Ionians)—the
Greeks who under Alexander the Great invaded India in 326
BC. The book cannot therefore be dated before the fourth
century. It is most likely that an early story of the Bharata
(Kuru) clan was elaborated with the account of the Pandava
brothers in the period 400 to 200 BC. During the period 200

BC to AD 200, the epic may have been rewritten with its present emphasis upon the god Krishna. There are indications that various additions were made to the story even after AD 200.

The main story of the *Mahabharata* serves as a string holding together numberless episodes, moral lessons, and legends. Stripped of its interpolations, the epic tells of the great civil war in the kingdom of the Kurus, in the region about the modern city of Delhi.

THE STORY OF THE *MAHABHARATA*

The *Mahabharata* is essentially a battle between duty and rebellion, between order and chaos. It deals with the dispute between two sections of the Kuru clan whose capital was at Hastinapur. The conflict arose over the right of succession to the throne. Dhrtarastra, the eldest son of the king, was born blind and so, according to custom, was not eligible to rule. His younger brother Pandu therefore became king, but he came under a curse that if he had sex he would die. He therefore gave up his kingdom and retired to the Himalayas as a hermit, leaving Dhrtarastra on the throne.

The two wives of Pandu did, however, conceive by supernatural means. His wife Kunti was given a *mantra* by a sage by which she conceived. Thus, all the sons of Pandu have quasi-divine origins. The sons of Pandu are known as the Pandavas, and are called Yudhisthira, Bhima, Arjuna, Nakula, and Sahadeva. When Pandu died, his 5 sons were still children, and were taken back to Hastinapur to be educated with the 100 sons of Dhrtarastra.

All the princes were educated by two Brahmins, Drona and Kripa, in the use of weapons. The five Pandavas soon became skilled in the use of the weapons, but it was Arjuna who excelled in every respect. As a result, the Pandavas became the focus of jealousy of the sons of Dhrtarastra. Duryodhana, the eldest of the Dhrtarastra, befriended a young man called Karna, who developed the skills of a warrior even though he was not thought to be of the warrior caste (Kshatriya).

While they were still completing their education, the blind king Dhrtarastra appointed Yudhisthira, the eldest of the Pandavas, as heir to the throne. The sons of Dhrtarastra, led by Duryodhana, resented the Pandavas and plotted against them. In one plot they attempted to kill them by setting a house on fire, but the Pandavas escaped and went to live in disguise. During this time, Arjuna won an archery competition, for which the prize was the beautiful princess Draupadi. She became the joint wife of all five brothers. It is at this time that they met Krishna, who was to become their great friend and helper.

The blind king called them back to their home country, and divided the kingdom between them and his own sons. The Pandavas built a new capital not far from what is now modern Delhi. However, this did not stop Duryodhana and his brother being jealous of the Pandavas. Duryodhana eventually invited the Pandavas to a great gambling match. He was helped by his uncle, who used loaded dice and so won every throw. Yudhisthira eventually lost not only his half of the kingdom, but his five brothers and their joint wife Draupadi. A dispute followed that led to a compromise in which all property was restored to the Pandavas.

There was a second great game in which the loser would be banished to the forest for twelve years, and would spend a year in hiding. Yudhisthira lost the second game as well. He and the other Pandavas, with their wife Draupadi, were banished for thirteen years. After the period of hiding, the Pandavas sent messages to the blind king demanding their kingdom be returned to them according to the promise. The sons of Dhrtarastra refused their claim, so both parties prepared for war. Both groups had many friends who gathered to their aid. Kings came from all over India, and even Greeks and Chinese took sides with one or other faction.

On the eve of the great battle, Arjuna, seeing the vast army and many of his relations about to fight him, was filled with remorse. He put down his weapons and turned to his charioteer, Krishna, for advice. It is the dialogue that occurred between them that forms the text of the *Bhagavad Gita*, and will be discussed in Chapter 10.

The battle lasted eighteen days, and resulted in the destruction of the huge armies. At last no important leader was left alive except the five Pandavas and Krishna. Yudhisthira was crowned king, and for many years he and his brothers ruled the kingdom in peace and prosperity. Finally, Yudhisthira renounced the throne and installed Pariksit, the grandson of Arjuna, in his place. The Pandavas, with Draupadi, set out on foot for the Himalayas where they climbed Mount Meru, the legendary centre of the world, and entered heaven.

The *Mahabharata* must be seen as the reworking of the Aryan way of life. The great battle of the epic is one that people would have liked to avoid, but they knew that it would lead to a new way of life for everyone. The old ways would end and something new would come in its place. The Pandavas represent the epitome of this new lifestyle, as they fulfilled their *dharma* despite all misfortune and cheating. Large numbers of people were killed on both sides, but a new and more dharmic way of life emerged.

The word *dharma* means more than is conveyed by the English word 'duty'. It includes discipline and the responsibilities of life that are considered essential for the support of the family and society. The application of Western ideas of 'good' or 'bad' to *dharma* is inappropriate as ethical associations do not apply. *Dharma* is that which must be performed. *Dharma* consists of sets of behaviour that apply to all creatures, including gods, demons, Brahmins and Untouchables. This is succinctly summed up by the *Mahabharata*:

> *Dharma* is that by which one is determined to act and by which all beings are sustained because they are determined by it.[3]

> Although pleasure and pain are transient, *dharma* is eternal. Therefore, one should not abjure *dharma*, whether for desire of pleasure, out of fear, avarice, or even if life itself is in danger. Life is essentially eternal and its objects, such as pleasure and pain, are transient.[4]

VARNA DHARMA

Already it has been noted that the words 'Hindu' and 'Hinduism' were given by foreigners to the people living on the other side of the Indus River. The people themselves refer to their religion as 'Sanatana-dharma', the ancient way of life. It is also called *varna-ashrama-dharma*, a term based upon the duties of a way of life founded on *varna* (caste or class) and *ashrama* (order of life). It is to these two important aspects of *varna* and *ashrama* that we now want to turn our attention.

Varna, or caste, is one of the few universals within Hinduism, but even this is being questioned by some today. First, it is necessary to distinguish between the four *varnas* and the many *jats* (see Figure 7.1). The *varnas* were the four hierarchically arranged divisions within Aryan society. At the head was the Brahmin, who was the teacher and priest, then the Kshatriya, the ruler and warrior, then the Vaishya, the merchant and peasant. The three higher *varnas* are known as 'twice born', the members of the Aryan élite. Finally in the social structure are the *Shudra*—the labourers. 'Untouchables' are outside the system altogether. The division of the various functions of the *varna* has tended to be ideal rather than real.

In a village one may not find all four *varnas*, but one will find several *jat*. A *varna* is better considered as a class or an estate, while a *jat* is a specific caste. A particular village may contain the following mix of households: three Brahmin, twelve Thakurs, twenty-four Kurmis, twelve Potters, five Camars (leather workers), and six Dhobi (washermen). The type and proportion of *jat* vary widely across India. The *varnas* therefore act as a universal reference map for the *jat* with regard to the various areas of India.

The key issue concerning caste is that a person is born into a particular *jat*. This ascribed social status is unchangeable in this life. As we have seen in Chapter 5, the doctrines of *samsara* and *karma* are basic assumptions of the Hindu worldview. *Samsara* is the cycle of birth and rebirth to which all souls are subject. *Karma* is the effect of previous deeds or actions. It is as a result of *karma* that a person is born as a bird, an animal, or a human being. As a human being, *karma* determines which caste you are born into. In Hindu thinking, it is impossible to separate the law of *karma* from the concept of caste, as the latter is the obvious outcome of the former. Western advocates of reincarnation have tried to make this separation because although *karma* appeals to them, they find the notion of caste obnoxious. However, this is to wrench an important aspect from an integrated philosophical system, and produce a system that is essentially inconsistent. To debate, as some Western young people have done, whether

Jat (caste)	Traditional occupation	Varna
Brahmin	Landowner & priests	Brahmin
Bhojki	Temple priests	
Rajput	Landowner & warriors	Kshatriya
Mahajan	Traders	Vaishya
Turkhan	Carpenters	Shudra
Lohar	Blacksmiths	(some may claim
Sonyar	Goldsmiths	to be higher
Nai	Barbers	caste)
Kumhar	Potters	
Girth	Cultivators	
Dumna	Basket-makers	
Chamar	Tanners	Untouchables
Bhangi	Sweepers	

Figure 7.1. Idealised Indian Social Categories

(The listing gives a sample of the various *jats* that may be found in an Indian village.)

Madonna is a reincarnation of Marilyn Monroe merely because they are blonde singers is to misunderstand the basis of *karma*.

Caste and kindred

A caste is a social group isolated from others due to concerns about purity and pollution. The two most important causes of pollution are considered to be touch and sexual intercourse. The caste system therefore gives means by which people retain their social distance within a wider social system. Caste may be characterised by three features.

First, separation, which reveals itself in two major aspects: endogamy, and food restrictions. With regard to endogamy, members of a particular *jat* will only marry their daughters to associated caste members. As marriages are arranged by parents, they ensure that the bride and groom are of the same caste and have a similar social status. With regard to food restrictions, castes will be restricted not only in the types of food they will eat, but also as to with whom they may eat. This is made visually obvious at feasts and festivals when different castes sit in separate groups.

The second characteristic concerns specialisation in respect of occupation and trade, by which a social group may remain distinct from others. For many centuries, sons have followed in the occupation of their fathers. Caste members should ideally follow the traditional calling of their caste, but changing economic circumstances have caused certain occupations to become redundant. As a result, certain castes have been obliged to turn to alternative occupations.

Certain occupations are regarded as ritually neutral with regard to pollution, and by far the most important in rural India is agriculture. In rural India, the greater proportion of the population is involved in farming to one degree or another. However, even here discrimination persists.

The specialisation is even seen in the arrangement of the village. The Brahmin families have their houses to the east to face the rising sun, while the low caste are grouped together on the west side. The middle class of artisans cluster together near the centre of the village.

Third, in all parts of India, the various castes form themselves into a hierarchy of local status and respectability. Certain crafts and occupations are regarded as essentially impure and hence are a source of pollution to higher castes. The hierarchy is confused by the fact that members of lower castes may become more wealthy than those of higher castes. Some writers have therefore sought to distinguish between secular and ritual status. The situation is, however, far from simple, as Professor Dumont seeks to describe:

> Unfortunately, there has sometimes been a tendency to obscure the issue by speaking of not only religious (or 'ritual') status, but also 'secular' (or 'social') status based upon power, wealth, etc. which Indians would also take into consideration. Naturally Indians do not confuse a rich man with a poor man, but as specialists seem to become increasingly aware, it is necessary to distinguish between two very different things: the scale of statuses (called 'religious') which I name hierarchy and which is absolutely distinct from the fact of power; and the distribution of power, economic and political, which is very important in practice but is distinct from, and subordinate to, hierarchy. It will be asked then how power and hierarchy are related to each other. Precisely, Indian society answers this question in a very explicit manner. Hierarchy culminates in the Brahmin, or priest: it is the Brahmin who consecrates the king's power, which otherwise depends entirely on force (this results from the dichotomy). From very early times, the relationships between Brahmin and the king or Kshatriya are fixed. While the Brahmin is spiritually or absolutely supreme, he is materially dependent; while the king is materially the master, he is spiritually subordinate.[5]

Dumont therefore accepts one scale of statuses that he calls a hierarchy, or ritual ranking, and another of social influence. The second is integrated within the hierarchial ranking of the *varnas*.

Finally, there is the characteristic of economic interdependency. The *jat* make up an interdependent system that serves the needs of the whole society. In practice, a Brahmin family will always get the pots they need from one potter family, and may act as priest to that particular family. The result is that a patron-client relationship develops. In some areas, this relationship is even used to support loans. However, with the growth of manufacturing industries and cash wages, the economic interdependency is diminishing.

Intra-caste relations

It is not only important to understand how castes relate to each other, but one must understand the implications of being a member of a caste. A local *jat* has a twofold function with regard to an individual member: to control and to conciliate. Caste membership requires the person to follow the rules and customs of the particular community. The caste rules are usually governed by an assembly of elders called *panchayat*. If there is no village *panchayat*, matters are dealt with either at an informal meeting or by common consent.

Whatever the method, caste control is rigorously enforced at the local level. This control is important so that the behaviour of a member does not damage the status of the caste as a whole. The *panchayat* is concerned not only with control, but also with social harmony. Where there is a dispute between fellow caste members, the *panchayat* will mediate.

For the individual, caste dictates his whole way of life.

> Thus the practice of caste dictates to each member customs to be observed in the matter of diet, the observance of ceremonial uncleanness, and whether he may, or may not marry or remarry a widow. It prescribes to some extent (or at least limits his choice of) ritual to be observed at birth, initiation, marriage and death. It may state, for instance, whether or not his ears shall be bored, and if so in how many places. With regards to the individual the function of caste is to predetermine his pattern of behaviour to a very considerable degree of nicety, leaving much less to individual choice than is usual in a casteless society.[6]

No individual can change his ritual status. The doctrines of *samsara* and *karma* require that an individual is born into a

caste appropriate to his past life actions. An individual growing up in an Indian village quite naturally acquires the way of
life of his family and caste. He will always eat, marry, and
behave in the manner prescribed by his caste. He will realise
that others behave in different ways according to their particular caste rules. Some castes he will consider more pure,
and superior to his own, but others he will look down upon as
polluting.

The conscious awareness of caste background is both universal and important in all areas of Indian society. The government has tried to deal with the disadvantages faced by
many 'Untouchables' by a practice of positive discrimination.
'Untouchables' gain certain preferences for university places,
but even so, many lower castes still complain of the discrimination which they experience in the colleges.

ASHRAMA DHARMA

Just as Aryan society was divided into distinct castes, the life
of an individual man was divided into four independent
orders, or *ashramas*. For a male, each *ashrama* brought its
own specific duties. In classical Hinduism, the *ashrama*
developed into distinct stages in a man's life.

Brahmacharya

Boys of the three upper *varnas* are initiated into the first stage
with the ritual of the sacred thread. The ceremony signifies a
second birth, and the initiates are called 'twice born'. This is a
very ancient ritual that goes back further than the time that
the Aryans entered India. A similar ritual was found among
the Zoroastrians of Iran. The ideal age for the ceremony varies
according to *varna*—eight for a Brahmin, eleven for a
Kshatriya, and twelve for a Vaishya.

This first stage is considered a student stage when the
Vedas and rituals are learned. Although the initiated boy is
still a minor, he has acquired the status of an Aryan and
should prepare himself in the knowledge of the ancient lore.
Today, few boys actually attend the traditional schools, pre-
ferring the Western schools that will enable them to gain the
qualifications necessary for future employment.

Grihastha

Today, it is considered that once a young man has gained skills and obtained a job, he should marry and enter the second stage. Getting married and having children is regarded as a sacred duty to continue the family. A householder is expected to celebrate festivals, offer hospitality, give charity, and look after aging parents.

Vanaprastha

The third stage is known as *vanaprastha-ashrama*, which literally means 'forest dwelling'. According to tradition, when a man's hair turns white, and he sees his grandchildren, he should become a hermit. He should hand over the running of the household and his business to his sons. He would then be free to leave his home and family to become a hermit devoted to religious pursuits. Generally, this practice has fallen into disuse, and is considered only as an ideal.

Sannyasin

Before death there is yet another stage, but this is optional and very few men enter it. One who does, as a very old man, leaves his hermitage and becomes a *sannyasin*. He will perform his own funeral rites and thereby renounce all ties with the world, his family, and his possessions. He takes to being a wandering holy man begging for food. He gives himself to meditation and yoga. When he dies, he is buried, because he has already himself performed the funeral rites of cremation.

The situation for a woman is markedly different than for a man. A woman, according to most traditions, is always a minor under the authority of a man. As a girl she is under the direction of her father, as a wife it is her husband, and as a widow her sons. The general view of women in the *Mahabharata* is that she should devote herself to her husband. 'She should devote herself to his service placing him higher than the gods.'[7]

Leslie, after her detailed study of the role of the Hindu woman, writes:

This devotion is described in two ways: serving and

obeying one's husband as one's guru: and worshipping him as one's only god. No other description could carry a greater weight of religious commitment and spiritual authority in the Hindu context than these.[8]

A wife should ideally follow her husband in death by lying with him on his funeral pyre. The practice of *sati* is now illegal, although cases do still occur.

This scheme of *ashrama-dharma* was never more than an ideal that few people would actually follow. However, it provided a framework around which people could structure their lives. The ancient religion that the Hindu calls *varna-ashrama-dharma* provided a pattern of duties and responsibilities for a distinctive way of life.

AIMS OF LIFE

Dharma provided a guide for the conduct of the Aryan people as they merged with the indigenous societies of the subcontinent. In addition to *dharma*, the Aryans accepted three other basic aims to life: *artha*, *kama*, and *moksha*.

Artha was the earning of money by honest means so that a man could provide for his family. A king, as head of state, was also required to follow patterns of specific behaviour to ensure that his kingdom would thrive.

Kama was the enjoyment of life. This included the sensual delights of sex, and led to the writing of books such as the *Kamasutra*. This book gives detailed instructions on erotic techniques, aphrodisiac recipes, and charms. The place of this book in the general context of the Hindu way of life has been lost on most Western readers, who tend to regard it as pornography.

Moksha is liberation from the cycle of successive births and deaths. This was mentioned in Chapter 5 in the context of the law of *karma*.

Hindu spirituality must never be considered separately from the way of life of the Hindu people. The religious diversity expresses itself in a complex social system. Although many religious ideas have been imported into the West, it is important to note those aspects that have not been advocated. Indian culture has been characterised by a rigid social system that has determined not only who one marries, but where one lives, and what occupation one follows.

As the Hindu scholar Balbir Singh writes in his book on *dharma*:

> When Draupadi questions the wisdom of her husband in following *dharma* in spite of the numerous hardships it caused, his only answer was that he did so not because of the expectation of recompense, but because his will had become irresistibly established in it. Since the ultimate truth we can so conceive of is *dharma* itself, man must make it the governing passion of his life if he wants to realize it in its fullness.[9]

Dharma produced a way of life in the eighteenth century that contained many things the British found repugnant. Zaehner writes in his classic text on Hinduism:

> Apart from the caste system, however, and the inhuman abuses it had given rise to, there were many other Hindu practices equally hallowed by *dharma* that would have been considered inhuman in most other parts of the globe, the encouragement of widows to sacrifice themselves on their husband's funeral pyre, the marriage of children long before they reached the age of puberty, enforced widowhood, and temple prostitution.[10]

Not surprisingly, many Christian missionaries could not remain silent in the face of such practices. Today, most Hindus realise the inhumanity of such practices and agree with the laws of the Indian state that forbid these acts. Many educated Hindus seek a *dharma* within their own consciences, but the social structure of *dharma* is still an integral part of Hindu life.

Western visitors, when they travel through India, are outside of this social system. They fail to appreciate the social pressures that the ordinary person faces. They do not realise the responsibilities of *dharma* that may often be neglected, but are always there as an ideal in the mind of every Hindu. Many Westerners in their search for spirituality have been like the magpie collecting gems from here and there. In the midst of this spiritual activity *dharma* has been rejected, and yet it is an integral part of Hindu spirituality.

Other aspects of Indian life that have been overlooked relate to the villages of India. There, in the poverty of the tens of thousands of villages scattered throughout the land, is found an amazing variety of religious belief and practice. It is to this subject that we must turn our attention.

Notes:

[1] V.S. Sukthankar, *On the Meaning of the Mahabharata* (Asiatic Society: Bombay, 1937), p 32.

[2] C.R. Deshpande, *Transmission of the Mahabharata Tradition* (Indian Institute of Advanced Study: Simla, 1978), p 3.

[3] Balbir Singh, *Dharma: Man, Religion and Society* (Arnold-Heinemann: New Delhi, 1981), p 33.

[4] *Ibid*, p 73.

[5] I. Dumont, *Homo Hierarchicus* (Paladin: London, 1972).

[6] J.H. Hutton, *Caste in India* (Cambridge University Press: Cambridge, 1946), p 98.

[7] Deshpande, *op cit*, p 90.

[8] I. Julia Leslie, *The Perfect Wife: The Orthodox Hindu Woman According to the Stridharmapaddhati of Tryambakayajvan* (Oxford University Press: Delhi, 1989), p 322.

[9] Singh, *op cit*, pp 73–74.

[10] R.C. Zaehner, *Hinduism* (Oxford University Press: Oxford, 1983), pp 148–149.

CHAPTER 8

Gods, Ghosts and Spirits

A LMOST 80 PER CENT of the population of India live in villages, and therefore it is not surprising that scholars have had a growing interest in the local expressions of religion. As Ursula Sharma comments, 'Anyone who studies Hinduism in its village context is liable to be more immediately impressed by the diversity of its local forms than by their unity.'[1]

This diversity of religious practice in the villages of India raises some major questions. First, some European scholars of the nineteenth century were much impressed by the philosophical aspects of Hinduism, and wished to down-play those elements of village practice that they found repugnant. The worship of crude stone images, sacrifice, and the suicide of widows appeared to conflict with the depth of philosophical speculation found in the *Upanishads* and other ancient writings. Christian church leaders also spoke of 'Hinduism' as the world's oldest religion, the most tolerant, and the most spiritual. To draw a distinction between what the European considers 'real Hinduism' and 'corrupt Hinduism', as found in village India, is a false way of studying the religious beliefs of any people.

As Simon Weightman writes:

> To use the word Hinduism is to perform an act of
> closure: that is to draw a circle round all the diverse
> phenomena and state that everything inside the circle

will be called Hinduism in contrast to the contents of other circles which might be called Buddhism or something else. Its place in this semantic field gives it an external definition. The ancient Hindus had no cause to set up such a semantic field. To do this is not to claim that the various elements enclosed within the circle coalesce to form some integrated whole or unity: it is simply to state that all these elements are compatible with the term Hinduism.[2]

A second question raised is: To what extent do these various aspects of religious life form any system? No universal analysis can be identified. The only possible way of presenting a representative picture is to attempt to identify broadly applicable patterns, although these may not be fully exemplified in every village. The world of the villagers of India is one also populated by spirits, ghosts, demons, witches, and magic. These things touch the reality of living in a small village, with all the personal struggles that may be encountered.

Why do things go wrong? What is the cause of suffering? Secular society considers misfortune to be a matter of probability, or the nebulous term 'an accident'. Westerners do not ask the fundamental question of 'why' the misfortune has occurred, but only 'how'. Philosophical Hinduism seeks to answer the question 'why' in terms of the law of *karma*. Although the villagers of India may accept *karma* as an explanation for other people's misfortune, for themselves there are causes that seem more real and relevant. A distinction is made between suffering that is humanly motivated and that from non-human agencies. Most typically, the former is attributed to sorcery, and the latter to capricious spirits outside human control.[3]

SPIRITUAL COSMOLOGY

All scholars who have studied village Hinduism have remarked on the bewildering array of village deities. Simon Weightman has proposed that these may be classed into four ranks.[4]

At the highest level there is a general belief in an absolute, impersonal Godhead, which is shared by villagers throughout the subcontinent. This reality is usually associated with the idea of Brahman, and often named Bhagvan (the Lord). There is almost no religious ritual directed to Bhagvan because Bhagvan is regarded as beyond reach. Fate is considered to be controlled by Bhagvan, but often the two are equated in the thinking of the villager.

At the second level is the supreme reality embodied and worshipped as the gods, the *devas*. These deities are the major gods of Hinduism that do the work of Bhagvan. They are pan-Indian deities (Siva, Rama, Krishna, Ganesa, Durga, and so on) whose stories are recorded in the great Sanskrit texts. The ceremonies and festivals of these gods are regular calendar rituals believed to be essential to preserve the social order.

Theoretically, individuals may choose to worship which-ever deity they will. This is a teaching known as *Ishtadeva*. Regarding the everyday life of the villagers, these second-level deities are not generally worshipped, as they are considered remote and preoccupied with running the universe. It is for this reason that people turn to the *devatas*.

At a third level are the regional gods, which Weightman calls *devatas* (godlings) or *gramadevatas* (guardian deities). O'Malley writes of them as follows:

> Taken all in all, the minor deities constitute a most extraordinary medley, being deified forces and natural phenomena, deified heroes and also blackguards, spirits of ancestors, spirits of both malevolent dead and the benevolent dead, spirits of different diseases etc. Some have no local habitation, image or symbol. Others may be represented by a stone, a lump of clay or a wooden post, or they may haunt trees, hills, rivers and rocks.[5]

Most of the *devatas* either have a specific function, or are associated with a particular group, and have the general func-tion of serving as guardians to the village. An important class of *devata* is the female spirits called *matas*. *Mata* means 'mother', and is an important cult throughout India. In the south, blood sacrifices are still offered to the mother goddess, who is often represented by a simple standing stone.

Finally, at the lowest level are the undomesticated demons and *bhut*. As with the *devatas*, these spirits are more local in character, and if pressed, villagers would say that they are 'our gods'. The general term for this variety of personalised, local spirits is *bhut* which literally means a 'being'. The primary distinction between *bhuts* and *devas* is that the *bhuts* are believed to have a direct and manifest action in the affairs of the village.

Any attempt to classify the vast army of *bhuts* is beset with difficulty, and notions about certain *bhuts* vary between localities. A particular name may be applied to different *bhuts* by neighbouring localities, or different names applied to the same *bhut*. In addition, ideas of human ghosts have merged with the belief in local demons and deities.

Village *bhut* tend to reflect the village social structure, with explicit caste distinction. Each *bhut* is the champion of his social group, and represents their ideal role in society at a spiritual level. The most powerful male *bhut* is the *brahm*, or brahman ghost, who can cause syphilis or leprosy. The people of a caste do not view their *bhut* as dangerous, impure or punitive, but honour him and the caste specialist who is possessed by the *bhut* at rituals.

POSSESSION

Before one can understand spirit possession within the Hindu context it is first necessary to attempt to appreciate the phenomenon of possession itself. Spirit possession embraces a wide range of phenomena. Even with an introductory reading of literature on possession in Hinduism, one sees a great variety of manifestations. It would be easy for the secular observer to classify some as psychiatric illnesses and others even as physical sicknesses. However, this is to miss the point. As Lewis writes, 'It is not thus for us to judge who is and who is not really possessed.'[6] If someone is, in their own cultural milieu, generally considered in a state of spirit possession, then he, or she, is possessed.

No matter how bizarre possession behaviour may seem to the outside observer, within the local culture it is a culturally normative experience. Possession must therefore be defined in the terms of the local community and not those of the Western observer. This is the general definition of possession that we will use.

Recent literature has continued to distinguish between trance and possession. Trance is considered as a state of altered consciousness, whereas possession is a culturally defined theory of trance and sickness. However, as Lewis has shown, trance and possession regularly occur in a similar context. Recent writers have therefore spoken of some forms of possession as an altered state of consciousness. Michael Harner, for example, has discussed the possession of the shaman in this way, and has argued for his social value as a healer.[7]

Within possession phenomena a distinction is often made between that which is regarded as related to a good or bad spirit by the local community. A more useful distinction can be made based on how the people involved regard the possession. Do the people consider the possession to be helpful or harmful for the society? All possession is considered dangerous, but some can be useful. Possession of a person by a ghost or spirit which results in illness is widespread in India, and is generally considered harmful. On the other hand, shamanistic healers—often called ojas in India—are possessed by a spirit in order to heal.

Allied with this distinction is the belief that possession may be either involuntary (uncontrolled) or voluntary (controlled). Involuntary possession is considered to cause harm and affliction, and it is often spontaneous. Voluntary possession is practised by the oja to attain the necessary power to heal.

AFFLICTION

We will turn first to the affliction that can be caused by a *bhut*. Certain places are reputed to be frequented by *bhut*, and the people who linger in their vicinity put themselves in great danger. *Bhut* are commonly found around graveyards, ancient ruins, empty old houses, caves, isolated fields, latrines, ponds, and rubbish pits. It can be seen that these are places of potential physical danger. A comparison is parents in Britain warning their children not to play in an abandoned house because it is unsafe.

Bhut are most likely to attack a person at night, or at

midday in the hot season.[8] These are times when a person does not normally move about. To do so demonstrates unusual or irregular behaviour which is likely to be charged with danger.

Many devices are prescribed in folklore to protect persons from *bhut*. These include amulets worn around the neck and arms, and black marks made on the forehead of small children. Protection from *bhut* is seldom perfect and many persons, particularly women, are believed to be possessed by these malignant spirits.

It is well known that the best protection against *bhut* is not to be afraid of them. 'It is believed that a *bhut* seldom takes forcible possession of anyone who does not fear it, or who does not believe in *bhuts*.'[9] Fear of *bhut* usually arises from a guilty conscience. When an individual first feels fear, then the *bhut* has gained power over him.

It is also believed that a *bhut* seeks vengeance on the family of the person who caused him, or her, trouble in life. It may 'live' in the family, causing death and misfortune. Possession is suspected if a series of misfortunes have befallen anyone, or there is doubt about the cause of sickness or death. Care is therefore taken to maintain social harmony. Thus, belief in the *bhut* may be considered as acting as an instrument of social control within the family and society.

There are various degrees in which *bhut* affliction is manifest. Sometimes an individual shows mild possession by behaving in an odd manner. Full possession results in trance, behaviour change, and glossolalia. The spirit is considered to 'ride' or 'adhere' to its victims.

The following account is an example of possession in Shanti Nagar, a village near Delhi.

> The first really noticeable symptoms of spirit possession were when Daya complained of feeling cold and began to shiver. She was moaning slightly and breathing hard. The mother-in-law and one of the daughters helped Daya lie down and piled about six quilts on her. She moaned and talked under the quilts; then she lost consciousness. The ghost had come.... When she began to return to semi-consciousness, she made a high wailing

sound which seemed to announce the presence of the ghost. The three relatives again had the girl sit up. The mother-in-law asked, 'Who are you?' The ghost replied, 'No one.' The relatives repeated the question, and then the ghost said, 'I am Chand Kor.' They asked the ghost what it wanted. The ghost said it would not leave until it had taken Daya with it.[10]

The most extreme forms of possession are described by villagers in north India by the Hindi verb *kheln*, which means 'to play'. The most noticeable sign of active possession is the rapid shaking of the hands from the wrist, which, according to Planalp, appears to be a culturally-patterned symbol of 'playing'. The possessed person often moves his, or her, head from side to side in a spasmodic manner. The *bhut* speaks through the victim, usually in a normal tone, but sometimes slower than normal and more hesitantly. After recovering, the possessed person remembers nothing of what occurred in the interim period.

Various methods of exorcism are employed by the villagers to expel the *bhut*. Most of the methods used involve shock and various hurtful activities. These may include beatings, pulling the hair, burning pig's dung, shouting insults, and dropping a concoction of mustard oil, chillies, and black pepper into the victim's eyes. One can understand that a *bhut* will hasten to find a more comfortable abode.

If the possessions continued, it would indicate that a permanent cure was beyond the power of the villagers, and so a healer would be called.

THE OJA

There are many different types of shamanistic healers, and they spread beyond the standard description given by Eliade as a person who experiences mystical flight during the healing rite.[11] Here we will use the term 'oja' to distinguish the broader identity of practitioners who give advice and heal by becoming possessed by a spiritual being.

In contrast to harmful possession, with the oja, possession is considered helpful by the society. Possession is controlled, and the oja can ask his particular spirit-helper to possess him whenever he desires. To achieve the state of possession, a certain amount of ritual usually has to be performed.

Many oja perform the ritual on regular occasions, most often once a week. The oja first bathes to become ritually pure. The spirit is then worshipped. This is followed by the performance of rituals, that vary in character across India. The oja may even drink large quantities of liquor or inhale the smoke of hemp while chanting endlessly. Finally, the spirit is asked to come upon the oja, who then goes into a trance. Frequently, the oja dresses in a manner characteristic of the spirit, and the spirit speaks through him to the gathered company.

The reasons why a person becomes an oja are many. A man usually receives a 'call', in a dream or a vision, in which a deity asks him to become his or her devotee and to treat people through his or her power. Often the person has suffered a long period of sickness before finally being cured by the particular deity. Others may take the role for profit, status, or family tradition, or a mixture of all motives.

A novice oja usually obtains the sponsorship of a practising oja, who becomes his guru. The novice worships the deities of his guru, learns *mantras*, and generally helps the guru.

The actual method of exorcism depends upon the particular oja. The possessed person is usually seated, and the oja squats in front of him or her. Sometimes he draws a circle or square on the ground, and moves his right hand slowly over the diagram. While doing so he will mutter *mantras* learned from his guru.

The oja requires an object for concentrating the possessing spirit. Many use cloves, which are broken in two and placed on the ground. The oja addresses the *bhut* in a polite but firm voice, and asks it to leave its victim. The *bhut*, speaking through its victim, usually requires an offering, such as some sweets, a garland of flowers, or a goat.

Some *bhut* are more stubborn than are others. If the *bhut* is reluctant to leave, possibly requiring a more substantial gift, the oja will cajole and bargain with the *bhut*. He may even cause his patient physical discomfort in order to make the spirit less comfortable within the person. Eventually, the *bhut* expresses its willingness to leave.

Sometimes the possessing *bhut* may pretend to be a *deva*. A skilled oja would find out the truth through his own spirits. The oja usually denies that he needs payment for his services. However, the oja's own spirit should be given a substantial gift to remove the *bhut* by force.

Although shamanism is focused upon healing rites, the oja may also take the role of an oracle and give advice. The spirit possessing the person is therefore able to communicate to members of the community. During a ritual, people come to ask advice of the deity. This tends to be for practical matters such as sickness or theft. The spirit then enters into dynamic discussion with the local people, giving pieces of moral advice with practical guidance.

The oracle is usually possessed by a local spirit and has certain idiosyncrasies. When the spirit possesses the person, he may perform distinctive acts. For example, in south India, the oracles may be carried while standing on the blades of two swords resting on the shoulders of a couple of men. During possession, the oracle has certain peculiarities, such as a change in voice, trembling body, and different bearing. The spirit will expect and be given the respect due to a *devata*.

EMBODIMENT

Possession by a *bhut* must be distinguished from a physical manifestation by *devas*. The former is more specifically possession, whereas the latter is regarded as embodiment or divinisation. Trance seldom occurs in this case, and the person, usually a guru, is regarded as the embodiment of the divinity.

Embodiment requires that at a certain time and place divinity may be perceived within the limits of a manifest form and, as such, becomes the focus of devotion. This immediately leads to the perplexing problem of how an infinite divinity may be restricted to the limits of a material form. For embodiment to occur, there needs to be the concentration of the entire cosmos into a particular image. Some scholars have therefore described this as a 'cosmic implosion'.[12]

The phenomenon of 'embodiment' is best considered with reference to both image worship and the divinisation of human beings. It must be remembered that this concept is complex, and care must be taken not to overgeneralise, as it involves a multitude of regional and historical variations.

It is more accurate to speak of 'image' rather than 'idol', as the material object is literally considered to become the image of the deity. Such an embodiment within an image is different from that of an incarnation or *avatar*, because it is a material entity which becomes divinity. As such, it is not considered merely a visual manifestation of deity, nor even a symbol of the deity, but the image actually becomes deity. The image therefore becomes the locus of the 'cosmic implosion'.

Hindu images are usually classed into aniconic and iconic. Iconic images are those that seek to represent the form or manifestation of the deity, such as an image of Rama. The manifestation is considered no different from the reality itself. The images can have fantastic forms with many heads and arms, with blue or vermilion colouring, and animal parts based upon Hindu mythology. As such, they are supposed to stretch the human imagination towards the divine by bringing earthly realities together in an unearthly way. These images may be regarded as visual theologies. Aniconic images, on the other hand, are those that have no such distinct form and may simply be a small standing stone.

The importance of images is exemplified within the *bhakti* tradition, where devotion is given to the image of the devotee's particular deity. It does not matter which deity the person follows, but the image itself serves as an instance of God's presence. The image will therefore be bathed, fed, and worshipped. This, in part, explains the devotional bathing of the image of Krishna that is performed by members of the Hare Krishna movement.[13]

Common sense would predict that some images will be less durable than others. Some images are therefore considered *nitya*, eternal manifestations, whereas others are *naimittika*, occasional embodiments. An image may also be considered to be dormant until 'revived' by ritual into the embodiment of the deity again. The divinity is considered to descend into the image at the request of the devotee and through the performances of the rituals.

When divine images are made, the eyes are frequently the final part to be carved or painted. Even after the spiritual life of the image is established, there is often a final ceremony of ritually opening up the eyes. When a devotee goes to the temple to 'see' the image, the aim is not only to see, but to be seen. The gaze of the image meets that of the worshipper, and that exchange of vision (*darsan*) lies at the heart of much Hindu worship.[14]

In the case of the embodiment of a human being, the deity is believed to become personified in an existing personality. Two examples of personages may be identified: the holy man, and the *sati*.

1. Saint (swami)

Sahajanand Swami (1781-1830) is worshipped by his followers as having been a manifestation of Krishna. It needs to be stressed that he is not considered to have been a vehicle for God's presence, but an actual embodiment of the supreme divinity. He both served divinity and embodied the very deity he served. The saint is considered 'eternal' in his divinisation, and so is viewed as the incarnation of deity by his followers. Another aspect of the idea of divinisation is that it may be transmitted to the devotees of the saint. In this sense, embodiment appears similar to Weber's concept of 'charisma'. This concept will be considered at greater length when the subject of the guru is discussed in Chapter 18.

2. Sati

Another path by which a human may become divinised is that of *sati*. Here, the very meritorious nature of the act is considered so great that the woman is divinised. The woman has chosen to become a deified eternal wife. Often people will build a shrine on the site of the burning.

The British colonial officers were also recipients of such honours. In the eyes of the villagers, they must have appeared as equal in power to the local *devata*. O'Malley tells the story of Captain Pole, who apparently was a great hunter and freed his district from the danger of tigers. After his death, both to propitiate his spirit and to invoke his continuing aid against wild animals, offerings were made at his tomb consisting of brandy and cigars.[15]

In conclusion, it must be stressed that possession and embodiment are important aspects of the life of the villagers of India, and cannot be overlooked as 'mere superstition'. They are as much a manifestation of the spirituality of India as is the teaching of the *Vedas* and *Upanishads*. The spiritual cosmology of the people provides at least a partial explanation of why things go wrong and how they may be dealt with. Another strategy is to be found in the heavens with the subject of astrology.

Notes

1 Ursula Sharma, 'The Problem of Village Hinduism: "Fragmentation" and integration', in Whitefield Foy (ed), *Man's Religious Quest* (Croom Helm: London, 1978), p 51.

2 Simon Weightman, *Hinduism in the Village Setting* (Open University Press: Milton Keynes, 1978), p 8.

3 L. Caplan, 'The popular culture of evil in urban south India', in David Parkin (ed), *The Anthropology of Evil* (Blackwell: Oxford, 1985), p 112.

4 Weightman, *op cit*, pp 26–36.

5 L.S. O'Malley, *Popular Hinduism* (Cambridge University Press: Cambridge, 1936), p 36.

6 I. Lewis, *Ecstatic Religion* (Routledge: London, 1989), p 40.

7 M. Harner, *The Way of the Shaman* (Bantam Books: Toronto, 1976).

8 J. Planalp, *Religious Life and Values in a North Indian Village* (University Microfilms: Ann Arbour, 1976), p 646.

9 *Ibid*, p 646.

10 A. Stanley and R.S. Freed, 'Spirit Possession as Illness in a North Indian Village', in J. Middleton, *Magic, Witchcraft and Curing* (Natural History Press: New York, 1967), p 297.

11 Mircea Eliade, *Shamanism* (Routledge & Kegan Paul: London, 1974).

12 J.P. Waghorne and N. Cutler, *Gods of Flesh: Gods of Stone* (Anima Books: Chambersburg, 1985).

13 W.H. Deadwyler, 'The Devotee and the Deity: Living a Personalistic Theology', in *ibid*, pp 69–88.

[14] Diana Eck, *Darsan: Seeing the Divine Image in India* (Anima Books: Chambersburg, 1985).

[15] O'Malley, *op cit*.

CHAPTER 9

Astrology

ONE ONLY HAS to walk through any town or village in India to be impressed by the numbers of astrologers. They sit in some shady corner of the market with their books and charts. The more renowned have their own consulting rooms, the walls of which are covered with charts and pictures of the various Hindu deities. The client sits before the astrologer as he builds up a horoscope and gives his advice. Astrology is part of the everyday life of the people of India. Before taking any important decision, the astrologer is consulted. He provides guidance for marriage, children, profession, and the crucial issues of life.

National newspapers include notices seeking to arrange marriage. Often there is a request for a horoscope, and in almost all cases the astrologer will be consulted before the marriage is agreed.

> An alliance invited from well settled Nair boys with good family background for a fair, beautiful, home-loving graduate, 23, Nair girl. Please apply with all particulars and horoscope. Box H, *Times of India*, Bombay.

To understand the role of astrology one must recognise the important polarity that exists within the thinking of most Hindus between auspicious and inauspicious. Times for carrying out particular undertakings are not considered to be of equal likelihood in producing a successful outcome. The time of an undertaking is therefore of crucial importance, and some method is needed to distinguish which times are auspicious and which are inauspicious. To determine an auspicious time for a particular undertaking, a person will turn to astrology or palmistry.

THE HISTORY OF ASTROLOGY

The history of astrology goes back far into the history of the human race. It seems that from these early times, humans have looked at the stars and sought for patterns and explanations of the movements. The discovery of astral omens is known to have been commonplace among the Chaldeans of the Babylonian empire before the Aryans entered the Indus valley. In the emerging civilisation of Babylonia, these ideas became formulated into increasingly elaborate systems of reference. In the period of the eighteenth to sixteenth centuries BC, a cuneiform text, *Enuma Anu Enlil*, was written, devoted to celestial omens.

To the Hebrew people in captivity, God spoke through the prophet Jeremiah in the sixth century BC:

> Do not learn the ways of the nations or be terrified by signs in the sky, though the nations are terrified by them (Jer 10:2).

These omens were common throughout the Assyrian empire in the seventh century BC, but they lost their popularity following the Persian invasion of the area. However, in the fourth century BC, several new texts were written in an attempt to find the correlations between celestial phenomena and terrestrial events. These ideas spread to the surrounding areas. A papyrus of lunar omens has been found in Egypt dated about 500 BC. A Greek text including much of the content of *Enuma Anu Enlil* has been found in the writings of a fourth-century BC Greek astronomer called Eudoxus of Cnidus.[1]

Although the history is still obscure, it appears that Greek mathematicians began to interpret Babylonian ideas in terms of Platonic and Aristotelian theories concerning the earth as the centre of the universe. The Greek philosophers assumed some correspondence between the macrocosm (universe) and the microcosm (humanity). The Greek astrologers adopted the Babylonian idea of dividing the orbit of the planets into twelve equal parts. These sections were to become the signs of the zodiac, with the names that are still common in the West today. Each of these signs was assumed to have a special relation to a part of the human body.

The planets revolve from west to east, and the zodiac appears to rotate daily about the earth in the opposite direction. Thus, from a given spot on the surface of the earth, the motion of the zodiac appears as a succession of signs rising one after the other above the eastern horizon. The Greek astrologers regarded the one that is the ascendant as the first place (or 'house'), the one following it as the second, and so forth. Knowing the time and place of birth of a person, the astrologer is then able to compute the localities of the seven planets with regard to the zodiac. This method of drafting a horoscope has been the general procedure since about 100 BC.

The first traces of Mesopotamian omen literature, including the material in *Enuma Anu Enlil*, spread to India some time in the fifth century BC. During this period, the Persian empire occupied much of the Indus valley.[2] Reference to these ideas is found in Buddhist texts of the period, and it is possible that Buddhist missionaries were instrumental in carrying this material to China, Japan, and southeast Asia.

Greek astrology was further transmitted to India in the second and third centuries AD by several Sanskrit translations of Greek texts. The best known text is *Yavanajataka*, made in about AD 150. It is therefore not surprising that the techniques of Indian astrology are not unlike those of ancient Greece. Several Greek loan words have become common in Sanskrit through astrology. As Basham writes, 'In the solar calendar the months are named after the signs of the zodiac, which are literal or nearly exact translations of their Greek originals.'[3]

While the astrological techniques were transferred quite readily, this was not so with the Greek philosophical principles. The Indians modified the system to take into account their ideas of caste, *karma*, and *dharma*. Some scholars believe that there may have been an earlier form of Indian astrology that divided the heavens into twenty-seven 'lunar houses' (*nakshatras*). The mixing of the various traditions led to an elaboration of the Hellenistic system that was eventually to make Indian astrology one of the most complex systems.

By the seventh century, the Syrian astronomer Severus Sebokht knew of the greatness of Indian astronomy and mathematics. Both Greek and Indian forms of astrology entered Islamic civilisation in the eighth and ninth centuries. The Muslim ruler of Baghdad employed an Indian astronomer, and many Sanskrit texts were translated into Arabic.

In India, astrology has traditionally been considered as originating from divine revelation or yogic insight. Indian interest in astronomy dates back at least to Vedic times, when the building of the sacrificial altar required astronomical information. This is not surprising as the Vedic gods are associated with astral deities. Agni, for example, is the god of the sun and fire.

Astrology has long been one of the branches of Vedic studies. The *Rg Veda* frequently describes days as 'auspicious'. This is not because some days in the calendar are better than others, but depends upon whether the gods choose to make a day auspicious.

> May Indra, Visnu, Varuna, Mitra, Agni, who do wonders, produce auspicious days (RgV 5:49:3).

Especially in the villages of India, there is an almost endless list of omens that are regarded as auspicious or inauspicious. For example, to have a vulture perch on the ridge-pole of your house is considered particularly calamitous.[4] I well remember our cook in India being shocked at a crow momentarily touching my wife's head. This he considered was very inauspicious, and he was therefore not surprised that soon after the incident we returned to UK because of sickness in the family.

Even today, all Hindu families, except the most Westernised, have an annual almanac. These are produced in vast numbers, and not only contain the phases of the moon and position of the stars, but auspicious and inauspicious times are specified. In recent times it has been concerning journeys that the question of the auspicious hour has become most important. Ellis Shaw tells the story of how he tried to help a sick man get to hospital for an operation. The man was a diabetic and was suffering from an unpleasant ulcer on his leg. Shaw offered to make the church car available to save him the difficult twenty-mile journey to hospital. The car was sent across in the afternoon, but the man refused to travel until 3 o'clock in the morning when the time for travel was auspicious. The ulcer required an operation from which the man died.[5]

Mainstream Indian astrology speaks of one or more original revelations, which were handed down from guru to disciple. Tantric astrology, on the other hand, claims that the revelation was given directly by Siva himself by yogic insight.[6] Dr Nemicandra Sastri has argued that this resulted from the Tantric concept of correspondence between the macrocosm and microcosm. 'As in the body, so in the universe.'[7] In other words, there are planets within the human body that are exactly like the planets of space. Tantric yoga gives knowledge of the planets within the body, and so whatever is discovered within must be equally applicable to the physical planets. Tantrism will be discussed further in Chapter 16.

Anthony Stone, after a detailed study, argues against the revelation model in preference for a historical 'growth model'.[8] From the early Vedic omens there was a mixing of zodiacal signs that produced an early system of astrology. Over a period, this developed into several complex systems, with detailed patterns for drafting horoscopes.

ASTROLOGY AND *KARMA*

The unique contribution of Indian thought to astrology is with regard to *karma*. This may well have been the reason astrology became so popular among Indian gurus. If the law of *karma* is so certain, then there may be ways in which its influences can be predicted. As we saw in Chapter 6, a person is born in a caste and state according to his, or her, *karma*. There is, therefore, a sense of fatalism when things happen. A life of good deeds will lead to good planetary influences in one's future birth. Consequently, astrology is a useful tool in gaining an insight into one's own life.

All the effects revealed by a chart are deemed to be the

results of one's *prarabdha* or past *Karma* that has begun to yield fruits. Hence these fruits of *Karma* constitute a person's nature, tendency and mental and physical peculiarities. However much man may try to get over these peculiarities, he finds that his efforts are no match for his 'nature' or destiny. For there is a debt that he owes to nature. In other words, man cannot fight shy of reaping the fruits of what he had sown previously, of which, no doubt, he is not presently aware. All relationships, good and bad, all ailments, severe and trivial, are the effects of debts due to nature.[9]

Once particular events of life are attributed to *karma*, it is a short step to the assumption that anyone predicting the future will naturally be thought of as revealing *karma*. The Sanskrit name for an astrologer means 'one who knows fate'. The adoption of the *karma* model of astrology leads logically to a problem. On the one hand, there is the issue of fate arising wholly from past *karma*, and on the other hand, there is the practice of choosing auspicious times. How may these two issues be reconciled?

The solution adopted by the Indian astrologers was to consider *karma* to be of two kinds, which may be called 'strong' and 'weak'. Strong *karma* is fixed by the birth horoscope. Weak *karma* may be modified by right actions. The *Vasantaraja* states:

> If a man relies on fate to deal with a snake, fire, poison, thorn etc., always leaving action far behind, he will not see much working of fate there! Intelligent men obtain their heart's desires by their own efforts. Those who rely on fate are like men who burn their feet in a forest fire.[10]

A common example given by astrologers is that of two seeds that are planted in the earth. They are planted in the same soil, given the same warmth and moisture, and yet they develop differently. Here the seed represents *karma*, and fate is the unseen cause that leads to the differing results from the same human effort.

A further issue resulting from *karma* is that a person does not have just one day of birth. Every rebirth will have its own horoscope. The question of whether a person had a first birth was discussed by Indian philosophers long ago. They concluded that there was no first birth. Each person therefore has an infinite number of past births.

ASTROLOGY AS SCIENCE

Throughout India, astrology is regarded as a science, at least in the mathematics of its predictive aspects. Young men study for several years in the university at Benares to graduate as astrologers. Others spend years learning astrological knowledge from gurus. For others, astrology is passed on from father to son over generations.

Celestial influence

Many theories have been proposed to explain the workings of astrology. One that has been most frequently advanced is that the heavenly bodies have a direct physical influence upon life on earth. This is a common theory in India. Astrologers usually believe that some particular deity has given them the power to understand this science and predict events.

In recent years, scientists have found many influences resulting from astronomical phenomena. For example, the eleven-year sunspot cycle coincides approximately with cycles in climate. Countries in the northern hemisphere show more than the average number of births in May and June, and less than the average in November and December.

Scientific tests made on astrological predictions have never been conclusive in their results.

> An American commission under the chairmanship of the astronomer Bart J. Fox of Harvard University, after having declared its readiness to test all cases submitted to them by astrologers, concluded that not a single one of the influences attributed to the stars by so-called serious astrologers could be demonstrated. Similar conclusions were reached by a Belgian committee, set up in 1949 by the Rector of Ghent University, which consisted of 30 reputable scientists belonging to various fields.[11]

Social role of astrologers

Western scholars have rejected any ideas of celestial influence, and have commented on the social role played by the astrologer in Indian society. He is like a family counsellor to whom one goes for advice and counsel. The Indian astrologer has time to listen to people, and allow them to express their feelings. In doing so, people come to see the issues in new ways. In this way, the astrologer plays a similar role to a Western psychiatrist.

The clients understand that there is usually a degree of ambiguity in all predictions, but they seek to apply relevant pieces of information to their situation. They recognise that the horoscope may not be fully correct, but the sheer fact of sharing the problem with another person lifts the emotional load. This itself is worth the cost of the consultation—for a labourer this may be two days' salary.

Most Indians build up a close relationship with their astrologer. Wealthy people may have several astrologers, each specialising in different subjects. For important decisions, it is not uncommon for people to visit another astrologer for a second opinion.

Synchronicity

Another explanation of astrology has been put forward by the Swiss psychologist Carl Jung (1875-1961). This model applies not only to astrology, but also the Chinese system of divination called 'I Ching'.[12] Jung proposed the idea that from the unconscious mind there may emerge knowledge that influences events. The classical example is that of one of his patients who was speaking of her dream about a golden scarab beetle. Almost immediately following this account, a very similar type of beetle flew into his office room. Jung's interpretation of the incident was that the patient's unconscious knowledge of the future controlled the content of the dream.

Jung recorded a study that was made on the horoscopes of 180 married couples. According to Jung:

> Marriage is a clear-cut fact, although its psychological content shows every conceivable variation. According to

the astrological view, it is precisely this fact of marriage that expresses itself markedly in the horoscopes.[13]

From the figures was derived a table of frequencies of married partners according to astrological conjunctions and opposition.

Jung concludes from these observations:

> An interesting point is the confirmation of the traditional astrological and alchemical correspondence between marriage and the moon-sun aspects... whereas there is no evidence of any emphasis on the Venus-Mars aspect.[14]

Even so, Jung has to acknowledge the randomness of the results:

> To a statistician, these numbers cannot be used to confirm anything, and so are valueless, because they are chance dispersions.[15]

Most Western psychologists now discount Jung's ideas of synchronicity, but it is important to see how this notion is becoming more accepted at a popular level in the West. The writings of Carl Jung are being reproduced in large numbers in a popular format. The scientific accreditation that is popularly given to the Jungian school of psychology is therefore promoting the wider acceptance of astrology and various methods of divination.

ASTROLOGY TODAY

In India, astrology remains firmly entrenched in the lives of the ordinary people. Chaudhuri, in his text on Hinduism, writes:

> In a Hindu, faith in his horoscope was far stronger than his faith in any god or goddess or even God, and this was evidenced in every act of his life. If a particular prediction in a horoscope came untrue that made no difference,

for it could always be explained away by assuming an error in giving the exact time of birth.[16]

Astrology remains of importance for every issue of life, whether it is buying a car, marrying a daughter, or offering a Vedic sacrifice.

In the West, Newtonian physics advocated against the theories of astrology, and astrology generally fell into disrepute. However, there have always been a few who continued to practise astrology, capitalising on an air of mystery. One of the most important European astrologers was Michel Nostradamus, a Frenchman of the sixteenth century. His most celebrated work was published in 1555, and consists of 10 sections, each with 100 parts. The language is strange and obscure, with an ambiguity that characterises much of astrology. According to his followers, he predicted such events as the rise to power of Napoleon, the League of Nations, and the invention of submarines. In recent years his writings have gained a new popularity.

With the growing Western interest in Hindu thought, the Indian system of astrology has grown in popularity in the West, along with other systems of astrology. In 1990, a survey of British adults showed that a quarter dismissed astrology as 'complete nonsense'. Two-fifths thought that it was a 'bit of fun, and something rings true', and one in five said 'there might be something in it'. However, over half said they had looked at a horoscope in the past seven days, and only one in six said they never looked at horoscopes.[17]

	Men %	Women %	All %
'I believe in astrology'	7	14	11
'There's something in it'	15	25	20
'It's a bit of fun'	34	44	39
'It's complete nonsense'	37	14	25
'Don't know'	7	3	5

With the emergence of the New Age movement, there has been a renewed interest in divinatory methods such as astrology. This is not merely a renewal of interest in ancient techniques. The practitioners claim that astrology is a help for the realisation of a person's spirituality.

Notes:

[1] *Encyclopaedia Britannica*, vol 2, p 221.

[2] See Esther 1:1–2.

[3] A.L. Basham, *The Wonder That Was India* (Sidgwick & Jackson: London, 1988), p 493.

[4] Simon Weightman, *Hinduism in the Village Setting* (Open University Press: Milton Keynes, 1978), p 37.

[5] Ellis O. Shaw, *Rural Hinduism: Some Observations and Experiences* (CLS: Madras, 1986), p 36.

[6] Anthony P. Stone, *Hindu Astrology: myths, symbols and realities* (Select Books: New Delhi, 1981), p 132.

[7] *Ibid*, p 142.

[8] *Ibid*, pp 145–154.

[9] Ramakrishna Bhat, *Fundamentals of Astrology* (Motilal Banarsidass: Delhi, 1967), p 201.

[10] Stone, *op cit*, p 121.

[11] R. Lewinsohn, *Prophet and Prediction* (Secker & Warburg: London, 1958).

[12] C.G. Jung, *Psychology and the East* (Ark: London, 1978).

[13] C.G. Jung, *Synchronicity: An Acausal Connecting Principle* (Ark: London, 1987), p 61.

[14] *Ibid*, p 72.

[15] *Ibid*, p 68.

[16] Nirad C. Chaudhuri, *Hinduism* (Oxford University Press: Oxford, 1979), p 202.

[17] Peter Brierley, *Act on the Fact* (MARC: London, 1992), p 13.

CHAPTER 10

The Song of the Lord

THE 'SONG OF the Lord' (*Bhagavad Gita*) is the most well known of the religious texts of India. Translations of the *Gita* are widely available in most Western bookshops, and it is the only Hindu text that most Westerners read. It is frequently a text assigned for reading by the school curriculum for Religious Education. Recently, my teenage son came home from school telling of how his teacher had read portions of the *Gita* to his class in their form period.

The *Bhagavad Gita* makes up the last part of the great *Mahabharata* that we considered in Chapter 7. The main story of the *Mahabharata* is usually dated about 200 BC. The *Bhagavad Gita*, however, is generally regarded as a later interpolation dated between the second and fifth century AD. The *Bhagavad Gita* is not an easy text to interpret, but it may conveniently be divided into three parts. The first, Chapters 1 to 6, deals with the different ways in which a soul may attain liberation. The second deals with the nature of God, and ends with a great vision of deity in chapter 11. The third part introduces teaching of a god of love who seeks devotion. This latter theme was at the time of composition a new religious idea for Hindu thought.

To understand the teaching of the *Bhagavad Gita* it is necessary to place the text in its dramatic context of the *Mahabharata*. Arjuna, the leader of the Pandava army, is about to do battle with the Kaurava clan. He sees many of his family and friends on both sides of the battle, and realises that many will soon die in the conflict. Should he fight? As he lays down his weapons, it is his charioteer, Krishna, who answers him. Krishna is later revealed as a manifestation of the supreme being. The dialogue that takes place between Arjuna and Krishna makes up the major part of the text, and its purpose is to show that Arjuna must fight. This aim is not lost throughout the text, but in the discussion many deep issues concerning the nature of man and God are considered.

A SYNTHESIS OF RELIGIOUS THOUGHT

In the previous chapters we have followed the development of the two great streams of Indian thought. The first was theistic, with ideas of deity stemming from nature gods such as Agni and Indra. Within this system, the Brahminic priesthood performed the many elaborate sacrifices. In time, the focus moved from the deities to the sacrificial rites themselves, and with this shift came the increasing domination of the Brahmins.

The reaction to this domination of the priesthood appears to have led to more speculative thought, as found in the *Upanishads*. This impersonal trend was the second stream, fostered by a dissatisfaction with what were regarded as the mere externals of religion. This stream resulted in the development of many great philosophical concepts, such as *karma*, *samsara*, and *atman*. Within the *Upanishads*, a direct association is made between the *atman* and the basic principle of the universe, the supreme self.

In contrast, the theistic trend continued as part of popular religion. No record remains of such popular cults that the *Bhagavad Gita* presupposes. However, these cults appear to have been moving towards some ill-defined form of monotheism. The old gods of the *Vedas* appear to fade away, and Vishnu and Siva begin to be perceived as supreme deity.

The blending of these impersonal and personal trends within the *Bhagavad Gita* has led many scholars to speak of the occurrence of one or more radical revisions of the original *Bhagavad Gita* text. Worthington considers the text to be a brilliant synthesis of Hindu religious thought.

In the *Bhagavad Gita* we see Indian capacity for synthesis at its most inspired. In eighteen brief chapters is displayed a kaleidoscopic mingling of the two streams that over a thousand years have been contending for the Indian mind.[1]

Basham argues for three 'strata of the *Bhagavad Gita*'. The first 'main tenor being philosophical, explaining the nature of the cosmos and the higher state, referred to generally as Brahman'.[2]

According to Basham, the second stratum of the *Bhagavad Gita* introduces many ideas that are important to later Hindu thought: the doctrine of the three *gunas*, yoga, and the mystical impersonal absolute Brahman. In contrast, the third stratum is thoroughly theistic, and is spread throughout the earlier text. It is in this stratum that Krishna becomes the incarnation of Vishnu, and the *bhakti* doctrine of devotion to God is developed. 'It is the work of a literary genius,' writes Basham, 'who infused the rather pedestrian verses of much of the second stratum with a new life, intense and moving.'[3]

In the third stratum, Krishna, the friend and advisor of the Pandavas, is portrayed as the incarnation of Vishnu, the supreme deity. As God, Krishna underlies all things, including the impersonal Brahman of the second stratum of text. Once this point has been accepted, it is evident that the words of the *Bhagavad Gita* are not merely those of a god, but of the supreme reality. Thus, the followers of Vishnu (Vaisnavas) would accord the *Bhagavad Gita* even more respect than the *Vedas*.

Basham's theory of three stratum would explain some of the ambiguity and even contradictions which appear within the text. However, this synthesis of ideas is not considered by Hindus as a hindrance, but in practice to be its very strength and value because the ideas are increasing revelations. This illustrates how the Indian mind takes up new ideas, but does not need to lose the old. It does not flee from what might seem to be incoherencies, as does the Western mind which prefers logic and rationality, but it almost delights in the variety. Great truths, it would be argued, cannot be reduced to simple philosophical analysis.

THE NATURE OF GOD

The *Oxford English Dictionary* defines theism as, 'belief in the existence of a god supernaturally revealed to man and sustaining a personal relation to his creatures'. However, it must be remembered that this definition has been formulated from a Judeo-Christian context. One must be careful how the word is used when considering the Hindu perception of deity, as we shall see.

The pinnacle of the revelation of the *Bhagavad Gita* is found in chapter 11. At this point Arjuna asks if Krishna will reveal himself in his supreme form. Krishna gives him a 'celestial eye' with which he may behold his transfiguration (vv 5–11). Parallels may be drawn between the vision of Krishna and that seen by the apostle John of the resurrected Lord Jesus Christ.

The rest of the chapter is a vision of this supreme form of Krishna, revealed as the absolute. He appears with many mouths and eyes, carrying the symbols of all the gods, facing in all directions. The light was that of a thousand suns, and the whole world was united in the body of the ultimate deity. Arjuna is filled with awe at what he sees and breaks forth into a hymn of praise (vv 36–49).

The *Bhagavad Gita* reveals the supreme deity as having many transcendent qualities. Deity is the highest person (11:3), the great lord of power and the skilful use of it (11:9), god of gods (11:13), monarch universal (11:16), incomprehensible (11:17, 42), imperishable (11:18), changeless (11:18), beginning-middle-end (11:19), awesome (11:21), eternal (11:32). Deity is revealed as a god who is far above humanity and does not depend upon humans for sacrifices, as do the Vedic deities.

Not least among the attributes of deity are those of his ethical perfection. He is without fault (5:19), strictly impartial (9:29), and 'guardian of eternal law' (11:18). Besides righteousness, love is another important attribute. He is the 'friend of all contingent beings' (5:29). This great deity returns love to those who love him.

> In whatever way (devoted) men approach Me, in that same way do I return their love (BhG 4:11).

When Krishna reveals himself to Arjuna as the supreme being, Arjuna falls to the ground in terror, unable to bear the awful splendour. Krishna declares his love for Arjuna (18:64), and assumes the human form again. Love is a quality of personhood. The concept of a god who can love and delights to be loved is a theme that is presented in the *Bhagavad Gita*, and later becomes more fully developed within the *bhakti* tradition.

The deity described by the *Bhagavad Gita* is one who in his transcendent nature is supreme, majestic, and all-powerful. In this form he is also unknowable, as he passes the bounds of human thought and imagination. He is, however, a deity revealing those qualities characteristic of personhood. He is concerned about creation, and wishes to communicate to humanity, in this case as Krishna the charioteer. He is revealed not as some impersonal ethical force, but as one who is righteous and loving.

Chaudhuri summarises the teaching as follows:

> This God was omnipotent, omniscient, all-pervading, and yet not an abstraction. He was personal and even more than that: he was full God as well as full man.[4]

One of the most important new doctrines of the *Bhagavad Gita* is that of the *avatar*. An *avatar* is a descent, a coming-down, from the prefix *ava*, down, and the verb *tr*, to cross over.

> The *Avatar* is an appearance of any deity on earth, or descent from heaven, but it is applied especially to the descents or appearances of Vishnu.[5]

The manifestations of Vishnu first appear clearly in the *Mahabharata*, although the word *avatar* is not used. There is, however, no question about whether Krishna really is an *avatar*. In the great vision of the transfigured Krishna he is twice hailed 'O Vishnu'. The supreme deity is here revealing himself to humanity by taking on a material form. In this case he is taking the form of Arjuna's charioteer, Krishna, who appears as a normal human being who has been reborn many times (BhG 4:5).

The clearest statement of the *avatar* teaching in the *Bhagavad Gita* is found in 4:7–8.

> For whenever the law of righteousness withers away and lawlessness arises, then do I generate Myself (on earth). For the protection of the good, for the destruction of evil-doers, for the setting up of the law of righteousness I come into being age after age.

The *Bhagavad Gita* suggests, first, that deity has incarnated himself repeatedly with different forms. The Vaisnava tradition to which the *Bhagavad Gita* traditionally belongs usually recognises ten such *avatars*, as we shall see in Chapter 11, which follows. In contrast, Christianity knows of only one divine incarnation. Another difference is that the second Person of the Trinity, having taken human form, was crucified. Later Jesus Christ rose from the dead and ascended into heaven, but he has not discarded his human nature.

Second, Krishna identifies himself with the divine nature that stands behind the human form.

> For that a human form I have assumed fools scorn Me, knowing nothing of my higher state—great Lord of contingent being.

The *avatars* must be distinguished from the gods (*deva*, *sura*). Gods are higher beings, more akin to angelic creatures of Christianity and Islam. The *avatars*, on the other hand, are tangible manifestations of the supreme reality.

Third, deity incarnates himself to protect the established order. Deity takes material forms to re-establish *dharma* (righteousness) when *adharma* (lawlessness) is dominating. Usually this intervention results from some demonic disruption to the balance of the world order.

The parallels between the concept of *avatar* and that of the incarnation of Christ have led some to ask whether this teaching emerged as a result of contact with Christians.[6] Although this may be a possibility, there is no clear evidence. However, major differences are found between the theistic ideas of the *Bhagavad Gita* and the Bible, which are seen when one especially looks at the relationship of deity with creation.

Christianity teaches that God created the cosmos ex nihilo—out of nothing. In other words, there is a basic dualism with the existence of an eternal deity, and a created cosmos that includes the material world. The *Bhagavad Gita*, on the other hand, accepts the general position of the *Upanishads* that the cosmos constitutes a part, or limitation, of the supreme reality.

> Know too that (all) states of being whether they be of (nature's constituent) goodness, passion, or darkness proceed from Me; but I am not in them, they are in Me (BhG 7:12).

The process of creation is explained by Krishna as one of expansion and dissolution.

> All contingent beings pour into material Nature which is mine when a world-aeon comes to an end; and then again when (another) aeon starts, I emanate them forth.
> Subduing my own material Nature ever again I emanate this whole host of beings—powerless (themselves), from Nature comes the power (BhG 9:7–8).

It is necessary to recognise the two 'natures' of Krishna. The material nature (*prakrti*) is that of the world of experience, while the higher nature is that aspect of deity which keeps the world in being.

> In one of His natures, He is *prakrti*; in the other, He is the all pervading life-principle, i.e., on the one hand He is the material cause of the world, and on the other its instrumental cause. When therefore He creates out of *prakrti*, He is really only creating out of Himself.[7]

Although deity is the material basis of the universe which is itself a part of him, he in no way loses his transcendence. He is 'higher' than the world and it is pervaded by him. Even so, he is different from the material world. The embodiment of deity is an important concept within Indian thought, as we saw with the role of images in Chapter 8.

> In conclusion, we may say that the Deity as revealed in the *Bhagavad Gita* appears to be one who, though in His transcendent aspect He is essentially unknown, is revealed in His relation to the universe as Supreme Self or Person, possessed of wonderful powers and excellences. All that exists, matter and souls, form part of Him, and He in one aspect of Himself brings them into existence, pervades, governs and withdraws them into Himself.[8]

THE NATURE OF HUMANITY

There is considerable ambiguity in the *Bhagavad Gita* concerning the individual self (*atman*). The teaching of *karma* and reincarnation, discussed in Chapter 6, remain as foundation doctrines.

In response to Arjuna's declaration that he will not fight, Krishna teaches that the *atman* is indestructible. It does not die when the body is killed but transmigrates from body to body until it achieves final release.

> As a man casts off his worn-out clothes and takes on other new ones, so does the embodied (self) cast off its worn-out bodies and enters other new ones (BhG 2:22).

The permanent and essential element in all individuals is the one universal reality.

> Finite, they say, are these (our) bodies (indwelt) by an eternal embodied (self)—(for this self is) indestructible, incommensurable. Fight then, scion of Bharata (BhG 2:18).

Consequently, release is achieved when it is believed that no self exists in the body apart from the one universal self. The experience of individuality, suffering, activity, and change that seems to demand the existence of an individual self different from the permanent self is explained as due to the body.

> Material Nature, they say, is (itself) the cause of cause, effect, and agency, while 'person' is said to be the cause in the experience of pleasure and of pain.
> For 'person' is lodged in material Nature, experiencing the 'constituents' that arise from it; because he attaches himself to these he comes to birth in good and evil wombs (BhG 13:20–21).

Attachment to the body is the issue that causes rebirth into the material world. Knowledge andd conttrol are the prime means of winning release from the bonds of the body.

Besides this strict monistic view, one can also identify those passages in the *Bhagavad Gita* which suggest that the individual self is distinct from the supreme self. This is especially seen in those passages speaking of the rewards of loving devotion.

> However evil a man's livelihood may be, let him but worship Me with love and serve no other, then shall he be reckoned among the good indeed, for his resolve is right (BhG 9:30).

The doctrine of loving devotion to God is an important new doctrine in the *Bhagavad Gita*. The word used is *bhakti*, and means loyalty or devotion. A Vaisnava devotee often refers to God as 'Bhagavan', which is generally translated into English as 'Lord'.

By *bhakti*, the devotee may be assured of receiving God's grace. *Bhakti* does not require the costly sacrifices characteristic of the Brahminical rituals, nor the severe discipline of the yogi. *Bhakti* provides an alternative path to an advanced spiritual state. It usually involves long and frequent recitation of the name of God, as is practised, for example, by the Hare Krishna movement. However, *bhakti* is more than this as it requires of the devotee a constant consciousness and love of God.

The strict law of *karma*, with the slim hope of release (*moksha*), must have appeared impossible for most people.

Bhakti marked an important stage in the evolution of Indian religious ideas. The *Bhagavad Gita* tells us that even if a man of evil conduct devotes himself to Krishna alone, he will go to eternal rest. The Shudras and women have no right even to hear the *Vedas*, nor perform the rituals of the Brahmins, but they are free to develop an attitude of *bhakti* towards God.

> For whosoever makes Me his haven, base-born though he may be, yes, women too and artisans, even serfs, theirs it is to tread the highest way.
> How much more, then, Brahmans pure-and-good, and royal seers who know devoted love. Since your lot has fallen in this world, impermanent and joyless, commune with Me in love.
> On Me your mind, on Me your loving-service, for Me your sacrifice, to Me be your prostrations: now that you have thus integrated self, your striving bent on Me, to Me you will (surely) come (BhG 9:32–34).[9]

The great message of the *Bhagavad Gita* is the union of human beings with God.

The process of syncretism which so characterises the *Bhagavad Gita* results in broad religious tolerance. Krishna points out that the supreme being does not try to draw everyone to himself. He permits, and, in fact, takes delight in the many ways and illusions of mankind, and approves of every faith and creed.

> If any worshipper do reverence with faith
>   to any god whatever,
> I make his faith firm,
>   and in that faith he reverences his god,
> and gains his desire,
>   for it is I who bestow them (BhG 7:21–22).

Such religious tolerance allows a wide variety of religious belief and expression within the Hindu religious quest. Many people from the West have been attracted to this aspect of Hinduism in reaction to the bigotry and dogmatism they have seen within other major religions of the world. It must, however, be realised that this tolerance is only possible because humanity is seen as wrapped in *maya* (illusion).

THE ROLE OF THE *GITA* IN HINDU SPIRITUALITY

Historically, the *Bhagavad Gita* has played a pivotal role in the development of the theistic trend.

First, the *Bhagavad Gita* expresses an idea of deity that is both monotheistic and possesses the highest imaginable qualities of excellence. This has been the source of attraction for many Westerners, because the concept of deity compares with the highest revelations within Christian teaching, but without the moral restraints of the latter.

Second, the Vedic gods were generally perceived as nature deities requiring material tributes from humanity. The *Bhagavad Gita* reveals a supreme deity who is a god of devotion (*bhakti*). Although sacrifice and discipline seem to be a hallmark of this earlier form of *bhakti*, the way of devotion is open to all. *Bhakti* is therefore ranked higher than the ways of knowledge and sacrifice. These earlier ways are not rejected but are placed in a definite order of value.

The *bhakti* ideal was later to develop into a more spontaneous form. As Brockington writes:

> It might even be said that, by its stress on the happiness secured by detachment here and now, the *Bhagavadgita* begins the shift of emphasis in the theistic movement away from the idea of release (*moksha*) in some distant future to an immediate and direct relationship with the deity.[10]

Third, the *Bhagavad Gita* builds upon the philosophy of the *Upanishads* by accepting the notion of the individual self and its transmigration. The *Bhagavad Gita*, therefore has to provide a solution to two seemingly incompatible ideas. On the one hand, there is the notion of a personal deity who seeks the devotion of human beings. On the other hand, there is the philosophical principle of monism that assumes all things are part of the same ultimate reality. How, therefore, may one aspect of the illusion of *maya* show devotion to another? This is a problem that the Judeo-Christian tradition does not have to face because of the essential dualism in the nature of God and his creation.

Fourth, in the *Vedas*, Vishnu and Rudra (Shiva) are only of minor importance, but in the *Bhagavad Gita*, Vishnu is revealed as the ultimate reality, the supreme being. It is not surprising that Vishnu, especially as Krishna, became one of the major cults for worship in later periods.

In assessing the message of the *Bhagavad Gita*, it must be remembered that it was not essentially a philosophical thesis, but a work of devotional poetry. However, the theistic theme expresses itself strongly within the *Bhagavad Gita*. An essential part of this is the possibility of a personal relationship between deity and his creation (*bhakti*). The *Bhagavad Gita* therefore has, through the centuries, stimulated deep emotions within the heart of devotees.

The religious historian is interested in understanding what the text has to say within its historical context. The devotee, on the other hand, seeks for the spiritual meaning. Speaking of historians, Robert Baird writes, 'Exoteric meaning is his only realm, for the esoteric tradition is closed to him.[11]

The *Bhagavad Gita* has become the source of religious inspiration for many since it was first drafted, and possibly redrafted. It has been read from the context of many historical and cultural backgrounds not only within India, but throughout the world. The ambiguous nature of some of the text leads to a variety of interpretations. Therefore, it is not surprising that many have looked to the *Bhagavad Gita* for esoteric teaching concerning the nature of the ultimate reality.

Notes

[1] Vivian Worthington, *A History of Yoga* (Arkana: London, 1982), p 56.

[2] A.L. Basham, *The Sacred Cow* (Rider: London, 1989), p 86.

[3] *Ibid*, p 89.

[4] Nirad C. Chaudhuri, *Hinduism* (Oxford University Press: Oxford, 1979), p 264.

5 G. Parrinder, *Avatars and Incarnations* (Faber & Faber: London, 1970), p 19.

6 *Ibid*, p 117.

7 B. Kumarappa, *Hindu Conception of the Deity* (Luzac & Co: London, 1934), p 63.

8 *Ibid*, p 84.

9 R.C. Zaehner, *The Bhagavad-Gita* (Oxford University Press: London, 1973), p 286.

10 J.C. Brockington, *The Sacred Thread* (Edinburgh University Press: Edinburgh, 1989), p 59.

11 R.D. Baird, 'Swami Bhaktivedanta and the Bhagavadgita "As it Is" ', in Robert Minor, *Modern Indian Interpreters of the Bhagavad Gita* (State University of New York: Albany, 1986), p 201.

CHAPTER 11

The Divine Lover: Krishna

WHO IS KRISHNA? Religious historians have considered him to be an ancient hero, a king, or a teacher, who through the passage of time had become deified as a manifestation of the god Vishnu. For the devotee, problems of historicity are not too important; the great issue is that Krishna is *all*. Throughout the centuries, Krishna has been the focus of devotion, and perhaps it is not surprising that it is this aspect of Hinduism that has spread most widely into the West.

THE *AVATARS*

In the previous chapter, when discussing the *Bhagavad Gita*, the notion of the *avatars* of Vishnu was introduced. In the *Bhagavad Gita*, Vishnu is considered to take on his greatest incarnation as Krishna, but according to popular classification there are ten *avatars*. The gods and heroes composing the list were adopted by the Vaisnavites at different times, but by the eleventh century the general pattern had been fixed. An *avatar* may be total or partial, and in this way every great person may be thought of as a partial incarnation of Vishnu. The ten incarnations are, however, special in that the deity is believed to have become embodied to save the world from some great danger.

1. The fish (Matsya)

This myth has close associations with the biblical account of Noah's ark. The world was overwhelmed by a universal flood, and Manu (the Hindu Adam) was in imminent danger. Vishnu took the form of a fish and carried Manu and his family in a ship fastened to a horn on his head. He also saved the seven great sages and the *Vedas* from the destructive flood.

2. The tortoise (Kurma)

Many divine treasures were lost in the flood, including the drink *amrta* (ambrosia, nectar) which enabled the gods to preserve their youth. Vishnu took the form of a tortoise and dived into the waters. On his back the gods placed Mount Meru, and wound the great snake Vasuki as a rope around the mountain. The gods pulled on one end of the rope and the demons on the other. By a process of continually pulling and releasing, the spiritual beings churned the seas in the way that an Indian dairyman churns butter. From the churning of the water emerged not only the ambrosia, but various other treasures including the goddess Laksmi.

Basham writes, 'The story is probably a piece of very early folklore, but the identification of the tortoise with Vishnu is comparatively late.'[1] This myth illustrates the way in which Hinduism has absorbed many ancient legends, leading to the diversity and complexity of the religion. Another example of this in seen in the *avatar* of the boar.

3. The boar (Varaha)

This myth probably developed from a pre-Aryan cult of a sacred pig. The story is told of a great demon called Hiranyaksa who throws the earth once more into the depths of the waters. Vishnu this time takes the form of an enormous boar, kills the demon, and dives into the water to raise the earth on his tusk. The cult of this *avatar* was important during the Gupta period, and many representations of the boar are still seen in India.

4. Narasimha, the man-lion

Another demon managed to obtain a boon from the god Brahma, ensuring that he could not be killed by either day or night, inside or outside, or by god, man, or animal. The increasing power of this demon caused concern among the gods, and Vishnu was called upon to help. He took the form of half-man/half-lion as a pillar at the palace of the demon. At sunset, when it was neither day nor night, he attacked the demon at his doorway when he was neither inside nor outside.

5. The dwarf (Vamana)

The theme of a demon causing a threat to the cosmic balance is repeated in the story of the dwarf *avatar*. This myth is an elaboration of the three strides of Vishnu recorded in the *Rg Veda* and mentioned in Chapter 4.

The demon Bali practises severe asceticism and gains great supernatural powers which threaten even the gods. Bali gains control of the world, and Vishnu is called to help. Vishnu takes the form of a dwarf, and asks a boon that he should be given as much land as he can cover in three strides. The boon is granted by Bali. Immediately, the dwarf becomes a giant and takes three mighty strides. These strides cover the earth, the middle air, and the heavens. Only the lower regions are left to the demon.

6. Parasurama (Rama with the axe)

The first of the human *avatars* of Vishnu is that in which he took the form of the son of a Brahmin called Jamadagni. Jamadagni is robbed by the wicked king Kartavirya. Parasurama kills the king, but in revenge the sons of Kartavirya kill Jamadagni. The enraged Parasurama then destroys all the males of the clan. Although Parasurama is often mentioned in the literature, he is rarely worshipped.

7. Rama

The great story of the *Ramayana* has been referred to earlier, and it provides the themes for veneration of Rama. To his followers he combines the ideals of a gentle husband, brave warrior, and just king.

8. Krishna

Krishna is undoubtedly the most important of the *avatars*, and was considered in the previous chapter.

9. Buddha

This is considered by the Vaisnavites to be the last historic incarnation of Vishnu. According to Vaisnavite scholars, the deity became Buddha to delude the wicked by leading them away from the *Vedas*. In this way, the cosmic balance would be retained. Western scholars tend to regard this *avatar* to be a means by which the heterodox elements of Buddhism were assimilated into the Vaisnavite theology. In general, little attention is given to the Buddha *avatar*.

10. Kalkin

The final *avatar* is believed to come at the end of the age. Vishnu will appear as a man mounted on a white horse with a flaming sword in his hand. He will judge the wicked and reward the good.

The parallels with Christian symbolism in the book of Revelation are striking.

> I saw heaven standing open and there before me was a white horse, whose rider is called Faithful and True. With justice he judges and makes war. His eyes are like blazing fire, and on his head are many crowns.... Out of his mouth comes a sharp sword with which to strike down the nations (Rev 19:11–15).

Although most scholars do not consider the possibility of any Christian influence in this myth, the parallels appear too marked to neglect.[2] It seems likely that there was some inter-action with the teachings of the Christian community that had existed in southern India from about the first century AD.

KRISHNA MYTHS

From the period of the early Christian era until the fifteenth and sixteenth centuries there were changes within the Krishna stories. It is difficult to identify clear patterns of development, but one can recognise the importance of the Krishna stories as a focus of devotion. The myths in their final form are long and complex and only an outline can be given at this point.

Krishna's father was called Vasudeva, and his mother was Devaki of the tribe of Yadavas. His mother was the aunt of King Kamsa, and it was prophesied that he would be killed by Devaki's eighth son. Kamsa therefore attempted to kill all her children, but Krishna and his elder brother Balarama were saved. Kamsa, on hearing that the boys had escaped, ordered the death of all the male children in his kingdom. But the boys were smuggled away.

There are many stories about the wonderful things which Krishna did during his childhood. He performed miracles and killed demons. He also played many pranks, such as stealing his adopted mother's butter. He had many amorous encounters with the wives and daughters of the cowherds (*gopis*) who were especially attracted by the music of his flute.

One of the great stories concerns Mount Govardhana. Krishna is perplexed by the way that the villagers arrange a festival to honour Indra. He finally persuades them to abandon the celebration, which angers Indra. Indra, the sky god of the *Rg Veda*, then sends his troops—the storm clouds. The village is in danger of being washed away and so the people turn to Krishna. He lifts Mount Govardhana over their heads on the tip of his finger like an umbrella. The story seems to illustrate the rivalry between Krishna and Indra for the devotion of the villagers.

Kamsa finally finds him and tries to have him killed. Krishna then gives up his pastoral life and destroys his wicked cousin. With his followers, he establishes a new kingdom at Dvaraka in Kathiawar. The myths at this period of his life are many. He defeats wicked kings, overcomes demons, and attains 16,000 wives. He also fights alongside his friends the Pandavas, as recounted in the *Mahabharata*.

After the great war, Krishna returns to his capital. His chiefs start fighting among themselves, especially after they have been drinking. Krishna bans all drink, but allows it for the celebration of a great festival. Under the influence of drink, the chiefs start fighting, and the whole city ends in bloodshed. Even his favourite son is killed in front of his eyes. Krishna finally leaves the city and wanders in the forest.

While he is musing over all that has happened, a hunter mistakes him for a deer and shoots. He is hit in his one vulnerable spot and dies. With him dies the city of Dvaraka, which is swallowed up by the sea.

The stories of Krishna find parallels with many ancient myths of Europe and the Middle East. The similarity of the sound of the words 'Krishna' and 'Christ' may well have been the reason Vasco da Gama and his men celebrated mass in a Hindu temple at Calicut in 1498. There are striking parallels between the narrative of the Krishna legend and the biblical story of Christ.

1. Both are born in poor surroundings.
2. The parents of both have to flee with the child. (In the case of Krishna it is the foster-parents.)
3. There is a massacre of male children.
4. Both Krishna and Christ are manifestations of deity.
5. Both religions stress the need for complete devotion.

All attempts to find a link between the two stories have failed. However, Basham notes:

> Can it be partly inspired by tales brought by Christian merchants or Nestorian missionaries to the west coast of India in the Middle Ages? Most authorities would deny this, but we do not reject the possibility out of hand.[3]

Although there are similarities, there are also marked differences. Krishna is portrayed as a god of love, but this is manifested as a sensual relationship. He not only attracts the *gopis*, but the slender-waisted Radha falls in love with him. 'He romps with them in the fragrant forest, torments them with the sweetness of the melodies he plays on his flute, rouses longings and fulfils them.'[4]

The erotic aspect of the Krishna story is important in *bhakti* as it is seen as a picture of a person's devotion to god. Just as the sound of Krishna's flute called the wives of the cowherds from their beds, so God is calling humans to leave earthly things and turn to the divine. The illustration is similar to that found in the Song of Solomon. The relationship of human beings with God is like the love relationship of husband and wife.

Perhaps the greatest text recounting the story of Radha and Krishna is the *Gitagovinda* of Jayadeva.[5] The book was probably written in the twelfth century, and has become very popular for songs and dances. The story concentrates upon the erotic nature of their relationship, and the Victorian scholars refused to translate some portions as grossly immoral. Even today, many Indian *bhakti* gurus think that the Westerner is unable to go beyond the sexual and reach the spiritual essence of the text.

To the Western mind, the playful behaviour of Krishna appears strangely out of place for the behaviour of a great deity. This 'divine play', which is common to all the gods of the Hindu pantheon, is called *lila*, a Sanskrit word which means 'flickering of fire'. Because the gods have no needs and no desires, they are free from the law of *karma*. Their activities are 'play' (*lila*), and they themselves are merely players enjoying this playful activity aloof from the world.

The great blind poet, Sur Das, expressed the great love play of Radha and Krishna in his poems.

> Radha raises lovely splashes in the River.
> Saffroned breasts slip from her bodice,
>   across them her hair hangs wet;
> Blue-stoned earrings dangle at her cheeks.
> Her hips sway slowly, like elephant's;
>   a girdle swings loosely at her tiger-thin waist.
> The play goes on, in the waters of the Yamuna;
>   immersed in love, swamped with passion....[6]

In the *bhakti* cults of India, often the devotee seeks to create an erotic relationship with Krishna. The boundaries of gender are transcended, and the male worshipper behaves like a woman to Krishna in an erotic fantasy. There are many stories of Indian devotees who have succeeded in feminising themselves even to the point of castration.[7]

THE VAISNAVITE SECTS

Within the Vaisnavite tradition, many streams can be identified. It is tempting to call these 'sects' of Hinduism, but the word 'sect' tends to convey an image of a group that has digressed from the orthodox position. As we have seen, this is not the idea common to Hinduism. The *sampradaya*, as these groups are called, are better imagined as parallel streams spreading across a flat plain in the manner of the delta of a river. They have a common source, but there are many off-shoots from the main current.

In Vaishnava thought there are 4 major *sampradaya*, and possibly 139 subdivisions. We shall, however, look at just two important movements which emerged in the north of India, and were founded by Vallabha and Caitanya. Both these men lived during the troubled period of the breakdown of the Delhi sultanate and the establishment of Mughal rule in the early part of the sixteenth century.

Vallabha (AD 1478-1530)

Tradition tells that Vallabha was born in AD 1478 while his Brahmin parents were on pilgrimage from Andra Pradesh to Benares. The child was born prematurely, and thinking the baby was stillborn, the parents abandoned him. That very night Vishnu appeared to them in a dream telling them to go back to where the child lay, as his spirit had entered him. When they returned, they found the child alive and safe in a ring of protective flames. The child became an eager student, and at the age of seven he was said to be totally familiar with the *Vedas* and the *Puranas*. After his father died when he was eleven, he began the first of three protracted pilgrimages all over India. During these pilgrimages he had instructions from Krishna to go to Mount Govardhana, where he found an image that had mysteriously appeared. Soon he had a vision of Krishna, in which he was taught of the importance of complete devotion to Krishna. He then had the vision of Mount Govardhana, in which the arm of Krishna appeared through the top of the mountain. To the side of the mountain there appeared a mouth which was magically fed by the milk from a cow.

Vallabha claimed to be guided by Krishna to the various

sites at which the myths of Krishna took place. The ancient city of Mathura is considered as the birthplace of Krishna, and is regarded as having existed on the banks of the Jamna River between Delhi and Agra. The surrounding area of Uttar Pradesh is generally called Braj, and it is in this area that the events of the Krishna myths are believed to have taken place. At these sites Vallabha set up shrines that became the centres for devotion.

Vallabha recognised four main types of devotion: servant, companion, parent, lover. He himself favoured parental affection. As a result, many in the movement worship the child Krishna. The other common type is that of lover—the erotic—in which the devotee imagines himself as one of the *gopis* enjoying Krishna's nightly call on his flute. The other two forms are not common.

There is a fifth type of devotion, which runs counter to Vallabha's teaching. This is the devotion of quiet contemplation, which can be seen to conflict with the strong emotionalism of Vallabha. This fifth type of devotion has been promoted in the West by the Divine Light master, Guru Maharaj Ji, to which we will return in Chapter 18.

After some twenty years of preaching and teaching, Vallabha had a dream in which the Lord Krishna appeared to him and commanded him to marry. This was very unusual for a spiritual leader, but Vallabha was quick to obey, and from the marriage he had two sons. It was the second, Vitthalnath, who was to become an important leader within the movement. He succeeded his father in 1543, and continued to be very active in promoting devotion to Krishna. As a result, the movement has flourished and has become popular, especially among householders.

Later leaders of this movement took upon themselves the title and lifestyle of a maharajah. They also claimed to be living embodiments of Krishna and became involved in sexual relations with female devotees. The scandal culminated in a court case in Bombay Supreme Court in 1862.[8] However, the notorious incident did not affect the growth of the movement, which now has many followers in western India and especially Rajasthan.

Caitanya (AD 1486-1534)

An even more important figure than Vallabha was Caitanya. His story is parallel to that of Vallabha, but he appears to have been a more charismatic personality. He is attributed with many Vaisnava devotional songs in Bengali. These draw for their inspiration upon the strong emotions found in Krishna's relationships with the *gopis*.

Caitanya grew up in Nadiya, a town noted for its learning. He was the ninth or tenth child of a Vaisnava Brahmin, but only he and one older brother survived childhood. His brother became polluted and outcaste from the family while Caitanya was still young. Caitanya was instructed in the teaching of the Sanskrit scriptures and appears to have been contemptuous of the popular *bhakti* movement. However, the story is told that when, in 1508, he went to Gaya to perform memorial rituals for his father, he met an ascetic from south India. This man introduced him to a deep religious experience and initiated him into the worship of Krishna.

When he returned home to Nadiya, Caitanya joined a group of *bhakti* devotees. These devotees would meet every night to sing praises to Krishna, and eventually began to have periods of ecstasy during which they were possessed by the deity. It was during this time that Caitanya became noted as a charismatic leader of the movement, and composed many chants and songs which were to be spread around the Western world with the Hare Krishna movement.

> In the course of one of his ecstatic movements, Caitanya is said to have dived into the sea near Puri and to have died. His body was recovered and buried near Puri.[9]

One may ask questions concerning the historic identity of the sites identified by the devotees of the sixteenth centuries. In recent times, scholars have studied the area, but they can find little evidence for any historicity to the Krishna myth. Charlotte Vaudeville writes:

> From the materials so far collected and the evidence brought forward in the paper it may be doubted if any specifically 'Krishnaite' cult, other than a primitive form

of nature-worship (including hills, waters, cows, trees and snakes), combined with some form of Devi worship, existed among the rural (pastoral) populations of Braj before the arrival of the great Vaisnava reformers in Govardhan and Vrndaban at the beginning of the sixteenth centuries. It is probably to their disappointment with such primitive forms of worship that we owe the famous legend of the 'loss' and 'recovery'...of Braj.[10]

Irrespective of any historicity, for the devotee of Krishna it is the myth that is important and the devotion which is generated. The *bhakti* movement of Caitanya swept across northern India in the fifteenth and sixteenth centuries. Many Muslims were converted, which antagonised the Muslim rulers. For Caitanya and his followers, *bhakti* emancipated them from the religious laws and conventions: 'they danced ecstatically and sang; they were as if mad.'[11]

In 1975, the International Society for Krishna Consciousness (ISKCON) completed an impressive temple in Brindavan, a pilgrimage centre for devotees of Krishna for 500 years. This was the very site that Caitanya clairvoyantly proclaimed was that of Krishna's circle dance with the *gopis*. The ISKCON temple has attracted many Westerners to Brindavan, and the local residents have been quick to adopt the familiar salutation 'Hare Krishna!' We shall discuss the well-known movement when we consider the role of the guru in Chapter 18. First, we must consider the second great deity, Siva.

Notes:

[1] A.L. Basham, *The Wonder That Was India* (Sidgwick & Jackson: London, 1988), p 302.

[2] *Ibid*, p 307.

[3] *Ibid*, p 306.

[4] A.L. Dallapiccola, *Krishna: the Divine Lover* (Serindia Publications: London, 1982), p 14.

[5] Barbara S. Miller, *Love Song of the Dark Lord: Jayadeva's Gitagovinda* (New York, 1977).

[6] Dallapiccola, *op cit*, p 23.

[7] Sudhir Kakar, 'Erotic fantasy: the secret passion of Radha and Krishna', *Contributions to Indian Sociology* (new series), vol 19, no 1 (January–June 1985): pp 75–94.

[8] Dallapiccola, *op cit*, p 139.

[9] Dallapiccola, *op cit*, p 140.

[10] Charlotte Vaudeville, 'Braj, Lost and Found', *Indo Iranian Journal*, vol 18 (1976): pp 212–213.

[11] E. Dimock, 'Doctrine and practice among the Vaisnavas of Bengal', in Milton Singer (ed), *Krishna: myths, rites and attitudes* (East-West Centre: Honolulu, 1966), p 65.

CHAPTER 12

The Erotic Yogi: Siva

S IVA IS THE SECOND deity, considered by his devotees as the ultimate divinity. He is almost as popular in India as the god Vishnu. Siva has always been an enigma to Western scholars. Siva is perceived both as the great ascetic and the god of the erotic, creator and destroyer, life and death. Siva can only be understood in terms of paradox. Throughout Hindu mythology, from earliest times, the opposing strands of Siva's nature have been accepted as aspects of his one nature.

While the concept of Vishnu developed from the idea of lesser deities in the *Vedas* with the name Vishnu, the name Siva is not found in the *Vedas*. He is, however, often associated with the god Rudra, and his character perceived as developing from a mixture of many Vedic gods.

> From Indra, Siva inherits his phallic and adulterous character, from Agni the heat of asceticism and passion, and from Rudra he takes the very common epithet (Rudra), as well as certain dark features.[1]

In general, scholars think that these early Aryan deities have merged with elements of a non-Aryan fertility deity. The famous Proto-Siva Seal of the ancient Harappan civilisation was mentioned in Chapter 2. This seal reveals many characteristics of the god Siva. These various religious ideas appear to have coalesced to form a complex, ambiguous concept of deity that is worshipped by the name of Siva today.

THE CHARACTERISTICS OF SIVA

Siva is distinguished by a strangely ambivalent character which contrasts with that of the benevolent Vishnu. Siva is the lord of destruction who lurks in the places of horror, such as the battlefields and the cremation grounds. He is death and time which destroy all things. Yet from the destruction comes life.

> Siva can be described as the reconciliation of opposites—good and evil, auspicious and malignant, active and quiescent—but more exactly he is the expression of the ultimate nature of reality manifest in the world in the many apparent polarities of life and death, creation and separation, the ascetic and the erotic, which are however not separate states but mutually dependent pairs on whose inter-relationship the whole of life depends.[2]

The images of Siva show a variety of forms that contradict each other, but in this very contradiction his devotees find the greatest meaning. The complexity of the nature of Siva requires him to be studied in at least three poses: ascetic, Nataraja, *linga*.

The Ascetic

One most important aspect of Siva is his role as the great ascetic. High on the mountain slopes of the Himalayas he sits with eyes almost closed in deep meditation. He is the one who has renounced both the joys and pains of the world. He sits alone and is unmoved by the passions common to humanity.

Upon his head a crescent moon adorns the topknot of his matted locks, which tumble down onto his shoulders. In the centre of his forehead is a vertical third eye that is a symbol of the mystic's ability to perceive beyond the material world. His forehead is marked with three white lines, which characterise his devotees even today. He sits crossed-legged upon a tiger skin. His body is ashen blue due to the covering of ashes.

Around his neck and arm are entwined snakes, of which he is lord. He wears a necklace of skulls. At his side is his favourite weapon—the trident—and by his feet a begging bowl. Near him is often seen his mount, the bull Nandi.

Siva is the arch-ascetic seated in splendid isolation—an epitome of the teaching of the *Upanishads*. As a result of his deep asceticism he has the great mystic power of *tapas* (heat). Only such a great ascetic could perform his destructive role with dispassion. Siva destroys, but without either pleasure or pain.

In a later version of the story of Vishnu's *avatar* as a boar, Siva appears in the role of an ascetic who rescues Vishnu from his passions.

> Once long ago, when the Earth was in danger of drowning in the cosmic floods, Vishnu took the form of a boar and saved her. Siva then said to him, 'Now that you have accomplished the task for which you assumed the form of a boar, you must abandon that form. The Earth cannot bear you and is becoming exhausted. She is full of passion and she has become heated in the water. She has received from you a terrible embryo, who will be born as a demon harmful to the gods. You must abandon this erotic boar form.' Vishnu agreed with Siva, but he kept the form of a boar and continued to make love to the Earth who had taken the form of a female boar. Many years passed, and the Earth brought forth three sons. When Vishnu was surrounded by his sons and his wife he forgot all about his promise to abandon his body. The sons played together and shattered all the worlds, but Vishnu did not stop them, for he loved them, and his passion for his wife grew greater and greater. Finally he remembered his promise and begged Siva to kill him. Siva took the form of a marvellous *sarabha* beast and killed Vishnu and his three sons, and the essence of Vishnu was freed from the boar form.[3]

Vishnu is here seen deluded by his passion, and needing to call upon the great ascetic to enlighten him. Siva is the lord of the ascetic, and, as such, frightening in his powers.

Lord of the dance

In striking contrast, Siva is also conceived as Nataraja—the lord of the dance. This aspect is especially popular in south India, probably because it was here that dancing developed as an important part of religious observance.

The most common dance postures of Siva portray him performing his dance in a circle of flames (see Figure 12:1). The circle represents the flow of cosmic unity. The dance symbolises the glory of this unity of the universe, and yet at the same time reminds the devotee of its eternal flux. Life ebbs and flows. The cycle of creation runs its course and destruction follows. Just as the movements of the dancer are transitory and the moment is soon passed, the old gives way to the new. Nataraja provides a powerful image of the rhythm of the universe.

With one foot the dancing Siva balances on the dwarf of ignorance and forgetfulness that separates us from the understanding of true reality. The other foot is raised in a dance posture, almost as if it is showing the way out from the bonds of illusion (*maya*). The dancing Siva is portrayed with hair flowing and four arms, each in characteristic dance postures. In Siva's upper right hand is a small drum, representing sound as the first manifestation of the universe and symbolising the continual rhythm of creation. In his upper left arm is a ball of flame which symbolises the final destruction of the world as a corollary to the act of creation. The lower arms are postured in positions that seem to invite the devotee to follow, and point to the way of release from the bonds of ignorance.

Linga

Siva is perhaps most commonly worshipped as *linga*. It was this aspect that most shocked the early European visitors to India.

In about 1820 Dubois wrote:

> It is incredible, it is impossible to believe, that in inventing this vile superstition the religious teachers of India intended that the people should render direct worship to objects the very names of which, among civilized nations, are an insult to decency. Without any doubt the

Figure 12.1. Siva—Lord of the dance

obscene symbol contained an allegorical meaning, and was a type, in the first instance, of the reproductive forces of nature, and generative source of all living beings.[4]

The *linga* is represented as a short cylindrical pillar with a rounded top, which seem to be a survival of the phallic images found in the Harappan remains. The cult of the *linga* may well have been an important fertility cult of some of the non-Aryan people of the subcontinent which was incorporated into Hinduism. The ithyphallic (erect phallus) image on the Proto-Siva Seal is surrounded by animals, and may well be a prototype of Siva as the patron of the reproduction of man, animals, and plants.

In all temples dedicated to Siva, one finds an upright pillar symbolic of the *linga* and the focus of worship. Phallic worship has been common among Indian ascetics from earliest times. In the *Ramayana*, while on his way to Lanka to regain Sita, Rama erects a Siva-*linga* and worships Siva. The story also shows the ascendency of Siva over Rama, who was an *avatar* of Vishnu.

SIVA-SHAKTI

The paradox of Siva as being both ascetic and erotic is one of the greatest enigmas to Western observers. It has not been they alone who have been perplexed; the paradox has been a central issue of the myths and icons of Hinduism. Siva is permanently ithyphallic and yet perpetually chaste.

Parvati

A well-known myth of Siva is that of his marriage to Parvati, the daughter of Himalaya, who is the personification of the mountains. The myth is often told as the seduction of Siva.

The gods were troubled by the demon Taraka who was becoming too powerful and so disturbing the cosmic balance. It was prophesied that he could only be destroyed by the child of Siva and the daughter of the mountains. As Siva was continually involved in meditation, the prospect of his producing any offspring seemed very remote. Parvati, however, was very beautiful and went to wait upon Siva, and made many attempts to gain his attention. He was oblivious to all her efforts until Kama, the god of love, pierced Siva with one of his arrows. Like his Greek counterpart, Kama is depicted as a handsome youth, armed with a bow and arrow, but his bow is of sugar-cane strung with a row of bees, and his arrows are flowers. Siva opened his third eye, which released flames of power that burned up Kama.

Finally, Parvati decided to follow Siva in his asceticism. She removed her ornaments, and became a hermit on a nearby peak. It was in this role that Siva noticed her and fell in love with her. They were married at a great ceremony at which all the gods were present. Soon Parvati gave birth to the war god Skanda (Karttikeya), who, when he grew to manhood, destroyed the demon Taraka.

Ganesa

The second son of Siva and Parvati is one of the most popular deities in India and is known as Ganesa. A well-known story tells of how Parvati stationed Ganesa at her bedroom door to keep everyone out. When Siva came to her room, Ganesa also denied him access. Siva became angry and burnt the head off the body of Ganesa. Realising the distress he has caused Parvati, Siva sent out his servants to take the head of the first living creature that they found lying down facing north. The first animal they found was Airvata, the elephant of Indra. They therefore cut off his head and returned with it to Siva. Siva then fixed the head to the body of Ganesa, who once again came to life.

Ganesa became a great sage, and is known as the god of wisdom and learning. He is the patron of scribes, and often manuscripts are begun with the auspicious formula *Sri-Ganesaya namah*, 'Reverence to Lord Ganesa'. He is perceived as a cheerful and benevolent deity, who is worshipped at the beginning of new ventures to remove any unforseen hindrances.

He is represented by Indian artists as having an elephant's head on the body of a fat man. One of his tusks is broken, and his steed is a rat. Sweets are offered to his image in the temples. Most Western scholars tend to think that Ganesa is the survival of a primitive non-Aryan elephant god that has been absorbed into Hinduism.

Shakti

The myths of Siva and his consorts illustrate some important principles concerning the powers of celibacy. Hindu celibacy is different to that found in Buddhism. In Hinduism, celibacy pertains to withholding sex to conserve semen that is the source of vitality, health, and long life. Semen must therefore not be wasted or spilled, but harnessed for the increase of magical power called *shakti*. The extreme form is found in Tantrism, where the devotees have intercourse, but refuse to ejaculate. This subject will be returned to in Chapter 16.

Siva's power is based on his asceticism, which involves withholding semen, or turning the genitals inward. This contrasts markedly with the Buddhist monk who renounces sex in all its manifestations. The Buddhist monk is neuter, but not the ascetic Siva. The Buddha leaves his wife and child, cuts off his hair, and renounces the world. 'And this idea is represented in the castration symbolism of shaven head, while matted locks are a denial of castration.[5]

Siva castrates himself, but the severed penis reappears as the *linga*. He meditates for enormous lengths of time, and then is afflicted by irresistible and destructive sexual urges. In one myth Siva rapes the wives of ascetics in the pine forest.

> When the women of the Pine forest saw Siva begging in their hermitage they were overcome by desire. Only Arundhati, the faithful wife of Vasistha, resisted. All the others, old women and young girls, threw off their clothing and urged Siva to make love to them.... Then Siva left the house and wandered through the woods with the frenzied women, laughing and making love to them day and night for twelve years.... Then with a curse the sages caused Siva's *linga* to fall. The fiery *linga* stretched for many miles and landed in the body of Sati, but when it had plunged into the ground its divine energy was withdrawn from the universe, and the world became dark.[6]

Siva is the god of excesses, both ascetic and sensual. When his power, or *shakti*, is personified, it is always as a goddess. While Siva remains aloof from the world, Parvati is active, pervading creation as its underlying strength and power. In this activity she is identified with nature, whereas Siva is identified with pure spirit.

SAIVITE SECTS

As with the worship of Vishnu, one also finds many sects among the devotees of Siva. Like the followers of Vishnu, the Saivites consider their deity to be the ultimate high god, but they are tolerant of those of other traditions. The Saivites consider Vishnu to be an emanation from their deity, Siva.

One can see growth and development within the Saivite sects as they absorb local traditions, and interact with the emerging Vaisnavites.

Pasupatas

The earliest Siva sect has association with Lakulisa, who is not only regarded as an incarnation of Siva, but the author of their foundational text, the *Pasupatasutra*. Lakulisa may probably be dated in the second century AD. Pasupata temples have been found in most of India from as early as the seventh century. Lakulisa is represented in early traditions as a naked yogin with a club in his left hand and his penis erect. The most distinctive feature of the Pasupata sect is their code of training and initiation. The aspirant has to pass through five stages in the progress to union with Siva. In the first stage, he is attached to a temple, applies the sectarian markings, and goes around naked, or nearly so. During this stage he worships Siva with dancing, roaring like a bull, and laughing. In this way, he begins to acquire yogic powers. In the second stage, he leaves the temple, abandons the sectarian markings, and invites ridicule by foolish or indecent behaviour. The remaining three stages consist of increasing degrees of asceticism. Finally, the devotee lives in an isolated cave, abandoned house, or even a cremation ground, but at the same time he is considered to be mystically in Siva.

Throughout this period, the aspirant seeks purification from past *karma* with the aim of becoming divine. The ultimate goal is *moksha*—freedom from the world and unity with the nature of Siva. The practices advocated include shaking, falling, and animal imitation, and are reminiscent of Shamanism.

Kapalikas

The revulsion felt by many orthodox Hindus to the more extreme forms of Pasupata was even more evident towards the Kapalika sect. The sect appears to have originated in the sixth century in the Deccan, or south India, but spread rapidly to the north. Seventh-century Indian literature makes many references to them, in which they are accused of making human sacrifice to Siva.

They sought to worship Siva in his horrific aspect as Bhairava. They did this both through imitation and by propitiation. This included the performance of the extreme penance prescribed by the *Dharma-sastras* for the accidental killing of a Brahmin. The vow required the person to live in the forest, begging for food, while stating his offence and carrying the skull of the victim. Probably, the vow was considered powerful due to its extreme penance.

The Kapalika also imitated Siva in seeking to realise in sexual union the divine bliss of Siva and his consort. Licentiousness in matters of drink and sex were common.

The sect rapidly declined in the thirteenth century, and had virtually died out by the fourteenth century. Their decline was probably the result of the rise of the Lingayat movement.

Kashmir Saivism

Saivism of the Middle Ages was not only characterised by licentiousness; it did have an intellectual tradition. The Kashmir school of Saivism dates from the ninth century, when its greatest scholar, Abhiava Gupta, was producing some of his greatest writings. Siva is perceived as the *atman* indwelling all beings, as well as the universe as a whole. He is the 'experiencer', as distinct from that which is 'experienced'. Siva is the supreme reality, whose essence is pure consciousness, immutable and eternal. Siva's immanent aspect is as *shakti*, which is his creative energy.

Creation is therefore the self-projection of his consciousness, and Siva conceals himself by the power of *maya*. Due to *maya*, objects which owe their existence to his consciousness appear independent of it. The bondage of self is caused by ignorance of reality, and the continual realisation of one's identity with Siva brings release. The unreality of the phenomenal world is recognised by the devotees through a sudden enlightenment, rather like a conversion experience.

Lingayats

A fourth important Saivite sect is that of the Lingayats, founded by Basava in the twelfth century. Basava rejected image worship, the *Vedas*, and the Brahmin priesthood. The only symbol accepted by the sect is that of the *linga*, a small representation of which is carried by all the members. Basava established a new priesthood called the *jangamas*, and instituted complete equality among all his followers. Among other Vedic practices which Basava condemned was cremation, and even today his followers are buried.

Other developments

There are many other lesser schools of Saivism, some of which go to extremes. The Urddhabahus extend one or both their arms above their heads until they atrophy and become transfixed in an upright position. The Nagas go naked and smear their bodies with ashes.

In the Middle Ages, a cult developed that sought to synthesise the worship of Siva and Vishnu, and still does so under the name of 'Harihara'. 'Hari' was a title of Vishnu, and 'Hara' a title of Siva. Deity is worshipped as an icon that combines the characteristics of both gods.

At a similar period, there developed the idea of a trinity of gods: Siva, Vishnu, and Brahma. Brahma was the creator, Vishnu the preserver, and Siva the destroyer. This trinity, called 'Trimurti', impressed Western scholars by its similarity to the Christian concept of the Trinity. However, all the devotees of Trimurti tended to favour one of the three gods as high god. This cult was really an artificial form of religious expression and has had little real influence in India.

CONCLUSIONS

The god Siva epitomises the very opposite of Western ideas of God. He is a synthesis of contradictions, and, as such, challenges the notions of Western logic that flee from paradox, and look for analysis and order. The Hindu notion of Siva refuses to be subject to Western study. The great myths refuse to hold still for analysis, but continue in perpetual motion.

Perhaps it is this paradox that has, in recent years, drawn a few Western people to explore the Eastern pagan path of the Siva-Shakti.[7] There are two aspects of Saivite teaching which have spread more widely in the West, and these are yoga and Tantra. Before we can turn to these aspects we need to look at the third feature of modern Hindu expression. Along with Vishnu and Siva is the great goddess cult of Devi.

Notes:

[1] Wendy Doniger O'Flaherty, *Siva: The Erotic Ascetic* (Oxford University Press: Oxford, 1981), p 83.

[2] J.L. Brockington, *The Sacred Thread: Hinduism in its Continuity and Diversity* (Edinburgh University Press: Edinburgh, 1989), p 72.

[3] O'Flaherty, *op cit*, p 41.

[4] Abbe J. Dubois, *Hindu Manners, Customs and Ceremonies* (Clarendon Press: London, 1906), p 631.

[5] G. Obeyesekere, *Medusa's Hair: An Essay on Personal Symbols and Religious Experience* (University of Chicago Press: Chicago, 1981), p 38.

[6] O'Flaherty, *op cit*, p 102.

[7] Denny Sargent, 'Tantrika: The Divine Science of Siva and Sakti: The Union of the God and the Goddess', *Green Egg*, vol XXIV, no 92 (1991): pp 6–7.

CHAPTER 13

The Divine Feminine

I N RECENT YEARS, scholars have come to realise more fully the importance of goddess worship within the Hindu religious tradition. The cult of the mother goddess is found throughout the long history of the Indian people. At some times it is more prominent than others, but always it seems to run within the religious awareness of the people. No other religious theme provides such a rich mythology, and even in modern Hinduism the popularity of the goddesses is still notable.

HISTORY

The earliest indications of goddess worship relate to the archaeological discoveries of the Harappan civilisation. As was discussed in Chapter 2, many crude images of nude females have been discovered in the ancient cities of the Indus. Evidence does suggest the possibility of a fertility goddess cult, but care must be taken to avoid undue speculation regarding the actual nature of the people's religious beliefs.

David Kinsley draws the following conclusions about goddess worship in the Harappan civilisation:

> First, we can surmise simply on the basis of the great number of female images found that goddesses were known and probably widely worshipped or exalted in this culture. Second, primarily on the basis of three scenes depicted on seals we can surmise that a goddess

was known who was associated with vegetation and most likely with the fertility of the crops.[1]

Vedic goddesses

In our study of Vedic religion, we saw that the deities of the Aryans were mainly male deities, such as Indra, Agni, Soma, and Varuna. There are a few references to goddesses in the *Rg Veda*. Even so, Usas, the greatest of the female deities, is only on a par with the male deities of the second rank.

Usas is associated with the dawn, and reveals herself with the daily coming of light into the world. She is perceived as riding a chariot that bursts through the darkness. As such, she is the one who causes all living creatures to rise from sleep to life, and so sets all things in motion for the new day.

> Like a dancing girl, she puts on bright ornaments; she uncovers her breasts as a cow reveals her swollen udder. Creating light for the whole universe, Dawn has opened up the darkness as cows break out of their enclosed pen (RgV 1:92:4).[2]

Usas is an auspicious deity of light and wealth. She observes all the things that people do, and therefore is often described as the eyes of the gods. Although she sees both good and bad, she is rarely invoked for the forgiveness of human transgressions.

Prthivi is the goddess associated with the earth, and, as such, is coupled with Dyaus, the male god of the sky. Dyaus is often called father and Prthivi mother. They come together when Dyaus fertilises Prthivi with rain, and she nourishes all creatures that live on her (RgV 1:160). This metaphor is similar to that of Baal (sky) and Astoreth (earth) of Canaanite religion, which is condemned in the Old Testament.

Other Vedic goddesses are similarly associated with natural phenomenon. Saravarti is affiliated with the River Saravarti, which has now disappeared from the terrain of the Punjab. Ritri is the night. Her physical appearance is rarely mentioned, but she is generally regarded as a beautiful maiden, like her sister Usas.

Prthivi persists in later Hinduism, and becomes associated

with Vishnu, but few of the other Vedic goddesses survive. There is no reference in the Vedic literature to the goddesses such as Parvati, Durga, Kali, and Radha who are so important in classical Hinduism. Neither is there any evidence that the Vedic goddesses were perceived as manifestations of one great goddess, as is found in later Hinduism. It appears that a similar notion of polytheism, common to the Vedic male gods, was also found with regard to the female deities.

Post-Vedic period

With the Aryan migration into the subcontinent, goddess worship attracted little attention. The Aryan peoples were anxious to keep their cultural identity and not merely to blend with the indigenous population. However, interaction between the pastoral Aryan and the indigenous non-Aryan people occurred in many and various ways, as mentioned in Chapter 3. The indigenous goddess cults appear to have remained as an active part of the life of regional communities, and over time these were absorbed into the main Aryan traditions. This can be seen in the various local goddess deities common to the villages of India even today.

By the Middle Ages, the feminine deities appear to have become synthesised with the cults of the male gods in a process by which they became their wives or consorts. This absorption of regional goddess cults into the main stream of Hinduism appears to have encouraged the gradual Aryanisation of the indigenous people. Similarly, other deities became accepted as children of the divine marriages. One example of this process we have already considered with Siva and Parvati. At an earlier period, the family consisted only of three, Skanda (or Karttikeya) being their first child. Later, one finds that Ganesa is also associated with the family. Ganesa was probably the deity of a regional elephant cult.

A more sophisticated development was that in which the female deity was perceived as the potency of her male counterpart, as we saw with the Siva-Sakti relationship in the previous chapter. Here, the male deity is considered inactive and transcendent, while his female partner is active and immanent. By the fifth century, goddess worship was an important element of worship among all sections of society. Frequently at this time, the female concept of deity was perceived as one overarching female being called Devi (goddess) or Mahadevi (great goddess).

Before considering the broader notion of Devi, we will first look at the various goddesses as consorts of the gods. Hindu society is overwhelmingly patriarchal. Social structures are based on the relationship of males to males, and women find their place by their association with their fathers, husbands, and sons. The importance of goddess worship therefore raises many intriguing questions.

CONSORTS OF THE GODS

Hindu male gods have a distinct relation with at least one female deity (*devi*), who usually is regarded as his wife or consort. Vishnu is associated with Laksmi, and as the *avatar* Krishna with Radha, and as Rama with Sita. Siva is associated with Devi, Shakti, Sati, Parvati, Uma, Gauri, Minaksi, Durga, Kali, Candi, and Bhairavi.

Laksmi

Laksmi, whose name means 'fortune', the wife of Vishnu, is also called Sri. She is one of the most popular of the Hindu goddesses. Early texts associate her with various male deities, and especially with Soma after he performs a great royal sacrifice. From about AD 400, she has been regarded as the consort of Vishnu, and in this role is considered a model Hindu wife, obediently serving her husband as lord. Vishnu and Laksmi provide a picture of domestic order and marital contentment resulting from the interdependence between husband and wife.

The association of Laksmi with Vishnu is portrayed mythologically in the context of the churning of the waters mentioned in Chapter 11. In this event, Vishnu becomes the *avatar* Kurma—the tortoise. The important aspect of this myth is the way that the waters are churned to obtain valuable things, in the same way that one churns milk until it yields a richer substance—butter. Although the mythological aim of the churning is to obtain the ambrosia of immortality, Laksmi is seen as the miracle of water producing organic life.[3] There is a parallel here with the Greek myth of Aphrodite, who emerged from the waters of the sea.

Laksmi is usually portrayed as a woman of mature beauty, seated upon a lotus, and often holding a lotus in her hand. The lotus is a symbol of fertility and life emerging from the primordial waters. In this way, the lotus may be taken as the symbol of the entire created world. It will be remembered that the lotus growing from the navel of Vishnu marks the beginning of a new cosmic creation. The lotus is a common motif both in Hindu and Buddhist iconography. For gods, buddhas, or even human beings to be portrayed as seated on a lotus suggests that the being has transcended the limitations of the finite world and floats freely in the spiritual reality.

On either side of the image of Laksmi are found two elephants, who sprinkle water on her from their trunks.

> An ancient Hindu tradition says that the first elephants had wings and flew about the sky. In fact, they were clouds and showered the earth with rain wherever they went. These sky elephants, however, were cursed by a sage when they landed on a tree under which he was meditating and broke his concentration. Stripped of their wings, they henceforth had to remain earthbound.[4]

The elephants convey the notion of the fertilising power of rain.

Laksmi is worshipped throughout the year in a variety of festivals. The most important festival is held in late autumn, when she is thanked for fertility and good harvests. She is a popular deity with merchants, who identify her with prosperity.

> During this festival it is customary for people, especially businessmen, to worship their account books. It seems to be clearly understood by merchants that wealth will not arise without Laksmi's blessing or presence.[5]

Laksmi is also believed to incarnate herself as the wife of Vishnu in his various *avatars*. She is therefore worshipped as

Sita, the wife of Rama, and as Radha, the favourite of the youthful Krishna.

Sita

The *Ramayana* was written about the time of Christ, but there is no real suggestion that Rama and Sita are divine. Their association with Vishnu and Laksmi tends to develop at a later period, until in about the fourteenth century Rama is praised as the supreme deity. Sita attains her divine status through her relationship with Rama.

Although Hindus always associate Sita with Rama, they are also aware of an earlier deity of the same name. 'Sita' means 'a furrow', as made with a plough. She was perceived as the fertility of the soil brought to life by the rains. As in many ancient societies, there was an association between the manly vigour of the king and the fertility of the land. Thus, the association of the wife of a great king with fertile soil would appear logical.

Like Laksmi, Sita portrays the role of an ideal Hindu wife. Her every thought revolves around her husband, and his reputation, welfare, and desires are her primary concern. This is seen often in the *Ramayana*. When Rama is sent into exile, he plans to leave Sita in the city, but she pleads to be allowed to go with him. And when she is abducted by the evil Ravana, she keeps her mind fixed upon Rama.

The popularity of the worship of Rama means that Sita is also venerated. Sita is never considered equal to Rama even though in Rama temples her image is found next to that of her husband. Sita takes the role of an intermediary between the deity and the worshipper, and so she presents a model of the ideal devotee. In her loyalty she gains the ear of her Lord Rama and the answer to her requests.

Radha

In contrast to the role of the ideal wife portrayed by Sita, Radha's relationship to Krishna is adulterous. Although she is married to another, she is passionately attracted to Krishna, and abandons the social norms to pursue her love. The relationship occurs during Krishna's adolescence, before his part in the *Mahabharata*. The love affair takes place in the little village of Vraja in a setting of the cowherds and woods.

Radha's popularity develops primarily in the context of her devotion to Krishna. Her frenzied love for Krishna bursts all the social norms, and because of this she becomes a metaphor of the human devotee giving up all things for the supreme deity. This theme was most markedly developed in Jayadeva's *Gitagovinda*, a twelfth-century devotional text. The poem portrays Radha as one who is torn apart between her love for Krishna and her social responsibility. The love-sick Radha wanders out at night searching the woods for Krishna.

> When spring came, tender-limbed Radha wandered
> Like a flowering creeper in the forest wilderness,
> Seeking Krishna in his many haunts.
> The god of love increased her ordeal,
> Tormenting her with fevered thoughts,
> And her friend sang to heighten the mood.[6]

Although Radha never legally becomes Krishna's consort, she is perceived philosophically as his *shakti*. In some later texts she is perceived as one half of an androgynous figure, the other half being Krishna.

> In the beginning, Krishna, the Supreme Reality, was filled
>   with the desire to create.
> By his own will he assumed a twofold form.
> From the left half arose the form of a woman, the right
>   half became a man.
> The male figure was none other than Krishna himself; the
>   female was the Goddess Primordial Nature, otherwise
>   known as Radha.[7]

For some sects, the status of Radha is elevated to that of the cosmic queen, equal to, if not greater than, Krishna.

Durga

Turning from the consorts of Vishnu to those of Siva, we have already considered Parvati, one of the greatest goddesses, in the previous chapter. Durga is a very different mythological figure, and her prime function is to combat demons who threaten the stability of the cosmos. In this role she is portrayed as the great warrior queen, with many arms, each wielding a weapon.

In the *Vedas* there is no reference to such a warrior queen, but around AD 350 images of Durga began to become common in India. By the sixth century, she had become a popular goddess whose story is told in many texts. It therefore seems that Durga comes from a non-Aryan origin, where she was regarded as a goddess who protected the village from evil spirits.

There are many mythical accounts of the origin of Durga. The most common is that concerning the demon Mahisa. He had been granted a boon because of his great heroism. In response, he had asked that he would be invincible to all opponents except women. He was therefore able to defeat the male gods. As the angry gods met, they congealed into the body of a beautiful woman. Her face was formed from Siva, her hair from Yama, her arms from Vishnu, and so forth. Each of the male deities from whom she had been created gave her a weapon. This great goddess, endued with the weapons of the gods, roared with such might that the earth shook, and she defeated the mighty Mahisa.

Durga violates the model of Hindu women. She is neither submissive nor subordinate to a male deity, and she excels in those roles that are traditionally male functions. As a warrior, she can hold her own against any male. Durga does not give her power (*shakti*) to a male consort, but the reverse. It is she who takes power from the male gods to perform her own heroic exploits. Durga reverses the normal role for a female and therefore stands outside normal Hindu society as pictured in the *Dharma-sastras*.

Kali

Even more ambiguous than Durga is the goddess Kali. She is always described as terrible and frightening. She is black, with long dishevelled hair. She is usually naked and adorned with severed arms as a girdle, freshly cut heads as a necklace, children's corpses as earrings, and serpents as bracelets. She haunts the battlefield, where she gets drunk on the hot blood of her victims. Kali is the epitome of antisocial behaviour.

The earliest references to Kali in the Hindu tradition come from about AD 600. In the *Bhagavata Purana*, Kali is presented as the deity of a band of thieves whose leader seeks to achieve Kali's blessing in order to have a son. The thieves kidnap a saintly Brahmin youth with the intention of offering him as a sacrifice to Kali. However, the virtue of the youth burns the goddess herself, and, infuriated, she kills the entire band of thieves. She and her host of demons then decapitate the bodies of the thieves and drink their blood until drunk.[8]

The most famous myth of Kali is found in the *Devimahatmya*.

> Early in the battle the demons Canda and Munda approach Durga with readied weapons. Seeing them prepared to attack her, Durga becomes angry, her face becomes dark as ink. Suddenly the goddess Kali springs from her forehead. She is black, wears a garland of human heads and a tiger skin, and wields a skull-topped staff. She is gaunt, with sunken eyes, grasping mouth, and lolling tongue. She roars loudly and leaps into the battle, where she tears demons apart with her hands and crushes them in her jaws.[9]

This story illustrates the role that appertains to Kali as a personification of anger. Kali is the very embodiment of fury. She is the one who threatens stability and order. Although she is eventually tamed by Siva in the myth of the dance contest, she is never fully subdued. The iconographic representations of Kali and Siva nearly always show Kali as dominant. She is usually seen standing on Siva's body above his erect phallus. In this role she is very important in Tantrism, as we shall see in Chapter 16.

Kali is outside the moral order of Hindu society. Kali invites the one seeking for reality to move beyond the bounds of social order, and perceive the complete picture. She takes her followers from order to chaos, morality to anarchy, restrictions to total abandonment. Kali provides a figure that has fascinated many Western scholars with regard to the psychological issues which she represents.

MAHADEVI

Early Hindu tradition speaks of discrete goddesses, but during the medieval period there was a tendency to think of all goddesses as one. Sometimes Parvati or Laksmi were regarded as the supreme deity, or consort, and the other goddesses merely as manifestations. At other times, the various goddesses were considered merely the manifestations of one transcendent reality called Mahadevi.

Several important philosophical assumptions may be identified in the tradition of the Mahadevi. First, the ultimate, powerful, active reality in the universe is a female being. She has therefore been associated by Western pagans with the concept of Gaia.[10]

Second, Mahadevi is *shakti*—'power'. As mentioned earlier, *shakti* is understood to be the active nature of the godhead by which the universe was created. The male and female elements of divinity are seen as complementary poles of equal status. However, in the text exalting Mahadevi, the female *shakti* element is identified as the essence of reality, and the male element plays a subservient role.

Third, the Mahadevi is often identified with *prakrit* and *maya*. As such, she is identified with existence itself, or that which underlies all existent things. The emphasis is not on the restricting aspects of matter, but on the Devi as the ground of all existence. Because she pervades the material world, it takes on a positive quality. This is the reason for the positive attitude towards the world found in popular Hinduism.

Mahadevi may manifest two opposing features within her mythology: benign and terrible. As benevolent, she is like Vishnu, playing the role of protector and preserver, and is typically thought of as some exalted figure seated in heaven. She does, however, hear the cries of her devotees, and is quick to come to their assistance. On the other hand, Mahadevi also has a terrible form. Most texts extolling Mahadevi tend to focus upon this aspect, and affirm her manifestations as dangerous and bloodthirsty.

These two features teach her devotees that she is an

ambivalent being who is unpredictable in her activity. She gives food to nourish all life, and yet she takes life and causes decay. Life and death is the process through which the energy of Mahadevi is continually recycled.

The identification of Mahadevi with matter and the cycle of life leads to the association of the world with parts of her body. The oceans are her bowels, the mountains her bones, the rivers her veins, and the trees are her body hair. The sun and moon are her eyes, and the nether worlds her legs and feet. The earth itself is therefore the great goddess. This has been taken further in the modern cult of Bharat Mata (Mother India), in which Indians are called children of India and are expected to protect their mother without regard for personal wellbeing.

The Indian national anthem cultivates the theme of the motherland as a goddess.

> Thou art the ruler of the minds of all peoples,
> Dispenser of India's destiny.
> Thy name rouses the hearts of Punjab, Sind, Gujarat
>   and Maratha,
> Of Dravida and Orissa and Bengal.
> It echoes in the hills of Vindhayas and Himalayas,
>   mingles in the music of Jamuna and Ganges
>   and is chanted by the waves of the Indian Sea.
> They pray for thy blessings and sing thy praise.
> The saving of all people waits in thy hand,
> Thou dispenser of India's destiny.
> Victory, victory, victory to thee.[11]

THE GODDESS AS ARCHETYPAL IMAGE

The goddess concept within Hindu thought has stimulated the interest of Western psychologists, and especially Carl Jung and his followers. Jung observed that many recurrent images in the dreams and fantasies of his patients had affiliations with great religious myths. He concluded that below the personal consciousness there exists within the human psyche a transpersonal phenomenon that he called the 'collective unconsciousness'.[12] These universally inherited factors lack specific content, but predispose one to recognise or produce certain mythical ideas that are rooted in one's own life-experiences. These symbolic elements he called 'archetypes'. They may range from geometric patterns to heroic or divine personifications.

Among the chief archetypes encountered are those of the 'anima' and the 'animus'. The anima represents the collective image of femininity, which emerges as a result of the relationships a man has with various women throughout his life. This collective image of the feminine frequently expresses itself in dreams and myths. In myths, she may serve either as the guide for the hero or even the goal for his heroic tasks. She is commonly encountered as the consort of a male deity, enduing him with power. The parallel with the *shakti* notion is clear. The animus is the male equivalent. Jung argued that within the human psyche both the anima and animus are to be found, irrespective of sex.

Another important archetype, according to Jungian psychology, is that of the mother. She is especially personified as the mother goddess or, on a negative side, as the terrible mother or a witch. The figure of Kali is considered the most grandiose image of the terrible mother. She may also appear, however, in a variety of impersonal forms, such as a city, country, the moon, the earth, or deep water. The analogue with mother India as goddess is obvious, but it should be remembered that Jung was influenced by Hindu thought in formulating his psychology. Thus, one would expect Hindu myths to be reflected in Jungian concepts.

The images thrown up by the unconscious, whether positive or negative, are said by Jung to direct psychic energy away from dangerous regression towards symbolic equivalents. The individual will therefore be led forward in his, or her, personal development. Within secular society, human beings have lost the traditional images. What is required, says Jung, is a growth in one's awareness of the collective nature of primordial images and a differentiation of oneself from their suggestive powers. 'The most we can do is to dream the myth onwards and give it a modern dress.'[13]

Clearly, Carl Jung drew heavily upon the complex Hindu mythology of the goddess in his perception of the human psyche. His influence has spread far, both stimulated by, and itself stimulating, the modern feminist movement. Deity as goddess has become an important element within the Western pagan and Wiccan movement. Even the Christian church has had to struggle with the issues of how to conceptualise deity as male, female, both, or neither.

How is the Christian therefore to assess Jungian analysis? Perhaps it is best to quote the words of David Wulff following his investigation of the Hindu goddess in the light of Jungian psychology.

> Do we, then, accept Jung as our guide to these matters? The great majority of American psychologists have rejected his approach as 'mystical' and 'unscientific'. Scholars of religion, for whom these epithets carry far less the intended opprobrium, might be well advised themselves to approach Jung with caution.[14]

Notes:

[1] David Kinsley, *Hindu Goddesses* (University of California Press: Berkeley, 1986), p 219.

[2] Wendy Doniger O'Flaherty, *The Rig Veda* (Penguin: Harmondsworth, 1981), p 179.

[3] Kinsley, *op cit*, pp 26–27.

[4] Kinsley, *op cit*, p 22.

[5] Kinsley, *op cit*, p 33.

[6] Barbara S. Miller, *Love Song of the Dark Lord: Jayadeva's Gitagovinda* (New York, 1977), p 74.

[7] C. MacKenzie Brown, 'The Theology of Radha in the Puranas', in J.S. Hawley and D.M. Wulff (eds), *The Divine Consort* (Beacon Press: Boston, 1986), p 57.

[8] *Bhagavata Purana*, 5:9:12–20.

[9] Kinsley, *op cit*, p 118.

[10] David Burnett, *Dawning of the Pagan Moon* (MARC: Eastbourne, 1991), pp 91–93.

[11] Kinsley, *op cit*, p 183.

[12] Burnett, *op cit*, pp 111–128.

[13] Carl Jung, *Collective Works* (University Press: Princeton, 1953-79), vol 9, pt 1, p 160.

[14] David Wulff, 'Prolegomenon to the Psychology of the Goddess', in Hawley and Wulff, *op cit*, p 297.

CHAPTER 14

Sankara and the Vedanta

T HE ANCIENT WRITINGS of the *Upanishads* do not present any systematised philosophy, but contain a rich variety of ideas and speculations. Some of the notions are totally divergent one to another, and most of the implications have not been fully developed. In later centuries, various attempts were made to draft specific philosophies that would give a more coherent form to the religious ideas of the early Indian sages.

THE SIX SCHOOLS OF PHILOSOPHY

From as early as the beginning of the Christian era, there has been a theoretical classification of the various schools of Hindu thought. These are generally divided into those schools which accept the *Vedas* as authoritative and those that do not. The latter include Buddhists, Jainists, and various anti-religious materialists such as Carvaka (see Figure 14.1). The six schools accepting the *Vedas* are known as *astika*, and have been fitted into a scheme of three pairs.

I	Nyaya	Vaiseshika
II	Sankhya	Yoga
II	Mimamsa	Vedanta

The six schools address a variety of issues that are not merely theological in content. The first two pairs do not deny the authority of the *Vedas*, but pursue an independent line of

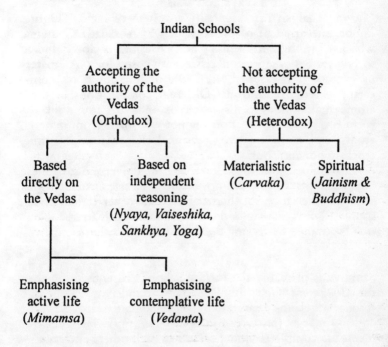

Figure 14.1. Classification of Indian Schools of Philosophy

approach to the problems of philosophy. The last pair argue that they are based directly on the *Vedas*, and develop their philosophies by interpreting the *Vedas* through commentaries.

Nyaya and Vaiseshika

Nyaya ('analysis') is essentially a system of logic. The first important exponent of this system was Aksapada Gautama, who lived in the third century BC. Vaiseshika is closely linked to Nyaya, but is more concerned with cosmology. All material objects, it is claimed, are made of four kinds of atoms: earth, water, fire, and air. Different combinations of these atoms make the various materials that are found in the cosmos. However, the world is not just made from material atoms, and there are five additional elements: space, time, ether, mind, and soul.

Vaiseshika claims that God made the universe out of these nine elements, but he did not create the basic elements. This school is therefore not theistic like some other Indian philosophies, but it assumes a dualism of soul and matter. Liberation is attained by freeing the souls from the other elements.

Sankhya and yoga

Sankhya is probably the earliest school and is mentioned in the *Bhagavad Gita*. Its legendary founder was the sage Kapila. It claims that the universe contains two types of entity—matter (*prakrti*) and souls (*purusha*). The two elements are completely independent of each other. *Prakrti* represents the basis of all material existence, but it does not consist of material elements alone. Under the influence of *purusha* the cosmos evolves, and the annals of the world are the history of this evolution.

An important aspect of Sankhya is its theory of evolution through the interplay of three forces, known as the *gunas*. Although the term is usually translated 'qualities', these *gunas* are more thought of as substances which compose matter in the way that atoms are understood to compose molecules in Western chemistry. This process of interaction has resulted in a pulsation of the universe over long periods, known as *kalpas*. Each *kalpas* lasts about 42,000 million years and represents a period of growth, followed by collapse. This model is widely accepted by the people of India.

The philosophical basis of yoga is the same as that of Sankhya, except that a personal deity is introduced into the system. The soul achieves liberation through the practice of yoga, because yoga purifies the consciousness so the true nature of *purusha* becomes evident. The subject of yoga will be discussed further in the following chapter.

Mimamsa and Vedanta

Mimamsa was originally a school of exegesis that defended the authenticity of the *Vedas*, claiming that these texts were self-existent and eternal. The system concentrated upon the practical implications of the *Vedas* with regard to ritual. Over the centuries, the school has lost much of its importance, and it is now the least significant of the six schools.

While the previous five schools of philosophy are now almost extinct and are of interest primarily to scholars, the Vedanta is still very influential. Almost all the Hindu teachers of recent times have been Vedantists and followers of the great philosopher Sankara.

'Vedanta' literally means 'the end of the *Vedas*'. Vedanta does not consist of just a single system because over the years scholars have interacted with the ideas of Sankara. There are therefore several streams of thought that differ quite radically from one another on certain basic issues. Here we shall consider only the three best known systems of Vedanta. These systems may be represented by their founder and primary exponent, but they take their names from their assumption about the ultimate nature of reality.

Exponent	Main Principle	Name of System
Sankara	Non-dualism	Advaita
Ramanuja	Qualified non-dualism	Visishtadvaita
Madhva	Dualism	Dvaita

One may simply summarise the three systems as if Sankara was veering to a monistic direction, Madhva veering in the opposite direction towards a radical dualism, and Ramanuja holding to a more central path.

SANKARA

Sankara is supposed to have lived from about AD 686 to 718.[1]
He was an orthodox Brahmin holding that the Vedic literature
was sacred and unquestionably true. His brilliance is shown
by the way he used logical argument to bring together the
apparently contradictory passages of the *Upanishads*. His
teaching soon became the standard philosophy of intellectual
Hinduism. It is, therefore, not without reason that his contribution to Hindu thought has been compared with that of St
Thomas Aquinas in Roman Catholicism.[2]

Levels of understanding

How does one know that the experiences of the physical
senses are true and real? In Western society, the question has
been totally dismissed with the assumption of empiricism.
Reality, it is assumed, is that which I perceive with my five
physical senses, and in these senses I trust.

Sankara, in contrast, approached the question in a very
different manner. He postulated two levels of truth. The
higher level is represented by the ineffable void, which can be
pointed to or hinted at, but never concisely expressed. The
other level is that which is generally experienced and is considered as one's everyday world. Sankara made use of the term
maya for the latter.

For example, a traveller in the desert may see a mirage of an
oasis. Although his senses detect the shimmering surface, he
knows that it is only an illusion of water. The perceptions,
given by one's physical senses, may not provide a true interpretation of reality. Similarly, argued Sankara, one must come
to realise that the world about one, which appears so real, is
but an illusion (*maya*).

The following humorous story, told of Sankara, illustrates
some of these points.

Sankara at a certain period was giving instruction in
philosophy and spiritual truth to a maharajah. The
prince however refused to believe the illusoriness of the
world, and so decided to play a trick on him. He got his
servants to release a wild elephant in the path of Sankara
one day as the latter was making his way to the palace

for his usual session with the maharajah. Sankara rapidly scaled the nearest tree. The servants recaptured the beast, and gingerly Sankara got down the tree and made his way to the palace. The king had observed his flight from the elephant from some bushes nearby, but was already back at the palace to welcome his distinguished young teacher upon his arrival. The maharajah was smug. 'You did not, sir' he remarked, 'think that the elephant was an illusion'. Sankara looked at the maharajah with a mild but pitying look. 'I see, sir, that you are still in the grip of ignorance', he replied. 'That was not me you saw flee from an elephant up a tree, but the appearance of me fleeing from an illusory elephant up an unreal tree.'[3]

For Sankara, *maya* is not literal illusion, but is one by analogy. Just as God is not literally a person, but may be understood as such by analogy. For the person seeing the mirage in the desert it has a subjective reality, and the person may shout, 'Water!' Likewise for us living in the world, our physical environment has a subjective reality.

Sankara justified this assumption with what has been called the doctrine of falsification. For example, I may see a long thin shape in the shadow and believe that it is a snake. I will continue to believe that it is a snake until some new experience occurs that contradicts that belief, such as if it fails to move when hit with a stick. I then realise that the shape is not a snake, but only a rope. Likewise, in the higher experience of knowing Brahman and relating my identity with the supreme reality, I must come to realise that what I once took as genuine is not so. My new experience contradicts, and so falsifies, what I used to take as real and natural.

> This whole world the illusion-maker projects out of this [Brahma],
> And in it by illusion the other is confined.
> Now, one should know that Nature is illusion,
> And that the Mighty Lord is the illusion-maker
> (Svet 4:9–10).[4]

Interpretation of contradiction

The concept of two levels of understanding provided Sankara with a means of resolving the problem of the apparent contradictions within the Vedic texts. The approach may be understood by comparing it with two methods that have been used to resolve apparent contradictions within the Bible. First, most evangelical Christians would say that the Bible is inerrant and conveys an everlasting truth. Any apparent contradictions can be solved by a better understanding of the context of the particular text. The problem is, therefore, to resolve them at the same level of truth.

A second method is that one can consider the Bible to be a human creation that merely reflects divine revelation. The problem then becomes which criterion to use to distinguish the divine from the human. One may, for example, consider the biblical account to be expressed in various forms of myths and allegories. It is therefore necessary to try to get behind the myth, as Bultmann attempts with his 'demythologisation'.

Sankara's approach is altogether different from either of these. He proposes that one may consider one portion of scripture as understandable at one level, and another portion understandable at a second level. Thus, if text A appears to contradict text B, this is because they are each speaking at different levels.

The consequence of this analysis is that practical religious ritual must fall within the lower level of truth. Thus, the Vedic sacrifices that are so important to the Brahmin priests are minimised. This explains why many Brahmin priests were quick to criticise Sankara's approach.

Cosmology

The two levels of understanding led to two distinct aspects of Sankara's cosmology. To the higher level he assigns the knowledge of Brahman, who is supposedly beyond description. In fact, there are three things that may be said about Brahman. First, Brahman is being, and is not merely a void. Second, Brahman is pure undifferentiated consciousness. Third, Brahman is bliss, because the realisation of Brahman is the supreme joy.

Corresponding to these three characteristics of Brahman

there are three allied aspects of mystical experience. First is mystic knowledge coming from contact with the ultimate reality. Second, there is pure consciousness from which worldly images have been banished. Third, there is the ultimate sense of bliss.

At the lower level, Brahman appears as personal creator. He is typically symbolised as either Siva, Krishna, Brahma, or Ishwara. In such forms Brahman attracts devotion and worship. Sankara himself wrote hymns in honour of Siva, Vishnu, and especially Ishwara. For him, Ishwara was Brahman seen through the veil of *maya*. In this way, the theory holds together the various manifestations of Hindu religious practice and encourages a tolerance of any religion. Thus modern Hindus have been able to work out a synthesis with Islam and Christianity.

Sankara's assumption of a strict non-duality does, however, cause a major problem. If there is only one ultimate reality (self, or *atman*), how do we understand the idea that somehow self resides in each one of us? The soul of man is, for Sankara, both identical with and subordinate to Brahman. To illustrate this relationship Sankara used certain analogies. For example, the soul is part of Brahman, as a spark is part of the fire. The soul may also be considered as a reflection of the divine, like the image of the sun in water. A more modern illustration would be that of a pot placed over a lamp. The pot has many holes through which the light passes. Looked at from the outside, there seems to be a multitude of small lights, whereas looked at as a whole, there is but one light.

Liberation

The root problem that humanity therefore faces is the inability to see the oneness of the divine self. This essential ignorance, called *avidya*, binds one to everyday life with its endless cycle of birth and rebirth. However, this does have the positive benefit of allowing the worship of divinity that should culminate in true knowledge. It is true knowledge, or *jnana*, that brings liberation and identity with the absolute.

As Sankara writes:

Neither by the practice of Yoga or of Sankhya philosophy, nor by good works, nor by learning, does liberation come; but only through a realization that Atman and Brahman are one—in no other way.[5]

This contrasts with Christianity where the basic problem is original sin, and not ignorance (*avidya*). For Sankara, 'salvation' is achieved through higher knowledge formed in mystical experience. In contrast, in Christianity salvation results from the grace of God through a personal faith in the Person and work of Jesus Christ.

One criticism of Sankara's philosophy concerns an explanation of the nature of suffering. He holds that suffering arises in human beings because they wrongly identify themselves with the body. One must identify oneself only with God (Ishwara). This must involve an attitude of indifference to others. It is for this reason that the highest form of goodness in Hindu thought is *ahimsa* (non-violence) rather than love.

Sankara's philosophy has an elegance and vitality that has caused it to have a lasting influence in Hindu thought. No wonder that the Vedanta system has come to dominate the thinking of most modern Hindu scholars, such as Vivekananda. It has therefore become the Western perception of Hinduism.

RAMANUJA

From earliest times in Indian history, there has been a devotional aspect within Hindu religion. This was seen to be an important element in the teaching of the *Bhagavad Gita*, mentioned in Chapter 10. However, in the seventh century AD, a strong surge of devotional expression began in the south of India, and spread to other parts of the subcontinent. This led to the worship of the great deities—Vishnu and Siva. It was out of this devotional movement (*bhakti*) that some of the greatest theistic thought of India emerged.

The *bhakti* movement of south India flourished among the indigenous people who were not pure Aryan. The new religious fervour therefore caused a potential threat to Brahmin orthodoxy, and a division between Aryan and Dravidian. The teaching of Sankara stressed non-duality. In contrast, the worship of God requires a distinction between the worshipper and the focus of worship. The result is that in Sankara's philosophy worship and devotion are in second place to higher knowledge. It was in this context that Ramanuja wrote, criticising the teaching of Sankara.

Ramanuja was a Tamil Brahmin, commonly believed to have lived from AD 1017 to 1137, some 200 years after Sankara. As a boy, he was trained by a teacher belonging to the Advaita school, but he rebelled against its extreme non-duality. Whereas Sankara regarded unity as excluding diversity, for Ramanuja diversity was involved in the very nature of the absolute who is personality. Even so, many features of the philosophies of Sankara and Ramanuja are similar.

Ramanuja's cosmology

Ramanuja was concerned above all to vindicate the reality of God as infinite personality. He therefore rejected the doctrine of *maya* as Sankara understood it. For Ramanuja, *maya* was the marvellous power of God manifested in the whole of creation. He, like Sankara, considered creation as divine play—*lila*. God can at once dwell in the world and remain free from its limitations and defects.

Ramanuja made use of the analogy of a body in his theology. The cosmos and souls involved in it are God's body. Just as the body is the instrument available to the soul, so the cosmos relates to God. There is, however, a problem. For humans, the body is not perfectly under the control of the soul. For example, although the eye can be blinked at will, it is not easy to control the rate of one's heartbeat. In contrast, God is considered totally in control of the divine body. The cosmos is therefore totally instrumental in the purposes of God.

Because the cosmos is totally dependent for its functioning on the purposes of God, it therefore follows that *karma* is an expression of God's will. Ramanuja took the body analogy a step further in applying it to the human soul. He argued that the soul contains within it a soul, known as the *amtaryamin*, or 'inner controller'. This doctrine provides an explanation of those passages in the *Upanishads* which speak of the divine within the heart that is tinier than a mustard seed. God is thus seen as the soul within soul, and not God being the individual soul.

As a result of this analogy of the body, Ramanuja is often classed as a pantheist. This is not, however, strictly correct. Ramanuja did not identify the material world with God. He always considered that God transcends the material manifestation. Also, his strong emphasis upon *bhakti* is a powerful criticism of the radical monism of Sankara. The philosophy of Ramanuja can only be regarded as a qualified form of monism.

Salvation

Ramanuja reversed the priority of devotion held by Sankara. For the latter, devotion of a personal type was merely provisional. More important were the spiritual insights that led to a complete loss of individual identity. For Ramanuja, it was the impersonal knowledge that was imperfect, and personal devotion was supreme. Salvation therefore means something radically different from the liberation of the Advaita.

Ramanuja told a story to illustrate his notion of the nature and destiny of the soul.

> A young prince once strayed from his royal home. He was taken care of by a brahmin who knew nothing of his identity, and instructed him in the teaching of the *Vedas*. When he was twenty-six, a man whose word he could not doubt informed him that he was the son of the ruler of the country, who was eager to see him again. When he heard this, the young man was overcome with joy. His father also, hearing that his son was alive, rejoiced greatly, and ordered him to be brought back home; and so at last the two were reunited.[6]

The story symbolises the divine nature of the soul and its alienation from God in the earthly life. When the truth about God is discovered, there is great joy as the soul is united with God. Although the highest state of bliss is permanent union with God, there always remains a degree of individual self-consciousness.

God was, for Ramanuja, a God of grace who seeks to unite

man with himself. This raises questions similar to those that have been debated in Christian theology concerning the sovereignty of God and the free-will of human beings. Ramanuja assumed that man is free, but he did not pursue the implications of the idea. In later centuries, his disciples have been sharply divided over the issue. The two schools of thought have tended to refer to themselves as the 'cat-principle' school and the 'monkey-principle' school. When a mother cat wants to carry her kitten to another place, she picks it up by the scruff of the neck. On the other hand, the mother monkey takes her little one on her back, and the baby has to cling on to her as it is transported to the destination. For the cat-principle, salvation is merely through the grace of God. For the monkey-principle, the soul must do something to arrive safely at salvation.

Ramanuja himself was content to postulate the saving power of *bhakti* as a response to divine grace. *Bhakti* can only become effective through the practice of meditation on the divine person.

MADHVA

The *bhakti* movement resulted in many systems of theology along the lines of that formulated by Ramanuja. One of the most important was that of Madhva, who went a step further than Ramanuja and maintained a doctrine of distinct dualism. Madhva was brought up in western India in an area that had been influenced by Jainism and, to some extent, Christianity. Both these religions make a distinction between souls and inanimate matter. It is likely that these religious traditions had an influence upon the Hindu community of the area.

Madhva was strongly antagonistic to the monistic teaching of Sankara. He looked upon Sankara as an incarnation of a demon who was sent to deceive human beings. In Sanskrit, as in Greek, the prefix 'a' means 'non', as in 'atheist' (non-theist). Madhva changed the name of Sankara's philosophy, 'Advaita' (non-duality), by removing the 'a' to produce the name 'Dvaita' (duality). In this bold stroke, Madhva made a sharp distinction between self and Brahman.

For Madhva, salvation was not considered to be union with God, but a drawing close to him in the contemplation of his glory. God saves souls by his grace, without which the strictest devotions would be of no avail. However, grace is only bestowed upon those who live righteous lives. For those who do evil, their souls become so weighed down by *karma* that they cannot rise. They will be expelled from the universe to a state of eternal damnation. Indian religious imagination was able to conceive some horrific view of hell. Dramatic pictures of these hells are often on sale in village markets.

Madhva was a devotee of Vishnu. He considered that all things are the manifestation of the creativity of Vishnu. Salvation comes through a recognition of whom God is. This realisation of God brings a continual flow of love to him that enables the devotee to conquer sin.

Madhva's theology was unique in another respect. He believed in a mediator between God and humans. This agent was Vayu, originally the wind god, whom he described as the son of Vishnu. The resemblance between Madhva's theology and Christianity is striking. Most scholars hold that Madhva was influenced by Christianity, no doubt through the Syriac Church of Kerala.

Many legends have gathered around the person of Madhva himself. As a child, he is supposed to have disputed with learned Brahmins in a temple; when he undertook asceticism, a voice from heaven proclaimed his greatness; he fed multitudes with a handful of food; he walked on water, and he stilled the raging ocean with a glance.

CONCLUSIONS

The philosophy of Sankara was, according to most scholars, the culmination of Brahmanism. His development of a system of monism, embodied in Advaita Vedanta, came to constitute the very essence of Indian thought in the following centuries. It is as a result of his efforts that Buddhism declined in India, and there was a renewal of Brahmanism. No wonder Sankara has captured the imagination of many Western readers.

Hindu thought has developed a rich and varied approach to the human predicament. Different religious leaders belong to different schools, and they are proud of such variety. When one turns to the study of great truths, they argue, no one theory can claim to explain all mysteries.

Notes

[1] Shankara, *Crest-Jewel of Discrimination* (Mentor Book: New York, 1947), p 7.

[2] A.L. Basham, *The Wonder That Was India* (Sidgwick & Jackson: London, 1988), p 328.

[3] Ninian Smart, *Hindu Patterns of Liberation* (Open University Press: Milton Keynes, 1987), unit 4, p 11.

[4] Robert Ernest Hume, *The Thirteen Principal Upanishads* (Oxford University Press: Delhi, 1990), p 38.

[5] Shankara, *op cit*, p 42.

[6] Sidney Spencer, *Mysticism in World Religion* (Penguin: Harmondsworth, 1963), p 43.

CHAPTER 15

Yoga

At about the middle of the nineteenth century Dr J. M.
Honigberger astonished the scholarly world with the
story of a yogi called Haridas. In the presence of
Maharajah Ranjit Singh and his court in Lahore, Haridas
put himself into a state of catalepsy and was buried in a
garden. For forty days a strict watch was kept over the
tomb. When the yogi was exhumed, he was unconscious, cold, and rigid. Hot compresses were placed on
his head, he was rubbed, air was forced into his lungs in
a kind of artificial respiration, and finally Haridas came
back to life.[1]

THIS STORY IS significant not only for the nature of the
remarkable feat, but because it represents one of the
many stories brought back to Europe by travellers,
colonial administrators, soldiers, and scholars in the nineteenth century. It was these accounts that led to the rise of
Sanskrit scholarship and Indian philosophy in the universities
of Europe. One can almost hear the gasp of amazement as the
Victorian scholars realised the sophistication of the teachings
of India. Nowhere was this greater than in the study of yoga.

Yoga is not easy to define. The word is derived from the
Sanskrit root *yuj*, which means 'to unite' or 'to link together'.
This root is the source of the Latin word *jungere* and the
English 'yoke'. The word conveys not so much the sense of
union, although it is used in that way in the *Bhagavad Gita*,

190

but rather, concentration (*dharana*) of mind. It implies the removal of all distractions, with the ultimate goal to unify the spirit in a supreme absorption (*samadhi*). The word 'yoga' has popularly come to describe every technique of asceticism and method of meditation.

PATANJALI

As was shown in Chapter 2, it is within the Harappan civilisation of the Indus valley that the first seeds of yogic practice are usually identified by modern scholars. The famous Proto-Siva Seal shows a man seated in the lotus posture characteristic of later yoga (see Figure 2.1). Years later, as some of the Aryan thinkers began to withdraw from the Brahmanic teaching of the *Vedas*, new philosophies began to emerge in which asceticism and yoga took a central place.

Yoga was developed in a variety of ways in the period after the *Upanishads*, but it was given its classical form in the *Yoga Sutras* of Patanjali. As Worthington correctly writes: 'The *Yoga Sutras* have had a most profound effect on the development and practice of yoga ever since they were first penned.'[2] About the author we know nothing, but he appears to have lived between 300 BC and AD 300. There is no definite proof of the date, but it was certainly after the writing of the *Upanishads* and early Buddhism. Patanjali himself acknowledges (YS 1:1) that he was merely publishing and correcting the doctrinal and technical traditions of yoga.

Patanjali essentially built upon Sankhya philosophy by adding a theistic component, with the belief in a supreme deity called Ishwara. Both Sankhya and yoga consider the world to be a manifest reality rather than being merely illusory. Nevertheless, the world only has this sense of reality because the 'self' is in ignorance of its true nature. When the last 'self' has found freedom from its ignorance, the very manifestation of creation will be no more.

'All is suffering for the wise man,' wrote Patanjali (YS 2:15). However, this does not lead Indian philosophers into despair, but to seek means by which liberation may be achieved. Patanjali did not teach that metaphysical knowledge alone would lead to liberation, but advocated meditation techniques. The *Yoga Sutras* essentially describe the use of the mental processes of mind and will to reach this goal. For Pantanjali, the techniques were not to achieve magical powers, but to reach a state of passivity.

As Eliade writes:

> One rejects this world and depreciates this life because one knows that there exists something else, beyond growth, beyond temporality, beyond suffering. In religious terms it might almost be said that India rejects the cosmos and profane life because she thirsts for a sacred world and way of life.[3]

Patanjali's definition of yoga was 'the abolition of states of consciousness' (YS 1:2). There are no limits to the number of states of consciousness, but Patanjali placed them into three classes.

a) Illusions—dreams, hallucinations, confusion, etc.
b) Awake—'the totality of normal psychological experiences—everything felt, perceived, or thought by the profane man, who does not practice yoga.'[4]
c) States induced by yogic methods.

According to Patanjali, each of these classes has a corresponding science or group of sciences by which experience is governed. Within their set limits, the various experiences are recalled. The aim of Patanjali's techniques is to abolish the first two categories of experience and replace them with the extra-rational experience of the yogic state.

Patanjali taught that there are eight disciplines that are necessary in yoga.

1. *Yama*—restraint, abstention from harming others
2. *Niyama*—observance, physical and mental purity
3. *Asana*—physical exercise
4. *Pranayama*—breath control to gain mastery of vital energy
5. *Pratyahara*—withdrawal, detachment from sensuality
6. *Dharana*—concentration, fixing the mind on a single point
7. *Dhyana*—meditation

8. *Samadhi*—self-collectedness, being able to see the object
of concentration as it really is.

These 'eight limbs', as they are called, form the framework
for most yoga systems even today. By themselves they form a
system known as Raja yoga. Patanjali acknowledged within
the *Yoga Sutras* that he was describing nothing new. He was
merely publishing and correcting practices well known in the
circles of Indian ascetics.

The importance of Patanjali's work was to advance a mystic tradition to the level of a system of philosophy. More than
this, it had an understanding of the human psyche that was
not to be achieved in the West until the development of depth
psychology in the twentieth century. It was to be a major
formative influence upon the ideas of Carl Jung. The great
perception of yogic thought was that by ascetic techniques
there could be a unifying of the states of consciousness.

SCHOOLS OF YOGA

Patanjali briefly mentioned the possibility of yogic techniques
developing paranormal abilities. Yet he was not interested in
these, and viewed them as a mere byproduct. Tantrism, however, saw the cultivation of these powers as a worthwhile end
in itself. It was probably as a result of this movement that
many reactions occurred, leading to a variety of systems of
yoga having their subdivisions. The major systems that may
be encountered by a Westerner are: Tantrism, Hatha, Jnana,
Karma, Bhakti.

Tantrism

Patanjali had, in general, ignored bodily processes, and especially sexual intercourse. Frequent sexual intercourse was
regarded as resulting in a loss of spiritual power. The Tantric
text, on the other hand, made prolonged sexual intercourse a
route to enlightenment. This was seen as a possible route to
reality. Prolonging the sexual act, it was claimed, generates a
flow of sexual energy between the two partners so that both
begin to experience the ultimate oneness of reality.

Most orthodox Hindus were scandalised by these ideas.
However, Tantrism had an impact on Buddhism, especially in
Tibet. Tantras give much attention to magic, spells, and rit-

uals. We shall consider this form of Tantrism further in the following chapter.

Hatha

Tantrism emerged in the seventh century, when its interest in the body brought about a new realisation of the close link between physical and spiritual power. Tantrism probably stimulated a new development known as Hatha yoga.

The word 'Hatha' (pronounced hat-ha) is made up of the syllable *ha*, meaning 'moon', and *tha*, which means 'sun'. Yogis believe that two warring impulses are set in motion every time we breathe. The 'moon' impulse (*prana vayu*) begins in the heart and ascends to the brain. The 'sun' impulse (*apana vayu*) starts at the solar plexus and heads downwards to the anus. The discord between these contrary pulls causes the restlessness we experience in mind and body.

Hatha yoga tries to harness these two sets of currents, and by making them unite to still both body and mind. The person would then be free to concentrate upon his, or her, true self. The breathing exercises are all designed to create the uniting of these two currents. What then happens is that the concentration of energy is pushed down to the base of the spine. Here there is situated one of the seven *chakras* (spiritual energy centres) of the body, and the entrance of the *sushumna*, the central spinal canal (see Figure 15.1).

For most people, the *sushumna* is never opened, as long as they live. By directing energy through the *sushumna*, the yogi suddenly finds that spiritual life has become all at once much easier. Not only may he go directly to Patanjali's stages six, seven and eight, but a whole range of spiritual options open themselves to him.

The British Wheel of Yoga concentrates heavily upon Hatha yoga, as do most Western textbooks on the subject. Hatha is considered valuable for all forms of physical and emotional problems. Hittleman gives tables listing posture to deal with the effects of arthritis, backache, constipation, headaches, respiratory illnesses, and weight control.[5] However, many yogi regard Hatha as merely the preliminary exercises to be gone through before real yoga starts. Hittleman writes that the reader who undertakes his programme seriously can

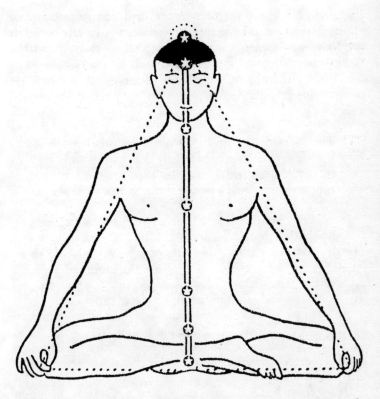

Figure 15.1. The seven *chakras* (spiritual energy centres) of the body

also expect to 'prepare the physical and subtle bodies for the esoteric objectives of Hatha yoga.'[6]

Jnana

Jnana yoga is the yoga of wisdom, and consists of mental effort. This is one of the three systems of yoga attributed to the *Bhagavad Gita*: Jnana, Karma, Bhakti. Throughout the *Gita*, *jnana* (wisdom) is contrasted with *karma* (action). The word *jnana* is from the same root as the Greek *gnosis*. It is often thought suitable for people of an intellectual cast of mind.

> The Blessed Lord said: Of old did I proclaim the two-fold law (that holds sway) in this world—for men of theory the spiritual exercise of wisdom, for men of action the spiritual exercise through works (BhG 3:3).[7]

Jnana yoga involves meditation upon the Vedic scriptures, and thoughtful discrimination on the circumstances of life. The ordinary reasoning mind cannot achieve this, and so an intense state of frustration results. At this point of absolute despair the true self will reveal itself, and the person will jettison the logical mind in favour of direct experience.

An example of this method is the 'who?' inquiry advocated by Ramana Maharishi. The disciple begins by asking, 'Who am I?' He will see that every response made by his ordinary mind is merely a statistic about a being that has been manufactured by the self. The disciple continues to enquire until his ordinary mind has exhausted its responses. Only at this point of exhaustion will the disciple begin to perceive the true answer to the question.

Karma

Karma yoga is the yoga of work and everyday life. Like Jnana, it has its origins in the *Bhagavad Gita*, where Krishna reveals to Arjuna that work can be worship.

> But work alone is your proper business, never the fruits (it may produce): let not your motive be the fruit of the

works nor your attachment to (mere) worklessness
(BhG 2:47).[8]

This system of yoga, which consists of selfless action, takes
the ancient idea of *dharma* and makes its ramifications more
understandable. It calls for the performance of the ordinary
activities of daily life, but in a manner of detachment from
their fruits.

> For the Karma Yogi, then, the art of living lies in his
> performance of action, the discharging of his duties,
> without the intervention of ego, without self-involve-
> ment.[9]

The best known Karma yogi was probably Mahatma
Gandhi, a man with an incredible work rate. Sri Aurobindo
was probably the most influential writer of this school, but he
has few followers in the West.

Bhakti

Bhakti yoga is considered to provide a path for those persons
who are devotional in character. As we have seen in previous
chapters, *bhakti* has been important among the Krishna
Vaisnavites from the time of the *Bhagavad Gita*.

The two major techniques of Bhakti are visualisation and
the repetition of a word or phrase. Visualisation requires that
the devotee finds an image that is arresting and he, or she,
holds it in his, or her, mind. The image is formed internally,
but it may be reinforced through an external image that is
cherished by the devotee.

The repetition of a word or phrase is common in many
forms of yoga, and is known as a *mantra*. As Worthington
writes:

> The aspirant pays a great deal of money for a *mantra*,
> which is a single work or phrase in Sanskrit taken from
> an ancient stock. It is selected to suit the uniqueness of
> each individual, and has no particular meaning. It is
> given during a short initiation ceremony, and the medi-

tator must return for instruction each day for four days.[10]

Each *mantra* is considered the embodiment of a force that has been created by placing certain syllables in particular formations. Through the prescribed rhythm and number of repetitions, the yogi is believed to generate powerful vibrations that are absorbed into him. Hittleman writes, 'He effects Yoga (fusion) with it.'[11]

TRANSCENDENTAL MEDITATION

In the 1960s, a growth in the Eastern cults began to have great influence, and some young people began to look to yoga for mind-expanding experiences. Perhaps the most influential form of yoga was that called Transcendental Meditation, or TM. This is a form of Bhakti meditation. The founder of the movement was Maharishi Mahesh Yogi. He was born in central India in about 1918. After studying for a degree in physics, he became the favourite disciple of 'His Divinity Swami Brahmananda Saraswati', generally known as Guru Devi. Upon the death of Guru Devi in 1953, Mahesh retired to the austere caves of the Himalayas for two or three years. He emerged to take the title 'Maharishi' (Great Seer), and began to teach a yoga technique that he called 'Transcendental Meditation'. His reception in India was indifferent, and he decided to take his teaching to the West.

Maharishi came to Britain in 1958, and moved to the USA a year later. His movement was first known as the 'Spiritual Regeneration Movement', and in 1961 it was granted a certification of incorporation for education purposes. An unlikely catalyst proved to be the Beatles. George Harrison was the first to meet Maharishi, through his study of Indian music. The Beatles began to practise meditation, and suddenly the number of followers of TM exploded. In 1965 there had been only 220 meditators involved in TM, but by the end of 1968 there were over 12,000. By October 1972, 10,000 new meditators were being enrolled each month. In UK, the monthly figure (500 converts a month) compared with the number of baptisms of the established church (660 monthly).

As far as the Beatles were concerned, the dream turned

bitter. 'We were wrong,' the Beatles concluded, with John Lennon accusing the Maharishi of being a 'lecherous womaniser'.[12] It is believed that George Harrison was publicly denouncing him as the fool in the Beatles' song 'Fool on a Hill'. However, even in 1992, Harrison still had close links with the movement.

In 1975, Maharishi announced the 'Dawn of the Age of Enlightenment' and received nationwide publicity through his appearances. The Spiritual Regeneration Movement became the 'Science of Creative Intelligence', and the Maharishi presented an image of a psychotherapist rather than a guru. Although his close disciples heard him teach from the *Bhagavad Gita*, to outsiders he repeated, 'It's not a religion.' The following year, he claimed that Americans were being initiated at the rate of 15,000 per month, and more than 350,000 were trained in TM.

The movement has a world plan that consists of seven goals.

1. To develop the full potential of the individual.
2. To improve governmental achievements.
3. To realise the highest ideal of education.
4. To eliminate the age-old problem of crime and all behaviour that brings unhappiness to the family of man.
5. To maximise the intelligent use of the environment.
6. To bring fulfilment to the economic aspirations of individuals and society.
7. To achieve the spiritual goals of mankind in this generation.

In 1977, the movement ran into difficulty with the US Federal Court concerning whether the movement was a religious or educational organisation. By claiming to be an educational technique rather than a religion, the movement had been able to receive both federal and state funding. On 19 October 1977, US District Judge H. Curtis Meanor declared, 'No inference was possible except that the teaching of the SCI/TM and the *puja* are religious in nature.'[13] This resulted in an eighteen-month legal battle, resulting in the US Court of Appeals affirming this ruling. The movement began to face growing criticism, especially from Christians.[14]

TM relies upon the Bhakti yoga techniques of chanting *mantras*, but does not assume any personality of God. The *mantra* is given to the disciple at an initiation ceremony. Here, the initiate kneels before a picture of Maharishi's deceased master, Guru Devi, and places fruit and flowers on a handkerchief. The initiator then begins to sing songs in Sanskrit. After the *puja*, the teacher bows before the picture of Guru Devi and invites the candidate to bow beside his initiator. The teacher will then tell the person his *mantra*.

TM, as prescribed by the Maharishi, requires the initiate to sit with eyes closed in a quiet relaxed position for twenty minutes, both in the morning and in the evening. During these periods, the initiate continually repeats his, or her, personal *mantra*. No mental discipline is necessary except the repetition of the *mantra*. The mind is allowed to become totally passive, so relieving tension. Advanced meditators claim to have mastered the art of levitation. Photographs of such levitations have been made public. However, offers of $10,000 to witness such an act have gone unclaimed. The nearest that has been demonstrated is what amounts to disciples bouncing around a room filled with cushions while in a cross-legged position.

In 1991, Maharishi Mahesh revealed to the world, via his followers, knowledge of the 'natural law'. This claims to be the association between sounds used in 'Vedic science' and modern mathematical models of quantum mechanics known as the 'superstring' theory. The 'discovery' was presented in a way that left most people blinded by science.

> In the unified quantum field theories of modern physics, the precise mathematical form of these fundamental laws is found in the Lagrangian of the superstring and the $N=1$ supergravity theories. In Maharishi's Vedic Science, these same fundamental laws — the Constitution of the Universe — are found in the eternal, self-referral dynamics of consciousness knowing itself.[15]

During the British elections of 1992, the Natural Law Party undertook a massive advertising campaign in which they claimed:

All candidates of the Natural Law Party have demonstrated greater orderliness of brain functioning, as indicated by increased EEG-coherence, and greater command of Natural Law indicated by their improved mind-body co-ordination in their achievement of Yogic Flying.... The ultimate goal of the Natural Law Party is for everyone to enjoy Heaven on Earth through the implementation of Maharishi's Master Plan to Create Heaven on Earth.[16]

TM has attempted to take traditional Indian mysticism and adapted it to a Western cultural context. It has been presented as a philosophy rather than a religion even though its roots are very much within the Hindu tradition. As a result of this form of interpretation, some of the leading companies and government departments have adopted TM techniques as a means for increasing the creative potential of their staff. There is, however, little or no objective proof of the effectiveness of these methods.

THE CHRISTIAN AND YOGA

After taking a seminar on the topic of yoga at a large Christian convention, I was immediately surrounded by many from the audience. Questions came thick and fast. The subject provoked great interest, but the views of the people present varied widely. On the one hand, there was a Christian couple who taught yoga at their local health centre, and on the other hand, there were people who regarded yoga as demonic. This illustrates the wide diversity of opinion found among Christians on this subject.

One may identify five main attitudes that Christians have taken concerning yoga. First, there is the view that all religions naturally include yoga. Adherents of this view would argue that all faiths, by the very fact that they are spiritual, are fundamentally devotional yoga. Yoga is not a discipline restricted to Hinduism, but is found in Buddhism, and in some forms of Sufism, as advocated by Idries Shah, for example.

Christopher Isherwood writes, 'There is no doubt that the great majority of believers, in all the world's major religions, are fundamentally bhakti yogis.'[17] Bhakti yoga, as we have seen, is an attempt to realise the true self by devotion to a chosen divine image. The aim is to escape from *karma*. The use of the word 'yoga' in this sense is so wide that it hardly means anything more distinct than 'spirituality'.

Second, there are those who regard yoga as the lost secret of Christianity. Maharishi Mahesh Yogi initially claimed that the world religions have failed because they have lost the techniques of yoga. There is no historical evidence for such an argument.

Third, some Christians have regarded yoga as an applied philosophy, not a religious system. As we have seen already, this is the argument presented by TM in recent years. Yoga and religion are considered as different entities that complement one another, as do science and literature. The US courts, however, after careful consideration of TM, could not see how yoga could be severed from its roots as a spiritual discipline of Hinduism.

Fourth, some hold the view that yoga is demonic. This has been the typical response of many evangelicals to the subject. Certain types of yoga, such as Tantric, do involve paranormal and occult phenomena. However, can the same be said about Hatha yoga? May this be used as a spiritual exercise? It must be remembered that Hatha yoga was essentially developed to facilitate other more advanced forms of yoga.

Finally, yoga has been considered a spiritual discipline that may be used by a Christian for his, or her, own spiritual development. The writings of Jean-Marie Dechanet, a French Benedictine monk, have been influential in promoting this view. He considers Christian yoga as simply a preparation for communion with God, an emptying of oneself to appreciate more fully the grace of God.

Dechanet recognises that not all forms of yoga may be used for Christian purposes.

> The essential point is to understand thoroughly and to admit *that it is not a question of turning a given form of Yoga into something Christian,* but of bringing into the service of Christianity and of the Christian life (espe-

cially when this is given up to contemplation) the undoubted benefits arising from yogic disciplines.[18]

Many Christians have sympathy for Dechanet's views, but have reservations. For example, if yoga is so important for spiritual development, why did Jesus not teach this, or some similar practice, to his disciples? If one regards Hatha yoga as merely a spiritual discipline that may be divorced from its Hindu origins, are there not other disciplines that would be equally effective? For example, yoga has been used as an exercise to develop physical fitness, but one can find isotonic schemes which produce the same results. Christians contemplating the use of yoga must ask themselves the question: What makes yoga special?

Hatha yoga was not developed to stand on its own, but as a preparation for Raja yoga. Dechanet recognises the dangers of Raja yoga, as well as other forms.[19] Can yoga be neutral? Almost all Christians would answer negatively, arguing that any benefits that may be gained from Hatha yoga can be achieved equally well through prayer and contemplation upon the Holy Bible.

The Bible does speak about meditation, but the implications are totally different from those carried within yoga. The Greek word used in the New Testament is *meletao*, which comes from the root 'to care for'. The word is translated in two ways: either to be diligent in religious practice, or to ponder or imagine.[20] There is no notion here of dissociation from the world, nor of absorption (*samadhi*) into the ultimate reality. The Bible continually speaks in terms of a relationship between God and his people.

Notes

[1] Mircea Eliade, *Patanjali and Yoga* (Schocken Books: New York, 1962), p 3.

[2] Vivian Worthington, *A History of Yoga* (Arkana: London, 1989), p 69.

[3] Eliade, *op cit*, p 18.

[4] Eliade, *op cit*, p 51.

[5] Richard Hittleman, *Yoga: The 8 Steps to Health and Peace* (Bantam Books: New York, 1978), pp 208–210.

[6] *Ibid*, p 111.

[7] R.C. Zaehner, *The Bhagavad-Gita* (Oxford University Press: London, 1973), p 161.

[8] *Ibid*, p 145.

[9] Hittleman, *op cit*, p 67.

[10] Worthington, *op cit*, p 184.

[11] Hittleman, *op cit*, p 55.

[12] Bob Larson, *Book of Cults* (Tyndale House: Wheaton, 1987), p 336.

[13] *Ibid*, p 333.

[14] James Bjornstad, *The Transcendental Mirage* (Dimension Books: Minneapolis, 1976).

[15] Advertisement, *The Independent* (16 March 1992): pp 16–17.

[16] Natural Law Party Manifesto, *The Independent* (20 March 1992): p 14.

[17] Swami Prabhavananda and Christopher Isherwood, *How to know God: The Yoga Aphorisms of Patanjali*, p 107.

[18] Jean-Marie Dechanet, *Christian Yoga* (Search Press: Tunbridge Wells, 1984), pp 17–18.

[19] *Ibid*, pp 15–17.

[20] W.E. Vine, *Expository Dictionary of New Testament Words*, vol 3 (Oliphants: London, 1940), p 55.

CHAPTER 16

Sexual Power: Tantrism

A NOTICE AT the entrance to the city of Rajneesh read, 'Shoes and minds are to be left here at the gate.'[1]
    The subject of Tantrism introduces terms, symbols, and ideas that are exotic to the Western mind. European scholars of the nineteenth century called Tantric images crude pornography, and yet their erotic symbolism engendered a strange fascination. The poetry of Tantrism uses terms that stretch the human intellect beyond the credible.

> Crazy is my Father, crazy my Mother,
> And I, their son, am crazy too!
> Shyama (the dark one, an epithet of Kali) is my Mother's name.
> My Father strikes His cheeks and makes a hollow sound:
> Ba-ba-boom! Ba-ba-boom!
> And my Mother, drunk and reeling,
> Falls across my Father's body!
> Shyama's streaming tresses hang in vast disorder;
> Bees are swarming numberless
> About Her crimson Lotus Feet.
> Listen, as She dances, how Her anklets ring![2]
> (*Bengali devotional hymn to Kali*)

In Tantric art, Siva and Kali are the major figures, but it is nearly always Kali who dominates the pair. She is the one shown standing or even dancing on Siva's prone body, stimulating his penis to erection. It is Kali who brings to life the wild sexual forces of Siva. Kali is dark, disruptive, intimidating, with ghastly habits. It is she who occupies a central place in Tantrism.

The term 'Tantra' is a name commonly given to the texts dealing with the esoteric practices of some Hindu, Buddhist, and Jaina sects. The word 'Tantra' comes from the root *tan*, 'to extend, to continue, to multiply'. 'Tantra would be "what broadens knowledge".'³ In the *Vedas*, the word 'Tantra' occurs in the sense of a loom, and so implies a method of doing or making something. Thus, Tantra came to mean the essentials of a religious system. In India, it is followed only by a small minority, but its exotic character has attracted greater interest in the West.

ANTIQUITY OF TANTRA

The origins of Tantra are unclear, but it has roots that go back to earliest times. Like the Vedic knowledge, Tantra was primarily a philosophical movement, somewhat akin to the old Pythagorean concept of 'philosophy'. It may best be regarded as a tradition that ran parallel to the main Brahmanical stream. Tantra enjoyed popularity among ascetics, and became a common movement throughout India. Buddhism and Jainism also accepted certain aspects of its beliefs and practice.

Tantrism appears to have developed at the social fringes of the Aryan peoples, especially in the regions of Bengal and the Himalayas in the north, and in the Dravidian area of the south. This may be considered a further example of the mutual interaction that occurred between the Aryans and indigenous peoples of the Indian subcontinent.

Many associated myths give an idea of a low caste origin. The emphasis tends to be on non-Aryan goddesses, including Durga and Kali, who were discussed in Chapter 13. Tantra may therefore have had its origins in ancient fertility rites. Eliade points to this as an indication of a goddess religion that was once common throughout the world. As we have seen, this was a feature of the religious beliefs of the Harappan civilisation.

Tantra shows similarities to the worship of Baal and

Asteroth practised by the Canaanites. They gave importance to ritualised sex with sacred prostitutes at the 'high places'. These practices permeated into ancient Israelite society and were strongly condemned by the Old Testament prophets.

The term 'Tantra' essentially denotes a particular group of post-Vedic Sanskrit writings, heterogeneous in content, and dealing with many secret practices. Most of these are dated about fourteenth to sixteenth century, and some even as late as the eighteenth century. It is unlikely that any of the Tantric texts predate the Gupta period. These texts show a more subtle idea of deity and philosophy, with its roots in non-duality.

Some advocates of Tantric philosophy look back to the *Vedas* for its origin, and so give the philosophy a degree of respectability. Both the *Rg Veda* and the *Atharva Veda* contain elements of magic and rituals. The *Atharva Veda*, especially, contains many charms and spells, but because it has been greatly Brahminised, it is difficult to distinguish which elements are Aryan and which indigenous. However, it is more likely that this association of Tantrism with the *Vedas* is merely one of back projection through the association of common themes.

Secular poetry and literature of the post-Gupta period is essentially antagonistic to Tantrism. The criticism is based upon two aspects. First, that it is unvedic in character. Second, that it is deliberately formulated to lead degenerates astray. Strong warnings are given to avoid even the more moderate of the Tantric sects.

CHARACTER OF TANTRA

All Tantric practices are considered repugnant by mainstream Hindus, who condemn Tantrism's orgiastic behaviour. However, Hindus do make two broad distinctions within Tantrism: the 'right-hand' (Daksinacara) and the 'left-hand' (Vamacara). The 'right-hand' tends to be the more moderate and therefore somewhat more acceptable to the ordinary Hindu. The 'left-hand' is considered more extreme and repugnant, with its focus upon the goddess Kali. In contrast, practitioners of Tantra consider the usual Hindu rites, though not wholly ineffectual, are only suitable for the ordinary worshippers of the goddess.

Tantrism is mostly concerned with practical methods, and lays little stress on religious theories. It does, however, have certain important concepts. First, is that the supreme reality has two aspects: Siva (male) and Shakti (female). Shakti is perceived as the 'cosmic force' that is elevated to the rank of a divine mother, who supports the universe and all its living beings.

The notion of the goddess implies that every woman becomes the incarnation of Shakti. Philosophically, the discovery of the goddess is considered by the authors of the Tantric texts as a new revelation of a timeless truth. The *Vedas*, with the Brahminic tradition, is considered inadequate for the contemporary world, and people need to return to the very source of life. The power of Shakti is identified with cosmic consciousness, since she projects the unity of male and female principles.

To realise this, Tantrism has developed a series of practices that break the usual taboos of Hinduism. The 'left-hand' path indulges in the five Ms, or *pancamakara*. These are as follows:

1. *Mamsa*—eating meat.
2. *Madya*—use of alcoholic drinks, drugs, and other intoxicants.
3. *Matsya*—eating fish.
4. *Mudra*—parched or fine grain. There is something within the preparation that makes one socially unacceptable.
5. *Maithuma*—sexual intercourse.

The act of sexual intercourse is symbolic of the Siva-Shakti concept. As such, it is considered a yogic discipline and not an erotic act. Sexual union is believed to create a state of heightened suspense, leading to the completion of all mental processes in a mystic sense of oneness with the basic reality of the universe. The fundamental principle of the 'left-hand' path is that spiritual progress is not achieved by avoiding desires, but by transforming them so that they become means of liberation.

As Ajit Mookerjee writes:

Sex is seen as divine in itself, and a source of a vital energy capable of acting with tremendous force on the physio-psychic state which in turn reacts on the higher cosmic plane.[4]

The *Guhyasamaja Tantra* states that through sexual union:

No one succeeds in gaining perfection by means of difficult and wearying exercises; but perfection can be easily won by means of satisfying all one's desires.[5]

This seems to give the impression that the Tantric path is easy, but in practice there are many long and arduous disciplines. The disciple must overcome the distinctions of duality between clean and unclean, sacred and profane. Like some spiritual hero, he is required to break his bondage to a world that is artificially fragmented. 'By affirming the essential worth of the forbidden, he causes the forbidden to lose its power to pollute, to degrade, to bind.[6]

Another important concept of Tantra is that the human body is believed to be a microcosm of the universe. The spinal chord represents the fabulous Mt Meru at the centre of the universe. The three main nerve connections running along the left, the right, and the middle of the spine represent the three sacred rivers—Ganges, Yamuna, and Sarasvati. The breathing process represents the passage of time.

Shakti is also called Kundalini, which is the Sanskrit word meaning 'coiled-up'. Kundalini lies serpent-like, coiled at the base of the spine. It frequently happens that an individual's Kundalini energy lies dormant throughout his, or her, entire life. The object of the Tantric practice of Kundalini yoga is to awaken this cosmic energy and allow it to move along the spinal chord through the *chakras* to be united with Siva. It is this union of Siva-Shakti that brings about the blissful realisation of non-duality.

Kundalini is often conceived as a coiled snake as in the *Yoga Kundalini Upanishad* (1:82).

The Divine Power,
Kundalini, shines

like the stem of a young lotus;
like a snake, coiled round upon herself,
she holds her tail in her mouth
and lies resting half asleep
at the base of the body.

In order for the Kundalini Shakti to be manifest, it must pass through the *chakras* that lie along the axis of the spine as consciousness potentials. The *chakras* are assumed to be situated not in the material body, but in the etherial body. They cannot therefore be studied by any physiological means.

Tantras commonly mention six *chakras*, though the number varies from text to text. Starting from the base of the spine, these centres are known as Muladhara, Svadhisthana, Manipura, Anahata, Visuddha, and Ajna. Sahasrara, the seventh, transcendent *chakra*, is said to be situated four-fingers' breadth above the top of the head (see Figure 15.1).

TANTRIC PRACTICE

Tantric practices vary according to the particular sect, and the teaching of one's guru. However, there are some common patterns.

Diksa

First, initiation is common to Hindu, Buddhist, and Jaina Tantrism and is frequently called by the term *diksa*. Although the revelation is intended for everyone, Tantrism requires an initiation that can only be given by a guru. It is the guru alone who can transmit the esoteric doctrine. *Diksa* is therefore essential, and consists of a one-to-one process between guru and disciple. Although several persons are frequently initiated at a time, this does not mean that group initiation is involved, but is usually done for convenience when the guru is renowned. During the ritual, each of the aspirants come to him separately, and he whispers a particular *mantra* into his ear.

Mantra

A *mantra* is a series of sounds for Tantric purposes. In the nineteenth century European scholars considered them to be a 'senseless mumbo-jumbo of words' because they could not identify any coherent meaning to them. However, this explanation was to miss the very purpose of *mantra*, which is twofold. First, sounds help the yogic practice of concentration. Second, they internalise the ritual liturgy. The word *mantra* comes from two Sanskrit roots, *man*, to think, and *trai*, to protect or free from bondage. *Mantra* is therefore thought that liberates.

Swami Sivanandra Radha points out that one of the greatest problems in concentrating the human mind stems from 'mental background noises'.[7] These are an accumulation of influences from the world around us, memories, and impressions that are triggered by associations. Swami Radha says that a *mantra* is able to help the mind focus on a point.

Sir John Woodroffe (alias A. Avalon) was the first non-Asian believer of Tantra to write on the subject. In his idealised perspective of Tantra, he states that *mantra* is not like prayer, nor is it things the worshipper wants to tell the deity. The *mantra* that is received at initiation is like a seed sown in the person's heart.

> ...*mantra* is a potent compelling force, a word of power—the fruit of which is mantrasiddhi—and is thus effective to produce monistic perception and liberation....[8]

Nyasa

Tantric disciplines include many meditative rituals and exercises that can be accomplished only with the help of yogic practice. This practice of *nyasa* is an identification of the worshipper with the deity. Initially, this requires the 'visualisation' of an image, into which the life breath of the deity is infused. Then the worshipper seeks to identify further and become himself enlivened with the deity. Almost piece by piece the devotee seeks to identify his body. As a Tantric maxim states, 'One cannot adore a god unless one is oneself a god.'[9]

Once received from the lips of the guru, the *mantra* is believed to possess unlimited powers. The *mantra* has the potential, with the proper recitation, to be that which it represents. Each deity possesses a *mantra* that is its 'seed', and so may become its very being. As Eliade writes:

> By repeating this *bija mantra* in conformance with the rules, the practitioner appropriates its ontological essence to himself, assimilates the god, the state of sanctity, etc., into himself in a concrete, immediate fashion.[10]

Mandala

A ritual peculiar to Tantra consists of constructing a *mandala*. The word literally means 'circle', but it is in fact a complex design comprising a circular border enclosing various symbolic shapes. The simplest *mandala* is the *yantra*, which is composed of a series of triangles. There are nine triangles in all, four apex up, and five apex down, surrounded by several concentric circles which are framed in a square with four 'doors'. The triangle pointing down symbolises the female principle Shakti, and the triangle pointing up, the male principle Siva. The *mandala* is considered to be an image, or model of the cosmos, in which the gods manifest themselves (see Figure 16.1).

Basham gives a picture of the typical Tantric ritual.

> Small groups of initiates met at night, often in a temple or private house, but also frequently in a burning-ground, among the bones of the dead. The group formed a circle, seated around the circumference of a large circular magical diagram (*yantra, mandala*) drawn on the ground. Though the members of the circle might include brahmans and outcastes, there was no distinction at the ceremony—all were equal, and no ritual pollution occurred from their contact.[11]

This mixing of castes is shocking to the orthodox Hindu. The ritual continues with the group indulging in the five Ms, the *pancamakara*. Meat and fish are eaten, alcohol is drunk, and even promiscuous copulation takes place. In the 'left-hand' path the instructions are carried out literally, but are taken in a figurative sense by the 'right-hand' path. Some groups may bring their wives to the circle for the purpose.

Figure 16.1. The Yantra Mandala

Asana

The ritual of *tantra-asana* is performed with a partner of the opposite sex. The ritual is usually performed in a solitary place at a time determined by a guru. The female participant is seen as the reflection of Shakti. The nude female is no longer regarded as flesh and blood, but as the goddess. Mookerjee writes, 'During sexual intercourse, the partners can experience glimpses of cosmic unity and transcend their feelings of individual separateness.[12]

It should be stressed that such practice is condemned by all orthodox Hindus, who regard it to be gross immorality. In the few cases known of by the writer of Westerners practising *tantra-asana*, severe emotional and social problems have resulted.

A parallel ritual is found in many European Wiccan groups. In the third initiation of Wicca, a circle is made in which the priestess becomes the incarnation of the goddess, and as such initiates the male. The priestess lies naked in the circle, and the man unites with her as the phallic lord.[13] This association is not surprising as Aleister Crowley, a major innovator of Western paganism, was much influenced by Tantric yoga.[14]

NEO-TANTRA

The most influential exponent of Tantra among Western people has been Bhagwan Shree Rajneesh. He urges his followers, 'Reclaim your freedom to love. Reclaim your freedom to be, and then life is no longer a problem. It is an ecstasy.[15]

Rajneesh Chandra Mohan was born at Kuchwada, in the state of Madhya Pradesh in India, on 11 December 1931. His father was a businessman. From 1944 to 1951 Rajneesh studied at Jabalpur and obtained a BA degree, and in 1957 he completed post-graduate studies in philosophy. From 1957 to 1967 he taught philosophy in two colleges, but finally resigned to devote himself to the spiritual regeneration of humanity.

In 1974 he moved to Pune, and bought a large bungalow as an ashram for his followers. His philosophical training and superb oratory attracted many Western followers. In six years he became very rich, and this caused him to gain many enemies. He was finally forced to leave India, and went to the

USA in June 1981. That year he bought a 64,000 acre ranch in Oregon, where he set out to build a Utopian commune of sannyasins.

By 1985, the movement listed nineteen centres in ten countries.[16] Rajneesh was worth seven million dollars, and owned seventy-four Rolls-Royces. The dream-city that he had claimed would be the only city in the world without crime was turned into an armed enclave. Rajneesh himself was in difficulties with the USA government over tax issues. On 14 November 1985, Rajneesh made a bargain with the US District Court to pay $400,000 in fines, and agreed to leave the country in five days. He returned to India, and a hostile reception. He vowed never to make a commune again.

Rajneesh's philosophy is anti-intellectual. His view of sex and mysticism is a deliberate combination of Tantrism and Jungian psychology. His basic assumption is that behind all the multiplicity in the world there is one reality that he calls God or Brahman. When many Westerners were turning to yoga to achieve unity with reality, Rajneesh revived the tradition of Tantra, and expressed it in a form immediately relevant to Western young people.

In his popular book, *From Sex to Super Consciousness*, Rajneesh argues that religions have so far condemned sex as sin. This has made people more sexual. He states that sex is divine. To turn sex into meditation there should be a total freedom of inhibition in sex. He therefore advocates total sexual licence.

> This is the tantric experience. Tantra says that you feel ecstatic only because something of your inner bliss flows to you. It is not coming from the outer woman, it is not coming from the outer man, it is coming from your innermost core.
>
> You have not known your deepest core. The first glimpse comes through total sex. Once known, the path can be travelled in other ways also. Just looking at a flower, you can be in the same ecstasy as when you meet with your beloved in a climax.
>
> If you remain aware you will come to know that sex is not just sex. Sex is the outermost layer: deep inside is

love and even deeper is prayer and deepest is God himself. Sex can become a cosmic experience. Then it is Tantra.[17]

The philosophy of Rajneesh is monistic, and as with all monistic teaching it cannot allow anything to be classed as evil. 'So tantra is not concerned with your so-called morality.[18] However, he did not hesitate to criticise other religious leaders. He accused Christian ministers of preaching sin to make people feel guilty, and so produce inferiority.[19] He also antagonised many Indians by condemning Gandhi for political mistakes.

How does one assess Rajneesh's attempt at worldwide spiritual regeneration with his monistic philosophy? The question may best be answered by considering his various communes, and especially those in Pune and Oregon. Internal power struggles resulted in the city becoming more like an armed camp. Rumours of gross sexuality were vividly illustrated when the BBC screened a documentary that had been filmed in secret at one of the meditation camps. Rajneesh himself had many girlfriends. One ex-*sannyasin* said that some women regarded sex with Rajneesh as 'the ultimate *darsan*'.[20]

Rajneesh finally fled from the centre at Oregon, and even the people of India did not want him. Many hurt and disillusioned individuals were left behind. An ex-disciple said, 'Rajneesh allows his disciples to sin as they have never sinned before, only he does not call it sin.'[21]

Notes

[1] Rajneesh, *Neo-Tantra* (Harper & Row: London, 1976).

[2] David Kingsley, *Hindu Goddesses* (University of California Press: Berkeley, 1988), p 120.

[3] Mircea Eliade, *Patanjali and Yoga* (Schocken Books: New York, 1975), p 175.

4 Ajit Mookerjee, *Kundalini: The Arousal of the Inner Energy* (Clarion Books: Delhi, 1982), p 59.

5 Eliade, *op cit*, p 180.

6 Kingsley, *op cit*, p 124.

7 Swami Sivanandra, *Mantras: Words of Power* (Timeless Books: Porthill, 1980), p 25.

8 A. Avalon, *Introduction to Tantra Shastra* (Ganeshan & Co: Madras, 1955), p 81.

9 Eliade, *op cit*, p 181.

10 Eliade, *op cit*, p 183.

11 A.L. Basham, *The Wonder that was India* (Sidgwick & Jackson: London, 1988), p 337.

12 Mookerjee, *op cit*, p 64.

13 Vivianne Crowley, *Wicca: The Old Religion in the New Age* (Aquarian Press: Wellingborourgh, 1989), p 235.

14 David Burnett, *Dawning of the Pagan Moon* (MARC: Eastbourne, 1991), p 74.

15 Rajneesh, *op cit*, cover.

16 Vishal Mangalwadi, *The World of the Gurus* (Nivedit Good Books: New Delhi, 1987), p 166.

17 Rajneesh, *op cit*, p 44.

18 Acharya Rajneesh, *The Book of Secrets* (Thames & Hudson: London, 1976), p 22.

19 *Ibid*, p 22.

20 Mangalwadi, *op cit*, p 162.

21 Mangalwadi, *op cit*, p 168.

CHAPTER 17

Reform and Renewal

THE PORTUGUESE SHIPS under the command of Vasco da Gama arrived at the west coast of India in 1498. They had travelled the long journey around Africa to discover the sea route to India. India had become used to invaders, but they had usually come from the northwest. Little did the people of India realise that these newcomers would initiate a chain of events that would have a profound influence on every aspect of their way of life.

After the Portuguese came adventurers from France, Holland, Denmark, and Britain. They established trading settlements along the coasts. Initially, these settlements were to provide bases for the Europeans to trade, but gradually they achieved a growing political influence over the surrounding areas. In time, these small settlements were to expand and become the vast metropolises of the twentieth century: Bombay, Madras, and Calcutta.

In the sixteenth and seventeenth centuries, the Mughal emperors unified the whole of north India (see Figure 17.1). This Muslim civilisation reached a splendour that had not been seen in the subcontinent since the days of the Guptas in the third to the sixth centuries AD. It was during the Mughal period that the world famous Taj Mahal at Agra was constructed. By the close of the seventeenth century, the Mughal empire was virtually at an end, and the European powers were ready to move into the political vacuum.

In 1701, the British East India Company was granted the

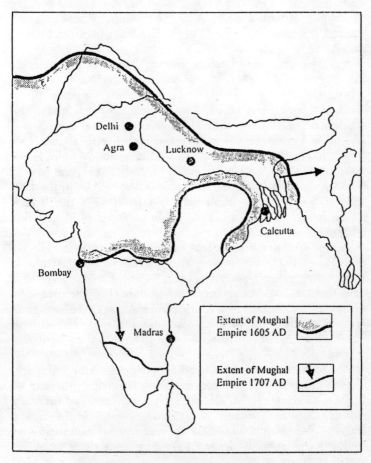

Figure 17.1. Extent of the Mughal Empire

territorial revenues of the area near Calcutta. Gradually, the company gained a greater role in the trade of the whole region of Bengal, and also in Tamil Nadu in the south. A dispute led to the battle of Plassey in 1757, in which Robert Clive gained undisputed influence over the area of Bengal. By 1788, Calcutta had grown to have a population of 250,000, and become the largest British base in Asia. The company was eager to expand and gain a monopoly of the rich trade between Europe and Asia.

By 1840, India had become Britain's most important trading partner. However, there was considerable discontent within the country. Tribal wars broke out with the Bhils, Kols, and Santals, as Hindu settlers invaded tribal lands. The economic conditions of the 1830s were such that there was a shortage of grain, resulting in rioting and dissatisfaction. This finally led to the rebellion of 1857. After a bloody fight, Delhi was taken by the British forces in November 1857, and later in the same month Lucknow. Because of the rebellion, the East India Company was abolished, and from 1858 the British government took over direct administration of the Indian empire.[1]

A new conqueror had come to India that was culturally far more alien than the former Muslim rulers. The Europeans were an aggressive people with a superior technology that gave them a marked advantage in warfare. For the orthodox Hindus, the British were conceived of as a ruling caste (*varna*), with their own culture and lifestyle. The British generally accepted this role, and rigidly kept to their Victorian way of life.

The British raj could not avoid having a major influence. Trade and government required an increasing number of Indians to act as clerks, minor revenue officers, and ordinary soldiers. English became the language of government and learning. Middle-class Hindu families began to send their sons to European schools despite the dangers of ritual impurity and Western ideas.

The East India Company was fearful of offending the Muslims and Hindus, and so at first forbad all Christian missionary activity in its administrative area. William Carey, for example, had to move from the British settlement at

Calcutta to the Danish settlement further inland.[2] In 1813, the growing evangelical conscience in Britain forced the company to admit Christian missionaries. From this time onwards, the number of missionary schools increased, and the call for social reform became stronger.

A very small community of semi-Westernised intellectuals began to form in Bombay and Calcutta. From this group, a variety of new ideas were to originate. These people began to look at their Hindu traditions and seek to interpret them in terms of the European knowledge they had been taught in mission schools. The result was a variety of new religious movements seeking to express Hinduism in a way that was relevant for the new age.

RAM MOHAN ROY (1772-1833)

The first reforming leader produced by these new communities was Ram Mohan Roy. He was born into a Brahmin family in Bengal, and was brought up as an orthodox Hindu. In his teens, he was sent to Patna to study the Qu'ran and to read Sufi poetry. He then went to Tibet to study Buddhism. Finally, he settled in Benaras to study the Hindu scriptures. Here he took a job with the British East India Company, and, in 1809, was appointed revenue officer. At this time he began to study the New Testament through contact with missionaries.

As a result of his studies, Ram Mohan concluded that original Hinduism was pure monotheism that accepted neither polytheism nor the worship of idols. Ram Mohan Roy therefore sought to reform Hindu life and practice. In 1811, he came in direct contact with the practice of *sati*. He was shocked when his brother's wife, in spite of her protests, was burned alive on her husband's funeral pyre. He actively campaigned for the abolition of the practice, which was eventually effected by Lord William Bentinck in 1829.

In an attempt to bring about a radical transformation of Hindu life and religious practice, Ram Mohan Roy founded the Society of Brahma (Brahmo Samaj) in 1828. The Brahmo Samaj was strictly monotheistic. It rejected image veneration and introduced a form of congregational worship similar to that of the Christian church.

The hall of worship had no images, statues, or pictures. Sacrifices and offerings were forbidden, and only prayers and hymns affirming one God were chosen. This unemotional form of worship was more like nineteenth-century Unitarian services than Hinduism. This is probably the main reason that the Samaj never gained popular appeal.

Ram Mohan Roy came to England in 1830, where he spoke to the Select Committee of the House of Commons on Indian issues. He died in Bristol in 1833 and was buried there. Although his movement gained few followers, it did provide a powerful inspiration for progressive movements in the wider Hindu society. The rising Hindu intelligentsia was now ready for prophets whose ideas, though subject to Western influence, were firmly rooted in the traditions of Hinduism.

DAYANANDA SARASVATI (1824-83)

The first reforming teacher holding strongly to classical Hindu ideas was Dayananda. He was born in Gujarat into a rich family who were ardent worshippers of Siva. When he was eight years old, he was invested with the sacred thread. Three years later, while he was keeping the night of vigil in the temple of Siva, he was shocked to see rats come and eat the sacred food that had been offered to Siva. He started to question how the all-powerful god Siva could allow unclean creatures to eat the food that was offered to him alone.

Soon after this incident both his sister and uncle suddenly died, leaving him pondering the question of death. His parents decided to arrange his marriage, but Dayananda left home and joined himself to a teacher. This blind swami (holy man), called Virajananda, taught him the *Vedas* for three years. In 1863, his teacher charged him with the task of spreading the Vedic faith. He then became known as Swami Dayananda Saraswati, and started travelling and teaching a new Vedic philosophy.

He began to use Hindi to reach the ordinary people who did not know Sanskrit. He met with leaders of Brahmo Samaj, but disagreed with their views. In 1875 he therefore established a new organisation, known as Arya Samaj (Society of Aryans), in Bombay. Whereas the Brahmo Samaj was a synthesis with Western ideas, the Arya Samaj represented a return to the past along more orthodox lines.

Even so, Dayananda's teaching was quite radical. He rejected all sacred scriptures but the *Vedas*. These he regarded to have been given by God millions of years ago, and considered them to be the eternal and complete revelation of God. He also interpreted the *Vedas* in a most unusual way, declaring that all the names of the many divinities were, in fact, alternative names of the one God. All references to animal sacrifices were considered merely symbolic. His great call to his followers was to go 'Back to the *Vedas*'.

Dayananda claimed that India was the fountainhead of all culture, material and spiritual. Sanskrit was the parent language from which all others have their origin. All cultures and religions were therefore based upon Vedic revelation. Thus, he saw the *Vedas* as the root of all scientific advances. This idea has been continued by the TM movement in the West with the concept of 'natural law'.

Dayananda accepted the doctrines of *karma* and reincarnation, but stated that the soul could not be lost in Brahman. He was against image veneration, polytheism, and animal sacrifices, as were most of the reformers. He condemned untouchability, child marriage, and the segregation of women.

Arya Samaj followers worshipped on Sundays, when they read the *Vedas* and received teaching on the texts. For the historian of religion, their most significant feature was that they were aggressive in their evangelisation. The Arya Samaj sought to convert both Christians and Muslims, as well as orthodox Hindus. They also introduced purification rites for Indians who had been converted to Christianity or Islam, and were now being reconverted. For the first time for centuries, Hinduism was taking the offensive. In the midst of direct Christian influence, middle-class Hindus were finding a new pride in their ancient traditions. This new tendency was encouraged by Madam Helena Blavatsky, the founder of the Theosophical Society.

RAMAKRISHNA PARAMAHAMSA (1834-86)

One of the most influential reformers of the nineteenth century was Ramakrishna. He was born into a poor Brahmin family in Bengal. He suffered from epilepsy and deep depression, but had a profound desire for spiritual reality. As a young man he worked as a temple priest in the Kali temple near Calcutta. Some time during this period, Ramakrishna was instructed in the Tantras by a female ascetic.

He regularly meditated before the image of Kali, and considered her to be his mother. As his biographer Advaita Ashrama writes:

> To Sri Ramakrishna the image of Kali was not inert stone but the Mother Herself. The Goddess wears a gorgeous Varanasi Sari (cloth) and is decorated with precious ornaments from head to foot.... The realization of God became the one absorbing passion of the young aspirant. He would shed profuse tears like a child at being denied the vision of the Mother and would burst out crying, 'O Mother! Where art Thou? Reveal Thyself to me.'[3]

Later, a monk learned in the Vedanta philosophy initiated him as a sannyasi and gave him the name Ramakrishna. Even so, he was always a mystic and never completely reconciled his beliefs in Advaita with his experiences. Towards the end of 1866, Ramakrishna began to realise the possibility of accepting all forms of religion as so many ways of reaching perfection. He therefore attached himself to a Sufi mystic called Govinda Ray. With his characteristic thoroughness, he applied himself to the practice of this new religion.

Seven years later, Ramakrishna came into contact with Shambhu Nath Mallick of Calcutta. Although he was not a Christian, he used to read the Bible to Ramakrishna, who thus came to know about Christianity. Ramakrishna felt a strong desire to come to a new realisation of the divine mother through this religion. He told the story of how one day, as he was looking at a picture of the madonna and child, rays of light began emanating from the figures into him. He realised that the Hindu ideas were being swept aside to be replaced by a deep regard for Christ and his church. For three days these ideas dominated his thinking, then on the fourth day, while walking in the town, he saw an extraordinary-looking man coming towards him. Immediately, he knew that this foreign-looking person was the Christ. The man came straight up to him, embraced him, and merged with him. At this point Ramakrishna lost consciousness, and is said by his disciples to have entered the state of *samadhi*. From this time, Ramakrishna was convinced that Jesus Christ was an incarnation of God.

As a result of this vision, he became firmly convinced that all religions were true and represented different paths to God. He held that they were not contradictory, but complementary, being suited to different outlooks. He taught that books on theology and philosophy gave instruction about God, but the most important thing was the actual experiencing of God.

Thus he used to say to his disciples:

> I have practised all religions—Hinduism, Islam, Christianity, and I have also followed the paths of the different Hindu sects. I have found that it is the same God towards whom all are directing their steps, though along different paths.[4]

A group of able disciples gathered around Ramakrishna, and these were to spread his message.[5] In this way, his fame spread all over India. He died at the age of fifty of throat cancer.

VIVEKANANDA (1863-1902)

The most important follower of Ramakrishna was Narendranath Dutta. He was born in Calcutta and graduated from the Christian missionary college. He was well instructed in Western philosophy and was influenced by the writings of Herbert Spencer and J.S. Mill. His conviction was that human beings are the masters of their own destiny and are able to achieve perfection by their own efforts. In 1882, he met Ramakrishna, and soon became his disciple. He was given a new name, and has become widely known as Swami Vivekananda.

For six years he devoted himself to meditation, and experienced visions. He was a keen student of the Vedanta, and was an able expositor of Vedanta philosophy. In 1893, he was sent by the raja of Ramnad to represent Hinduism at the Parliament of Religions in Chicago. His oratory gained him a responsive audience. Wherever he lectured he drew large audiences, and several Vedanta Societies were founded in the large cities. On his way back to India, he visited Britain and evoked a similar response. He did more than any other person to promote the study of Vedanta in the West.

Vivekananda accepted that all religions were true, but declared that Hinduism was the mother of them all. He taught that all the practices of Hinduism were essentially good, although some had become corrupted or were misunderstood. He held that there was no polytheism in pure Hinduism, and all Hindus were, in fact, worshipping the one divine person behind all the many images and titles. Following Madam Blavatsky, he declared that Hinduism was the oldest and purist of the world's religions, and India was the spiritual source for the nations. This argument, that older is better, has attracted many Westerners on their spiritual quest.

Vivekananda admired Western materialism, and wanted to see India become equally prosperous. However, he wanted to see such material prosperity coupled with the Vedanta philosophy of India. It was the duty of Indians to absorb from the West all that was good and useful in science and technology. In return, Hindus should teach the world true spirituality.

He established the Ramakrishna Mission in 1897, and founded a monastery near Calcutta. Although he disapproved of Christian evangelism, he modelled the work of the Ramakrishna Mission on Christian missionary patterns. He developed educational, social, and religious activities. The Ramakrishna Mission became a major force for spreading Hinduism beyond the borders of India. After a second extended visit to America in 1899 to 1900, Vivekananda died at the age of thirty-nine.

For centuries, Hindus have been subject to evangelism by Muslim and Christian missionaries. Vivekananda gave Hinduism a new sense of pride. The ancient religion of India could now hold its own with theologians of other faiths.

In India itself, the ideas of Vivekananda found few followers, and so made little impact on the general character of Hinduism. They did, however, influence the thinking of the small community of semi-Westernised Indians. It was from this group that the Indian National Congress was to find its main leaders. The teaching of Vivekananda not only fostered a new Hindu consciousness, but also political nationalism. This new spirit of nationalism caught the imagination of the people of India and spread throughout the nation. It was the next great reformer who was to succeed in introducing new religious ideas to the general population of India.

MAHATMA GANDHI (1869-1948)

Mahatma Gandhi was born on 2 October 1869, the son of the prime minister of Porbandar, a princely state in Gujarati. His parents were worshippers of Vishnu, and he grew up with the *varna-ashrama-dharma* philosophy. Gandhi was married to Kasturba when they were both thirteen years old. He therefore knew first-hand the problems of child marriage, and later strongly opposed it when he realised its dangers. When he was fifteen, his father died. This event was to have a lasting effect upon him.

Gandhi was sent to England, where he studied law. He was exposed to many Western writers, such as J.S. Mill, William Morris, Tolstoy, and Ruskin. He also was much impressed by the New Testament, and regarded the Sermon on the Mount as a pinnacle of the teaching of Jesus Christ. On his return to India, he practised as a lawyer for a time before going to South Africa. It was there that for twenty years (1893-1914) he worked as a lawyer. He fought for the rights of Indians working in South Africa in the face of apartheid. Here he organised Indian opposition, and first put to the test his weapon of non-violence.

Satyagraha is a religious technique which can be interpreted as the insistence on truth and non-violent acceptance of the consequences.[6] *Satyagraha* literally means 'truth force'. According to Gandhi, the four essential religious elements that make a true follower of *Satyagraha* are: truth, non-violence, self-control, and sacrifice.

The most effective *Satyagraha* was commenced in April 1930. The protest was against the Indian government's salt monopoly, which stopped poor people making their own salt from sea water. Gandhi gave notice to the viceroy of the

planned 'Salt March'.⁷ This began from his ashram at Sabar-
mati, and he walked with his followers the 241 miles to Dandi
on the west coast of India. In a symbolic gesture, Gandhi
picked up a pinch of salt from the beach, thereby breaking the
law. A month later he was arrested. Even when he was in
prison, his followers continued *Satyagraha* despite being
beaten by the Indian police. The British authorities in India
considered Gandhi's activities to be a political nuisance. For
Gandhi and many of his followers, this was a religious act that
eventually led to the independence of India.

Gandhi spoke strongly against the evils of untouchability,
and appealed to Hindus to remove this blot from their religion. His message of non-violence and social reconciliation
drew great suspicion from some of the orthodox Hindus, who
thought that his ideas would destroy Hinduism. On 30 January 1948, Gandhi was assassinated by a Brahmin member of
the Hindu extremist party. He died with the invocation to
Rama on his lips.

Gandhi's success with the ordinary people of India had to
do with the way he came to them as a *sannyasi*. As such, it was
quite natural for him to adapt ideas to a new situation. He
was, for the ordinary people, a great saint who had achieved
close contact with God. Earlier reformers may have laid the
foundations of a new Hinduism, but it was Gandhi who was
the real architect.

AUROBINDO (GHOSH) (1872-1950)

There is one other reformer who must be considered, the man
known as Sri Aurobindo. He was born into a rich family in
Calcutta, and after a primary education at a European convent
school in India, he was sent to England at the age of seven.
His education in England lasted fourteen years, and he finally
obtained a degree in classics at Cambridge University. He also
passed the entrance examination to the Indian civil service,
but was disqualified because he failed the riding test.

On his return to India, he was appointed Vice-Principal of
Baroda College, where he learned Sanskrit. In 1910, he joined
the independence movement, and started two new magazines.
He was imprisoned for a year by the British in 1908. This time
he used to study. When released, he went to the French

colony of Pondicherry to found an ashram. Despite all his years of Western education he was never accepted by the British establishment, and so returned to his Hindu roots.

Aurobindo claimed that his teaching stemmed from the *Vedas*, *Upanishads* and the *Bhagavad Gita*, and he actually wrote substantial works on the *Vedas*. In practice, his teaching was essentially based upon that of Sankara's Vedanta, to which he introduced the idea of *shakti*. He believed that *shakti* manifests itself as energy and matter, and that the latter is shaped by the former. *Shakti* is often equated to Brahman, who is the sole reality.

According to Aurobindo, the Brahman merges with the individual soul through Purna yoga (integral yoga). This form of yoga, which requires complete surrender to God, concentrates the divine energy. This frees human beings from their self-centredness and leads to ultimate bliss.

> The integral meets the religious ideal at several points, but goes beyond it in the sense of a greater wideness. The religious ideal looks, not only beyond this earth, but away from it to a heaven or even beyond all heavens to some kind of Nirvana.[8]

REFORMED HINDUISM

Hinduism has always been a religion that assimilates rather than excludes. During the last 150 years, Hinduism has had to interact with the vigorous ideas from the West. From among the Indian intellectuals who straddled the philosophies of East and West new developments have occurred and great changes have resulted. The ancient Hinduism is still there, but it is giving way to a new expression. This will not lead to some great religious revolution, but, as in the past, the old will make room for the new and all will move forward in the variety that is Hinduism.

With the rise of India to a nation of international standing, Hinduism has become a world force. Vivekananda's teaching of the Vedanta began an interest in Hindu spirituality for many in the West. However, in recent years it has been the gurus of India who have attracted the greater interest from Western seekers.

Notes

[1] Francis Robinson, *The Cambridge Encyclopedia of India* (Cambridge University Press: Cambridge, 1989).

[2] Pearce S. Carey, *William Carey* (Hodder & Stoughton: London, 1926).

[3] Advaita Ashrama, *A Short Life of Sri Ramakrishna* (Advaita Ashrama: Calcutta, 1968), p 24.

[4] *Ibid*, pp 65–66.

[5] Swami Nikhilananda, *The Gospel of Sri Ramakrishna* (Ramakrishna-Vivekananda Center: New York, 1958).

[6] S. Radhakrishnan, *Mahatma Gandhi: Essays and Reflections on His Life and Work* (George Allen & Unwin: London, 1939), pp 31–40.

[7] Ignatius Jesudasan, *A Gandhian Theology of Liberation* (Orbis: Maryknoll, 1984), pp 99–102.

[8] Quoted in Whitfield Foy, *Man's Religious Quest: A Reader* (Croom Helm: London, 1978), p 159.

CHAPTER 18

The God-men—Guruism

WHEN IN INDIA, I always felt sorry for the average Indian in his, or her, attempt to understand the Westerner. Apart from movies of James Bond, their main impressions came from the strange mixture of white people they saw on their streets. First, there was the missionary, whose presence in their country they had come to tolerate during the past two centuries. Second, there was the tourist, epitomised by the middle-aged American ladies wearing shorts as they ventured out of their hotels in search of souvenirs. Finally, there were those who had come in search of a guru. They were mainly young intellectuals who had become disillusioned with the materialism of Western society, and were looking for new spiritual leaders. From the initial trickle, the numbers have grown into many thousands of those who have come to India to seek reality and a spiritual guide.

The guru is an important part of Hindu spirituality. As Kabir, the fifteenth-century Indian mystic, wrote:

> In the midst of the highest heaven there is a shining light; he who has no Guru cannot reach the palace; he only will reach it who is under the guidance of a true Guru.

WHAT IS A GURU?

Several etymological meanings of the word 'guru' have been given. Some people have suggested that it derives from *gur* (to hurt, kill, eat, or go), with the noun-making termination 'u'. A guru is therefore one who kills, or eats up, the ignorance of his disciple and brings him to the light.[1]

There are different kinds of gurus, and they are not easy to place into neat categories. Even the definition of the word itself becomes somewhat ambiguous. The orthodox Sikhs limit the use of the term guru to God, Guru Granath to their scriptures, and Guru Panth to the sects that have arisen among them.

The Vedic literature makes no mention of the idea of 'guru', as may be expected with its emphasis upon priestly sacrifice. It is in the period of the *Upanishads* that the term developed the meaning of teacher. There were various types of gurus, who taught music, dancing, wrestling, and other skills. However, the most important guru was the one who taught spiritual truth. He was the one who helped the disciple come to a knowledge of true reality and leave the illusion of this world.

There are different perceptions of guruism, but three types of guru are usually recognised. The first view assumes that the guru actually is the absolute deity. In other words, the embodiment of divinity, as discussed in Chapter 8. The second view is the traditional monistic view in which the guru is considered further along the road of merging into the ultimate reality than is the disciple. The guru is like God, but he is not God himself. Finally, there is the dualistic view, in which the guru never becomes God or merges into ultimate reality. He, or she, may be worshipped as equal to God, but there is no claim that the guru is God. Swami Prabhupada of the International Society for Krishna Consciousness is an example of the latter.

The exalted position of the guru appears to have developed with the rise of Bhakti yoga. Because it was the guru who led the disciple to the spiritual revelation, he became divinity to the devotee. Sant Kabir (AD 1440-1518) wrote:

> Guru and God are both standing, whose feet shall I touch first? I shall touch yours O guru, for you revealed God to me.[2]

The guru therefore became the focus of devotion for the disciple. The supreme manifestation of that devotion is for the disciple to surrender himself totally to his master. The guru who takes this role is called a sad-guru, the teacher of reality. This is to distinguish him from other, perhaps lesser, types of guru.

The sad-guru usually has his own centre, called an 'ashram'. This is a term used for the Brahmin retreat centres where disciples are taught the *Vedas*. Today, the marble temples with guest houses for foreign visitors contrast with the forest retreats of the sages of the past. An ashram is supposed to be a place of peace, simplicity, and austerity, where one can experience God without facing the dichotomy between contemplation and action.

The study of the life history of a sad-guru often shows common features. As a boy, for most are male, he may be very religious and different from other children. When the time comes for him to marry, he will often refuse and leave home to travel to the holy places. Eventually, he will meet up with the person whose disciple he is destined to be. He will stay with his guru, in full submission to his will. During this time, his wisdom and esteem will develop. When his guru considers it time for him to leave, he will receive his initiation (*diksha*). Now the disciple may follow one of two paths. He may leave and set up his own ashram while retaining close links with his guru. Alternatively, he may stay with his guru, and when he dies, take over as head of the ashram.

The initiation of the disciple is the most important aspect of the relationship. It is a recognition by the guru of the spiritual worth of the disciple as he continues on the path towards liberation. The initiation often consists of the giving of a *mantra*, as mentioned in Chapter 15. The initiation can also involve a touch or a glance from the guru that provokes a sudden inner response. It may involve something of the guru's own divine power (*shakti*) entering the disciple. This may occur unexpectedly at their first meeting, or after some absence. As Brent comments, 'Such informality of initiation indicates what is essential—that something of the consciousness of the self-realized man should enter into the eager consciousness of his disciple.'[3]

The Western idea of a teacher is one in which the student receives knowledge almost as a commodity. The student is like a vessel that is filled by his instructor, while little reference is made to the nature of the vessel. Examinations assess what the student knows, and not the quality of his life. It is not important whether or not the teacher lives up to the instruction that he gives. In contrast, the guru shares his very life with his disciple, and epitomises the teaching. The guru *is* the teaching. What he does, what he is, is more important than what he says.

It is therefore the relationship between the guru and his disciple that is most important. There are various levels of discipleship. At the lowest level, there are those who come only on occasions to listen to the teaching of the guru, and spend most of their time in their daily work. At the highest level, there are those persons who make a complete commitment to live with their guru in the ashram. Chaudhuri writes:

> In fact, they become almost slaves of the gurus. They hang up portraits of the guru in their homes, and not only worship the guru as if he was the deity, but also sanctify their food by offering it first to the picture of the guru.[4]

One American young man called David explained his experience of living in the ashram in these words:

> And what they do here is you do your chores every day and you go sit in front of Swami Muktananda for a certain period of time a day. And I did that. And after a while I started feeling some very strange sensations in my head and body. A very thick, honey, warm feeling, a feeling that I'd call ecstasy. And say that I'd never felt ecstasy before; I thought that sex was ecstasy, but this is another level of ecstasy, a level terribly more gripping, amazingly enough. You just feel.... I have read other people's descriptions; someone who describes his feelings in front of Raman Maharishi and it's exactly the way he described it. He said it feels like your mind is immersed in a thick sea of honey.[5]

A genuine guru must be one who proves his spirituality by the frequency and intensity of his experiences. The disciple seeks to become like his guru.

The problem faced by most Western seekers of a guru is to distinguish the true guru from the false. Swami Krishnananda said that genuine gurus are rare.[6] One reason he gave for this was that people wanted to be gurus without first being disciples. The Indian ideal of a spiritual person is one characterised by simplicity, humility, and poverty. This contrasts with the advertisements of some groups proclaiming the greatness of their guru, or the sight of him travelling in a Rolls-Royce.

THE IMPORTANCE OF GURUISM IN INDIA

Many societies have used the discipleship model for training young people. In Europe, the apprenticeship scheme was common to most trades until recent times. Jesus Christ himself called twelve disciples with whom he lived and taught for three years. Some Christians have even used the model of the guru in their communication of the gospel. As Vandana writes, 'To a Christian, he says: "Jesus Christ remains your guru. I am but an upa-guru; a little guru." '[7]

The institution of the guru, however, is a particular product of Indian society, in which people may claim to be divine. Vishal Mangalwadi, in his book *The World of the Gurus*, suggests five sociological factors he considers are significant in the widespread acceptance of guruism.[8]

First, as we saw in Chapter 7, the life of a man in Aryan society was theoretically divided into four stages, or orders. The first was that of a student who lived under the guidance of a teacher who taught him the *Vedas*, astronomy, and mathematics. In the absence of printed books, the student was not able to evaluate his teacher's opinions, and he was required to learn by rote. He was expected to treat his master with the utmost reverence, and minister to all his needs. The teacher therefore attained the position of unquestioned authority.

Second, much of Indian spirituality is esoteric in character. The *Upanishads* express some of the secret knowledge which was conveyed from guru to disciple. Only at initiation was the all-important *mantra* given to the disciple. Because there were no objective reference points within the teaching, there was no method by which the guru's teaching could be checked. The way was therefore open for any charismatic figure to arise and start his, or her, own sect. The guru's own authority was derived directly from his own personal mystical experiences. The guru was therefore an indispensable authority.

Third, Mangalwadi argues that the guru in practice replaced the Brahmin priest as the spiritual authority. Within the caste system, the Brahmin priests, with their knowledge of the *Vedas* and sacrifices, were the exclusive spiritual leaders. With the gradual diminution of the importance of the caste system, the guru has replaced the Brahmin priest in some sections of society. Mangalwadi writes:

> The authority and worship of the guru is subtly replacing the authority of scriptures and of idol worship. The four classes are being reduced to two: initiates and non-initiates.[9]

The fourth characteristic of Indian society that has led to the growth of guruism was originally mentioned by Peter Brent.

> From almost his earliest days, and certainly from the age of four or five, the young Indian is expected to conform absolutely to his father's wishes and commands. So comprehensive is this discipline imposed and accepted, that for the rest of his life the average Indian is almost incapable of doing anything of which his father disapproves. In this situation, the guru can appear as a rescuer.[10]

The guru is the father whom the disciple has chosen. He has made a change in his allegiance from father to guru. He is taught to be non-attached, and so he is able to cut himself off from his family without guilt. 'He is the father who has been chosen; in this way, the disciple remains free in his bondage, bound in his freedom.'[11]

Mangalwadi writes confirming this analysis from his own experiences:

> In the ashrams of the Divine Light Mission at Hardwar

and New Delhi I have seen young men doing manual labour almost slavishly but happy. They cannot step out of the ashram, nor answer the questions of visitors (like myself) without permission. Yet they testify that they have peace and contentment now, which they didn't have before.[12]

Finally, Mangalwadi argues that Indian society is charac-terised by a repressive puritanism. The strict segregation of the sexes has often led to the repression of normal emotions. The individual is locked within the structure of family and society. There is not the freedom to express one's love as in Western society.

For the average and particularly the middle-class Indian, there are often only two directions he can go to prove he can love, and that he can be loved. One is towards homosexuality, the other towards the guru. (These are not, of course, mutually exclusive.)[13]

The intensity of love between guru and disciple is often the transference of the sexual urge. This may lead to an extreme licentiousness, or repression. We saw in the discussion of Tantrism in Chapter 16 that Acharya Rajneesh advocated sex as a legitimate means of salvation. On the other hand, Swami Prabhupada, for example, of the International Society for Krishna Consciousness, discourages devotees from getting married. If they are married, he allows sexual intercourse only once a month, on a night designated by the *Vedas* for fertility, and only after chanting for five or six hours.[14]

Gurus who once failed to evoke any noticeable response in India are now making a great impact in the West. C.V. Mathews considers:

Perhaps the only reason for this new wave of enthusias-tic acceptance in India is the unexpected acceptance and success guruism has met with in Western countries, among the white-skinned people. This reflects the old Indian colonial psychology that whatever the Whites do and believe must be good and noble, and therefore should be accepted and valued in India, too. This is what Swami Agehananda Bharati of Syracuse University calls the 'Pizza-effect' of guruism.[15]

THE SPREAD OF GURUISM

Although one may understand some of the sociological factors for the development of guruism in India, the issues become more complex in examining the growth of popularity by Western followers. The disadvantages of Indian social rigidity are contrasted with Western flexibility. Even so, the gurus, swamis, and bhagavans have had a major influence in the spread of Hindu ideas throughout the world.

It was in the 1960s that gurus began to be noticed in Europe and America. The Beatles' announcement of their devotion to Maharishi drew worldwide attention. Four American disciples of Sanskrit scholar A.C. Bhaktivedanta Prabhupada brought the International Society for Krishna Consciousness (ISKCON) to Britain from California in 1969. Beatle George Harrison directed them to Apple Studios for the recording of the hit song 'My Sweet Lord'. A generation that had become disillusioned with a materialistic worldview began to turn to a mystical worldview. They began to look beyond mere rationality, and guruism fitted well into this climate.

Various guru movements have already been mentioned in this book. The ISKCON was mentioned as an example of a modern movement focused upon devotion to the Lord Krishna. All the guru movements focus upon yoga and mysticism. In Chapter 15, we saw how Maharishi Mahesh Yogi spread the teaching of Transcendental Meditation. In practice, most modern guru movements are related to the teaching of Tantrism and Kundalini.

Roy Wallis has drawn a useful distinction between three types of new religious movements: world-rejecting, world-affirming and world-accommodating.[16] The world-rejecting movements are those that tend to be idealistic and seek to produce a new society. They are therefore community based. The members are usually people who have felt that modern society is purely materialistic, alienating the individual. Most of the core members are from middle-class backgrounds from which they feel they are escaping to form a new and better society.

An example of this type of movement is the International Society for Krishna Consciousness (ISKCON). Here the devotees seek to live out a 'Vedic lifestyle'. This requires the adoption of Indian dress, symbolism, and customs. The movement established its model agricultural community in West Virginia, USA, to 'show that one need not depend upon factories, movies, department stores, or nightclubs for happiness; one may live peacefully and happily with little more than some land, cows, and the association of devotees in a transcendental atmosphere of Krishna Consciousness.'[17] The cow is considered sacred, as in India, and the British section of ISKCON has established the first cow protection society in Europe.

This type of group has been criticised by certain sections of the media. Some claims are exaggerations, but others have been confirmed.

> Criticism has been levied at ISKCON on a number of fronts including accusations of brainwashing and deceptive fund raising activities. Some devotees, shocked by the behaviour of some of their erstwhile leaders, have left ISKCON, while still espousing Krishna consciousness; others have tried to keep the movement in order by remaining inside.[18]

This class of world-rejecting movements is more recognisably religious than the second type. World-affirming movements are those that help their members cope with the world and its current values. The emphasis here is upon the increased ability to succeed in Western society. It therefore includes the wide variety of practices of the human potential movement. In the world-affirming class movements the emphasis is upon the individual rather than the formation of a new community.

The religious nature of this type of movement is not immediately apparent. There is no abrupt change of dress, or lifestyle, that is characteristic of world-rejecting movements. People may commence by reading a book on self-development or yoga, and then go on to attend evening classes or weekend courses. Transcendental Meditation (TM) is one most important example. TM does not claim to be a religion, but a philosophy that enables the individual to develop his, or her, potential. Unfortunately, objective studies give no clear evidence that such promises are realised.

The flexible nature of this type of movement means that it draws upon distinctive spiritual aspects of various religious traditions that are applied to a Western lifestyle. There is therefore the opportunity for the mixing of various religious and philosophical elements. The term 'New Age' has been applied to many of these human potential movements, that are characterised by numerous teachers and gurus. Most people who would identify themselves with New Age thinking see themselves as seekers who are exploring new and exciting frontiers. Elements from traditional Hindu thought provide an important source for the continual development of syncretistic beliefs and practices.

The third type, according to Roy Wallis, are the world-accommodating movements. These movements attempt to accommodate their religious beliefs to the practical issues of daily life. In this class he includes some non-Christian movements, but the most important is the Christian charismatic renewal movement. Although one can identify various leaders of this movement, it would be stretching the definition of the word to call them 'gurus'.

Roy Wallis writes of the Christians in the charismatic movement in the following words:

> They typically consist of individuals who, although committed Christians before joining the Renewal Movement, felt something to be lacking in their spiritual lives, particularly an active experience of God's power working within them and within the church.[19]

This movement restores an experiential aspect to the spiritual life, and so provides meaning to religious practices that have become increasingly marginalised by Western society.

WHEN GURUS FAIL

The gurus of India have become the focus for the emergence of many new religious movements. Although the claims of these god-men are spectacular, in practice the truth is far different. Many who have left home and family to find their guru become disillusioned with a guru who has failed them.

Maharaj Ji

The spectacular rise and later fall of the Divine Light Mission has made it one of the most publicised guru sects in the West. The founder was Shri Hans Ji Maharaj, who as a young person was religiously inclined. He met and became the disciple of a guru called Dada Guru. The story is told that the day after he was initiated, while meditating, he lost body consciousness (*samadhi*) and realised the divinity within. Dada Guru appointed Hans Ji to be his successor, and he attracted many followers.

In the tradition of Sant Mat, guruship is hereditary. As his first wife did not bear him a son, Hans Ji married again, and his second wife bore him four sons, all of whom were claimed to be divine. It was, however, the youngest who was considered the one born as a guru. His father initiated him when he was six years old, and after about a month of meditation he came to realise his divinity. At his father's funeral, on 1 August 1966, when he was only eight years old, he declared himself to be the 'Perfect Master'. His mother and brothers prostrated themselves at his feet, with thousands of devotees present at the funeral.

A mammoth gathering was held in Delhi in November 1970, where Maharaj Ji declared that he would establish peace on earth. Six months later, he went on his first tour of the United States, Canada, and Britain. His mission had great success, and by 1973 the movement claimed to have 480 centres in 38 countries. His devotees declared him the saviour of the world.

Wherever Guru Maharaj Ji appears, His devotees flock to see Him and to touch His Lotus Feet. They shower Him with tokens of their love, because He is their Lord and Creator in human form and has given them True Knowledge.[20]

In December 1973, when just sixteen years old, Maharaj Ji married his twenty-four-year-old American secretary, Marilyn Louise Johnston. Throughout 1974, his mother attempted to keep her son on the right path, but his frequent visits to night clubs were soon impossible to hide. Division within the 'divine family' came to a head when his mother sought to enthrone her eldest son, Bal Bhagavan, in the place of Maharaj Ji. This led to a scandalous court case. In general, the Western followers sided with Maharaj Ji, while the Indian devotees accepted the leadership of Bal Bhagavan. However, the movement was in decline and now is only a fraction of its former size.

Maharaj Ji rejected many aspects associated with Indian traditions, and in the early 1980s adopted the name Elan Vital. He insisted that he was not to be worshipped as a god, dissolved the ashrams, and adopted a low media profile. By April 1989, according to Elan Vital's internal UK newsletter, there were 15,000 persons on the US mailing list and only 5,000 in the UK.[21]

Rajneesh

A similar failure occurred with the Rajneesh movement and culminated in the collapse of the Oregon commune in October 1985. This has led writers to look at the question: What happens to members when the central tenet or figure fails? Dr Arvind Sharma studied the case of the Rajneesh commune in Sydney.[22] After the October crisis of 1985, when Rajneesh fled the USA, the top five leaders of the commune left. Some of the members tried to continue the commune along democratic lines, but the commune failed and was closed in March 1986.

Sharma found that many members went through the stages of bereavement, with feelings of denial, anger, grief, and finally acceptance of the situation. Although some of the former members of the Rajneesh community left, others stayed in touch with each other and were mutually supportive through the following months. The trauma is most dramatically seen with the failure of world-rejecting movements because the members have made clear obvious breaks with their former lifestyle when joining the community.

Notes

1 Vishal Mangalwadi, *The World of the Gurus* (Nivedit Good Books: New Delhi, 1977), p 10.

2 *Ibid*, p 11.

3 Peter Brent, *The Godmen of India* (Allen Lane: London, 1972), p 17.

4 Nirad C. Chaudhuri, *Hinduism* (Oxford University Press: Oxford, 1979), p 303.

5 Brent, *op cit*, p 257.

6 Vandana, *Gurus, Ashrams and Christians* (Darton, Longman &.Todd: London, 1978), p 27.

7 *Ibid*, p 19.

8 Mangalwadi, *op cit*, p 16.

9 Mangalwadi, *op cit*, p 19.

10 Brent, *op cit*, p 287.

11 Brent, *op cit*, p 287.

12 Mangalwadi, *op cit*, p 20.

13 Brent, *op cit*, p 285.

14 Mangalwadi, *op cit*, p 106.

15 C.V. Matthew, 'Guruism: A Closer Look', *Areopagus* (spring 1988: p 48).

16 Roy Wallis, *The Elementary Forms of the New Religious Life* (Routledge & Kegan Paul: London, 1983), pp 9-39.

17 *Back to the Godhead*, vol 60 (1973): p 14.

18 Eileen Barker, *New Religious Movements: A Practical Introduction* (HMSO Books: London, 1989), p 185.

19 Wallis, *op cit*, p 36.

20 Editor, *Divine Light*, vol 3, no 3 (1973): p 1.

[21] Barker, *op cit*, p 178.

[22] Arvind Sharma, 'When Gurus Fail', *Areopagus* (spring 1988): pp 22–23.

CHAPTER 19

God Incarnate

I pity the Christian who does not reverence the Hindu Christ. I pity the Hindu who does not see the beauty in Jesus Christ's character (*Swami Vivekananda*).

I F ONE IS TO identify the single foundation principle of Christian teaching, it must be that Jesus Christ was the very incarnation of the invisible God. The parallel of this concept with the Indian belief in the *avatars* of Vishnu is too close to have gone unnoticed. Hindu scholars such as Ramakrishna embraced Jesus Christ as an *avatar*, and placed him within the Hindu religious system. In 1930, V. Chakkarai wrote an influential book which he entitled *Jesus The Avatar*.[1]

Does the Hindu spiritual tradition have a contribution to make to the Christian perspective of the Person of Jesus Christ? In this chapter we want to examine the various ways in which *avatars* are similar to the Christian understanding of Jesus Christ, and to clarify how Jesus is distinct from the Hindu god-men. We will commence by referring to one of the most outstanding examples of a living guru, the person of Satya Sai Baba whom some claim is 'the Hindu Christ'.

THE HINDU CHRIST—SATYA SAI BABA

Satya Sai Baba is perhaps the greatest living self-proclaimed guru in India. There are few homes and shops in south India that do not have a picture of Satya Sai Baba. He is worshipped by millions of devotees, including many important industrial and political leaders. Because he has not visited the West, he is not one of the most well known gurus outside India. Nevertheless, there could be as many as 10,000 of his followers in Britain, the majority belonging to the Asian community.[2]

The early life of Sai Baba is not easily established due to the amount of romantic legend that has developed about him. He was born in Puttaparthi in 1926, and it is said that a cobra was found beneath the child, a symbol signifying his royal status. He has two birthmarks that are regarded by his followers as physiological proof of his divinity. One is a circular mark on the soles of his feet, and the other is in the shape of a garuda bird on his chest. At the age of seven he began to compose religious songs, and soon afterwards started to perform miracles. The act of materialising objects from out of thin air has become his particular characteristic.

At the age of fourteen he fell into a trance, and would scream and sing religious songs. It seemed as though he had been stung by a scorpion, but one was not found. No doctor, astrologer, priest, or oja was able to cure him. Suddenly, on 23 May 1940, the boy regained normality and began materialising sweets and fruit for his family. He then announced that he was a reincarnation of Sai Baba of Shiridi, a master guru who had died in Bombay in 1918, with the declaration that he would reincarnate after eight years. He left his family and took the name Sai Baba, which loosely translated means 'saintly father'.

From that time onwards Sai Baba drew an increasing number of followers to himself. Baba claims that his miracles are his 'visiting cards' that draw people to him and instil faith into them. Every devotee has a story of Sai Baba's miracles, which he often performs before vast crowds. He claims that the miracles are only a means to the establishment of a new *dharma*, which is his aim.

Sai Baba's ashram was founded in a village just outside Puttaparthi in 1950, and is called Prasanthi Nilayam ('the Abode of Heavenly Peace'). This has become the centre of pilgrimage for thousands of devotees, and in 1966 it became a legal township. The five principles of his message are: truth, righteousness, peace, love, and non-violence. The greatest of these is love: 'Begin the day with love, spend the day with love and end the day with love: that is the way of God.'[3]

Sai Baba manifests what is known as 'Sai power'. This power is considered to be multiple in nature, with manifestations on physical, psychic, and spiritual levels. On the physical level he performs miracles, especially those of the materialisation of objects. At the psychic level Sai Baba claims such phenomena as telepathy, clairvoyance, and psychokinesis. In the spiritual domain he affects the human spirit, and thereby performs spiritual surgery and even resurrects people from the dead.

Satya Sai Baba has been scrutinised by many sceptical Western observers, including the American conjurer Doug Henning.

> The famous professional magician Doug Henning viewed a movie about Satya Sai Baba. He felt certain that he could duplicate all the cases he saw on the film with his magician's art. However, he considered Satya's feat of making a picture in a ring disappear and then reappear, to be beyond the skills of magicians. Henning also said that if Satya does produce objects upon demand, that this would be an accomplishment that no magician could duplicate.[4]

As his popularity has spread, a virtual industry in pictures and objects has developed about him. Along with the many Indian devotees have come those from the West looking for spiritual reality.

Satya Sai Baba proclaims that he is the embodiment of all aspects of God that have been manifested on earth. He is considered by his devotees to be the rebirth of Jesus Christ. On Christmas Day, 1972, he pointed to a lamb and said.

> The lamb is merely a symbol, a sign. It stands for the voice: 'Ba-Ba'; the announcement was of the advent of Baba.... The lamb is the sign and symbol of love. Christ did not declare that He would come again; he said, 'He who sent me will come again'. That 'Ba-Ba' is this Baba.[5]

Although many have been drawn to Sai Baba, there have been reports of corruption, manipulation, and homosexuality. Many of those who have entered the inner sanctum of Sai Baba have left saddened by a guru who failed them. Tal Brooke, an American devotee, shocked many of Sai Baba's followers when he published a detailed account of his experiences within the heavily guarded ashram.[6] Barbara Szandorowska tells a similar story and implies a satanic background.[7]

Is Satya Sai Baba the Hindu Christ? Many Indian devotees claim that he is, and so have a few spiritualist ministers in America. Some evangelical Christians, on the other hand, have suggested that he is more likely the Antichrist prophesied in the New Testament to appear at the 'end of the age' (Rev 13:13–18).

SIMILARITIES BETWEEN *AVATARS* AND CHRIST

Among the Jews of the first century AD, Jesus was called a rabbi and prophet. These titles were culturally significant to the Jewish people at that time. If one was to imagine that Jesus had been born in a Hindu context rather than a Jewish one, one could expect him to have been hailed as an *avatar*.

Professor Parrinder, in his study of god-men, lists twelve characteristics of *avatars*.[8] They are:

1. *Avatars* are real.
2. The human *avatars* take worldly birth.
3. The lives of *avatars* mingle human and divine.
4. *Avatars* finally die.
5. There may be historicity in some *avatars*.
6. *Avatars* are repeated.
7. The example and character of *avatars* is important.
8. The *avatars* come with work to do.
9. The *avatars* show some reality in the world.
10. The *avatars* are a guarantee of divine revelation.
11. *Avatars* reveal a personal god.
12. *Avatars* reveal a god of grace.

As Parrinder has pointed out, these characteristics of *avatars* share many features with the Christian doctrine of the incarnation of Jesus Christ. All may be applied to Jesus except for point 6.

Birth

The birth dates of the *avatars* are associated with special events and are often foretold in a similar way to that in which Jesus' birth was announced. Thirteen months before Chaitanya's birth, his father felt a divine light enter his heart and then pass on to his wife, who saw many gods worshipping her. Ramakrishna's mother dreamt that she was being possessed by a god.

We noted in Chapter 11 the striking similarity between the story of the birth of Krishna and that of Christ. Both were born of poor parents, and in both accounts there is a slaughter of innocents. In the case of Satya Sai Baba, special signs attended his birth, such as the cobra found lying under his bed, and musical instruments were supposed to have played by themselves.

Hindu religions do not have a doctrine of a virgin birth, as in orthodox Christian teaching. *Avatars* are considered to be 'conceived' in heaven and 'implanted' in an earthly mother. God-men are therefore considered to originate in heaven.

Life

During their earthly lives, *avatars* demonstrate their divine nature. Their omnipotence is shown by their ability to enter super-consciousness, and, in some cases, perform miracles. The miracles of Satya Sai Baba have aroused much interest and speculation about his identity. Satya's healings remind one of the acts of Jesus. For example, the touch of his robe, it is claimed, produces healing. Stories are told of Satya curing cancer, meningitis, blindness, and spiritual possession.[9] Satya claims to know all of the past, present, and future, including the time of his death in the year AD 2022 at the age of ninety-six.

The human aspect of the *avatar* is often shown through suffering and affliction. Ramakrishna was afflicted with cancer of the throat. The parallel with the suffering and crucifixion of the Lord Jesus Christ is often drawn by Hindus.

Revelation

God-men bring a revelation of the divine nature. Another parallel between Satya Sai Baba and the Christian theology of the Person of Christ is that both are considered part of a trinity. As Jesus is the second Person of the Christian Trinity, so Sai Baba is the second person of a trinity consisting of Shiridi Sai Baba, Satya Sai Baba, and Prema Sai Baba. The claim is made that eight years after the death of Shirdi, he reappeared as Satya in 1926. Furthermore, Satya claims that after he dies in AD 2022, he will reappear as Prema Sai Baba in Karnataka state, India. His devotees believe that this last manifestation will initiate the golden age.

Many god-men inspire eschatological expectations in the minds of their followers, and many *avatars* have been thought to be the apocalyptic *avatar* Kalki. In a like manner, the New Testament teaches the second coming of Christ that will bring in the end of the age and final judgement.

For these reasons, many Hindus believe that Jesus Christ was an *avatar* in a way similar to their own gurus. This association has its origin with Ramakrishna, who, in 1874, had a vision of Jesus Christ, and for him this validated Jesus as a spiritual master. The significance of Ramakrishna's vision was to place Jesus Christ on a par with Krishna, Rama, and other *avatars*. Near the end of his life, Ramakrishna gathered around him twelve disciples, and insisted that two of them had been disciples of Jesus in a previous incarnation. The similarity between Ramakrishna and Christ resulted in many people considering that he was an incarnation of Christ. In this way, there began a process which may be considered as the Hinduisation of the Person of Christ.

The path of Hinduisation took a further step with Satya Sai Baba. Previous god-men claim to have approached Jesus through mystical experience, or Christ-consciousness. Sai Baba claims to be a reincarnation of the historical Jesus, reporting things about Jesus recalled from a past life. Many of the miracles and sayings of Sai Baba are remarkably similar to those recorded of Jesus in the Gospels.

DIFFERENCES BETWEEN *AVATARS* AND CHRIST

The Bible uses various metaphors concerning the Person of Jesus Christ. One of the most useful for this current debate is that used by the apostle John at the beginning of his Gospel. He writes: 'In the beginning was the Word, and the Word was with God, and the Word was God. He was with God in the beginning' (Jn 1:1–2).

The concept of 'the Word', or in Greek *logos*, came from the Greek philosopher Herakleitos. *Logos* meant discourse, reason, logic and pattern. He asked the question: Is there *logos* to life? But he found no satisfactory answer. The Jewish philosopher Philo later made use of the term to explain Jewish thought in terms of Greek philosophy. Philo recognised the importance of 'the Word' to God in the act of creation, and argued that God created through the *Logos*. Later still, the apostle John applied the term to the Person of Christ, and so presented us with one of the most telling of biblical metaphors.

His uniqueness

The *Logos* existed with God before the beginning of space and time. This concept of a Supreme Being who created the universe out of nothing (creation ex nihilo) asserts that God exists separate from his creation. It is the Supreme Being that gives a point of reference for all creation. Because the Creator is distinct from creation, it is therefore reasonable to assume that there is an external reality that can be known and studied.

Some Christians have tended to overstress the transcendence of God, so that God has been perceived as totally other and therefore unrelated to creation. This tendency has given the perception of the universe as a closed system locked into a pattern of rational laws. The historic teaching of the church has always recognised a balance between the transcendence of God and his immanence in creation.

The *Logos* metaphor also provides an expression of the nature of the Godhead that is by definition beyond comprehension. The *Logos* does not make up the entire Godhead, but has a particular relationship with the other centres of personhood of the Godhead. Nevertheless, the divinity that belongs to the Godhead totally belongs also to him. The complexity of this notion has caused church theologians throughout history to struggle to formulate a doctrine of the nature of God. The orthodox teaching of the Trinity, one God in three Persons, is the model that has been endorsed by the church and perhaps most closely represents the teaching of the Bible.

Jesus Christ is the unique 'Son of God', revealed once and for all within space and time. He is the sole locus in human existence, where God's revelation and presence is to be found. The *Logos* became a man of flesh and blood. The early church, at the Council of Chalcedon, stated that the two natures of Christ, divine and human, were perfectly blended.

> ...one and the same Christ, Son, Lord, Only-begotten, recognized in two natures without confusion, without change, without division, without separation; the distinction of natures being in no way annulled by the union, but rather the characteristics of each nature being preserved and coming together to form one person and substance, not as parted or separated into two persons, but one and the same Son and Only-begotten God the Word, Lord Jesus Christ....

In contrast, Hinduism denies any exclusive belief in one unique incarnation. It advocates a continual descending of souls that are occasionally manifest as *avatars*.

His titles

Modern *avatars* emphasise their divinity through a variety of symbols and titles. As a manifestation of deity, they encourage people to love them as 'Baba'. The word 'Baba' means 'father', and the devotee is encouraged to enter a paternal relationship with his guru.

Jesus Christ used the Aramaic word 'Abba', meaning 'father', to refer to God the Father rather than to himself. The most famous statement is found in the Lord's Prayer. Here Jesus teaches his disciples to pray, 'Our Father in heaven, hallowed be your name, your kingdom come' (Lk 11:2). Jesus uses the term *Abba* to establish a filial relationship between the Father in heaven and his children here on earth. Baba, on the other hand, points to the role of the father that the *avatar* himself assumes. The letters 'a' and 'b' can be combined to spell either 'Abba' or 'Baba'. However, between the ideas carried by the two words there is a world of difference.

Another important symbol associated with *avatars* is that of the serpent. In India, the snake (*naga*) is regarded as part of God's essence, and is the symbol of the life energy that motivates birth and rebirth. The *avatar* and the snake are both manifestations of the one divine substance. They function harmoniously, demonstrating a mutuality between the god-man and the forces of nature. Most modern *avatars* show an empathy to the cobra. Satya Sai Baba's followers consider it significant that a cobra was found under his bed when he was born. He now sleeps in a bed made with a canopy in the shape of a hooded-cobra.

In contrast, both in the Old and New Testaments the serpent stands for evil, death, and chaos. From its first introduction in the Garden of Eden until its destruction in the book of Revelation, the serpent represents the forces opposed to the Creator. The *Logos* came as the destroyer of the forces of evil. 'The reason the Son of God appeared was to destroy the devil's work' (1 Jn 3:8).

His resurrection

As we saw in Chapter 6, Hinduism and Christianity have a totally different conception of life after death. The concept of *avatar* is related to that of reincarnation, in which a soul may come back to earth thousands of times. Satya Sai Baba claims to have been Jesus Christ in a previous life, and that is why he knows many details about the life of Christ.

The notion of reincarnation is totally foreign to the New Testament. The Jews believed in one life which was ended by physical death. The writer of the letter to the Hebrews is quite explicit when he says, 'Just as man is destined to die once, and after that to face judgement...' (Heb 9:27). Beyond physical death the Jews believed there was some shadowy existence from which they might one day be resurrected. The notion of reincarnation is never considered within the biblical texts. The goal of Hinduism, on the other hand, is the release from reincarnation, and a negative value is placed on preserving individuality after death.

The New Testament demonstrates that Jesus Christ was victorious over death. During his lifetime Jesus raised people from the dead: Jarius' daughter (Mk 5:35–43), the widow's son (Lk 7:11–17), and Lazarus (Jn 11:1–44). However, it is the bodily resurrection of Jesus Christ himself that is most significant. The New Testament records that between his resurrection and his ascension Jesus made 11 appearances within 40 days, both to his disciples and, on one occasion, to 525 people. Jesus then ascended into heaven with the promise that he will come again at the end of the age.

In his teaching, Jesus frequently associated his resurrection with the eternal life of his disciples. In John 11:25 Jesus says: 'I am the resurrection and the life. He who believes in me will live, even though he dies; and whoever lives and believes in me will never die.' In John 3:36, he says, 'Whoever believes in the Son has eternal life, but whoever rejects the Son will not see life, for God's wrath remains on him.'

His mission

The Hindu belief in the intervention of deity in human history through *avatars* is inherently different from the *Logos* concept. *Avatars* entered the world to destroy evil, and this required repeated *avatars*. The mission of Jesus Christ was to deal with the problem of human sin.

The Hindu understanding of the idea of sin varies widely. To some, sin is just committing bad deeds; to others, it is disobedience to one's conscience; to yet others, sin is non-existent. As we have seen, the main problem within Hindu philosophy is not considered to be sin, but ignorance.

The *avatars* possess a 'yogic consciousness' that assists in the spiritualisation of humanity. The various forms of yoga are the means by which one may attain transcendent consciousness and become united with God. Hinduism suggests that the individual soul has to discover its true identity and become one with the supreme soul.

The advocates of new physics claim that the 'Newtonian paradigm' resulted in a clockwork view of the universe, with humans being nothing but programmed robots. What attracts many to pantheistic monism is that they find in it a basis for asserting the dignity and value of human beings because, since everyone is an expression of the ultimate reality, each individual is divine. The position does have its difficulties. For example, if taken to its conclusion, monism removes the distinctive value of humans as opposed to other forms of life. All are either expressions of the one ultimate reality, or unreal creations of the mind. Further, the quest to realise one's own divinity leads to a selfish preoccupation that neglects the wellbeing of others.

In contrast with both the Hindu and secular view, the Bible teaches that human beings are formed by a special act of the creative power of God. The expression used in the Scriptures is that humanity is made in the 'image of God'. This immediately provides an answer to the basis of true humanness. Humans are not mere robots, nor are they expressions of divinity. The biblical teaching means that humans have a value that makes them distinct from the rest of creation. Human beings are not merely highly developed animals. People possess personality because God is personal, and we are able to love because God is love. Each individual therefore has his, or her, own worth and value. It was for this reason that Jesus Christ came into the world to die

Unlike the Hindu *avatars*, Jesus does not possess a yogic consciousness, but lived in simple obedience to his heavenly Father. His entire life was dominated by a total and overwhelming passion for God. He was therefore willing to offer his perfect life as an atonement for the sins of humanity. His death on the cross was not like the cancer of the throat experienced by Ramakrishna, but a deliberate act of vicarious sacrifice that was central to his mission.

Love and *bhakti*

The path of *bhakti* has been popular for many Hindus in recent centuries. As we saw in considering the *Bhagavad Gita*, there is a deep sense of seeking for a personal relationship with the divine. The emotion that *bhakti* elicits is a mixture of awe, fascination, and dependence. The similarity of *bhakti* with the Christian devotion to Christ led many scholars to speculate about the possibility of Christian influence upon Hindu thought. However, the term *bhakti* always occurs from the side of the devotee and is towards the deity. It is therefore inaccurate to equate this with the Christian concept of love, which is primarily the attitude that God takes towards his creation.

The *Logos* metaphor illustrates how the indescribable Creator, the ultimate meaning and logic, was manifest in human form. He may therefore be comprehended, appreciated, and adored. Devotion is given to him because he first loved us. This love was shown through his sacrificial death upon a cross.

The quest for peace (*shanti*) is a major aspect of Hindu spirituality. The Hindu way is one of detachment from the material world. The biblical way is one of knowing the peace of Christ in the situations of everyday life. Biblical spirituality has a reality of expression in the context of the physical world. The universe is not an illusion, but a habitation for humanity in which God has placed us to utilise the resources in a creative and responsible manner. Christianity presents a religion that has a reality in every dimension of human experience.

Christianity presents a picture of a God who takes the initiative in seeking those who have not yet turned to him. The divine Shepherd goes into the wilderness to seek a lost sheep. This contrasts with the Hindu image of a flock of sheep seeking guidance from the shepherd. As Daniel Bassuk concludes: 'Abba, the Christian God, loves to save; Baba the Hindu Avatar, saves who love.'[10]

Notes

[1] V. Chakkarai, *Jesus the Avatar* (Christian Literature Society: Madras, 1930).

[2] David Bowen, *The Sathya Sai Baba Community in Bradford: Its Origin and Development, Religious Beliefs and Practices* (University of Leeds monograph: Leeds, 1988).

[3] Vivayak K. Gokak, *Bhagavan Sri Sathya Sai Baba* (Asia Publishing House: Bombay, 1952), p 6.

[4] Daniel E. Bassuk, *Incarnation in Hinduism and Christianity* (Macmillan Press: Basingstoke, 1987), p 91.

[5] Samuel Sandweiss, *Sai Baba: the Holy Man and the Psychiatrist* (Birth Day Publications: San Diego, 1975), p 178.

[6] Tal Brooke, *Avatar of Night: The Hidden Side of Sai Baba* (Tarang Paperbacks: Delhi, 1982).

[7] Barbara Szandorowska, *Escape from the Guru* (MARC: Eastbourne, 1991).

[8] Geoffrey Parrinder, *Avatars and Incarnation* (Barnes & Noble: New York, 1970).

[9] Howard Murphet, *Sai Baba: Man of Miracles* (Macmillan: Madras, 1971).

[10] Bassuk, *op cit*, p 191.

CHAPTER 20

Through Other Eyes

There are a lot of people who want to interpret the present in the context of the past. Such people can't differentiate between an objective analysis and their own selfish outlook. Or, because of selfish motives they don't want to. But, if the present doesn't analyze the past on the basis of its own reality how can it benefit from past experiences? The present cannot return to the past, however glorious it may have been. All we can do is to try to understand it well. In fact, that's exactly what we need to do. Problems arise whenever the most scholarly can't distinguish between myth and reality (*Mahabarata*).[1]

T ERMS SUCH AS 'the Orient', 'the East', or 'India' have for centuries conjured up exotic images that fascinated the European. From this part of the world rare spices and beautifully crafted articles came on the camel caravans of Muslim traders. It was to reach India that Columbus sailed westwards some 500 years ago, but instead found the New World of the Americas. Other European explorers looked for a northwest passage around the Americas, and yet others followed the Cape route around Africa. The magnet for these explorers was the mysterious, exotic land of India.

In the previous chapter we examined the concepts of *avatar* and incarnation. These two doctrines summarise some of the central issues of the theological differences between East and West. However, there are other issues that underlie the theological discussion. These matters relate to the very perception that the West has of the East. It was Edward Said who first challenged the established Western attitudes towards the East in his stimulating book *Orientalism*.[2] What actually is our perception of India?

CONSTRUCTIONS OF INDIA

Europeans have constructed images of India out of many materials. They have used painted canvas and the written page to create stereotypes of this distant land and its peoples. As the West gained political control of the country, scholars began to write their own interpretations of the history of India. These constructs have been fashioned within the academic study of history, sociology, anthropology, and economics. In anthropology, Western scholars perceived themselves as 'civilised', with the task of studying non-Western people who, in consequence, became 'the primitive'. India was always seen as the exotic 'other', an object to be studied, controlled, and, for the missionary, converted.

Ronald Inden, in his perceptive study of Oriental constructions, identifies two main images of India that have been fabricated by Western thinkers.[3] These may simply be called the 'Rational' and the 'Romantic'. Such constructions are not restricted to India, but have also been written of Africa, Asia, and Latin America.[4] However, it is India and China that have provided images of old civilisations that compare with those of ancient Egypt, Greece, and Rome, from which Europe claims its cultural roots.

Rational

Sir William Jones (1746-94) is the person usually credited with first suggesting that Persian and the European languages were somehow related, and differed from languages such as Hebrew. Because he advocated the study of Eastern languages and texts in India, he and his colleagues were called 'Orientalists'. They were opposed by a group known as 'Anglicists', who argued that Western knowledge in English should displace that in Eastern languages.[5] The most notable of the Anglicists was James Mill whose book *History of India* influenced British policy in India. In contrast, it was Christian missionaries who were at the forefront of the translation of Indian languages.

Although the early Rationalists believed that the Indian and Chinese civilisations had arisen at the same time as that of the Near East, they held the view that these civilisations had essentially moved into cultural cul de sacs. Although they had been responsible for the invention of gunpowder, paper, and printing, they had no further contribution to make concerning the ongoing civilisation of humanity. These civilisations were considered irrational malformations of those of the Western Enlightenment. India and China were considered to have fallen behind the West as they stagnated in their erroneous ideas of reality.

Hegel, in Germany, was one of the foremost in constructing an Indology of Hinduism. He was seeking to account for the differences between societies in a world that was increasingly dominated by Europeans. He developed the distinction between the rationality of the European Enlightenment and the primitive mentality of other societies. In each society of the world, he assumed, different mental faculties predominated.

For Hegel, imagination (*Vorstellung*) was the mode of knowing for religion, while conceptual thought was the mode for philosophy. The imagination takes sensual images that it experiences or recollects, and associates them. Hegel considered imagination to be a lower form of thought, but one that continues after it has been superseded by rational thought. European reason is therefore contrasted with Indian imagination. Reason dominates imagination, just as the West dominates the East.

James Mill placed the Hindu civilisation at the lower stages of human evolution, the so-called 'barbaric' stage. India was represented as a civilisation dominated by the rule of the priests and ascetics rather than princes and governors. Inden considers that the most formative factor was the social organisation which the English called 'caste'. He writes:

> Caste, then, is assumed to be the 'essence' of Indian civilization. People in India are not even partially autonomous agents. They do not shape and reshape their

world. Rather they are the patients of that which makes
them Indians—the social, material reality of caste. The
people of India are not the makers of their own history.
A hidden, substantialized agent, caste, is the maker of
it.[6]

The metaphors that were commonly used of India were
those of 'the sponge' and 'the jungle', as mentioned in Chapter 1. These metaphors convey notions of the amorphous
nature of India as compared with the rational order that the
West was believed to possess. Hindu ideas, the Rationalists
claimed, lacked definition, enjoyed paradox, were mystical,
and internal. Western thinking, on the other hand, was logical, analytical, practical, and materialistic. The West had science and rationality; the East had myths and superstitions.
The West was forceful and masculine, while the East was
passive and feminine. In this way, India became regarded as
the opposite of the West; it was the inferior 'other'.

Romantic

Although the Rational view has been dominant, there has
always been an alternative view of India. This may be
described as romantic, spiritualistic, or idealistic perception.
This view argues that because India is distant, one is not so
subjectively involved, and so one can understand more accur-
ately. This view still sees India as the opposite—'the other'.
Where the Romantics differ is in the evaluation placed upon
Indian civilisation. The very features of Indian civilisation that
the Rationalists criticise as worthless, the Romantics consider
to be of greatest value. The ascetic practices, philosophies,
myths, and art that are rejected by the Rationalists are the
centre of study for the Romantics.

The great Romantics were first found among the German
scholars, where interest in pantheism developed as part of
post-Kantian idealism. Among these were Johann Herder
(1744-1803), Friedrich Schlegel (1772-1829), and Friedrich
Creuzer (1771-1858). They presented an image of an archaic
civilisation that expressed its religious knowledge in terms of
symbols and myths. This contrasted with Western rationality
and logic.

The most influential of the scholars holding to a Romantic view was Carl Gustav Jung (1875-1971). In his short article 'What India can teach us', Jung writes:

> Whatever the ultimate fate of the white man may be, we can at least behold one example of a civilization which has brought every essential trace of primitivity with it, embracing the whole man from top to bottom. India's civilization and psychology resemble her temples, which represent the universe in the sculptures, including man and all his aspects and activities, whether saint or brute. That is presumably the reason why India seems so dreamlike: one gets pushed back into the unconscious, into that unredeemed uncivilized, aboriginal world, of which we only dream, since one's consciousness denies it. India represents the other way of civilizing man, the way without suppression, without violence, without rationalism. You see them there side by side, in the same town, in the same street, in the same temple, within the same square mile: the most highly cultivated mind and the primitive.[7]

Jung was sympathetic to the Eastern emphasis on detachment and inner vision, and throughout his life was interested in the religions of the Orient. Following him were his disciples Joseph Campbell (1904-89) and Mircea Eliade (1907-86).

The Jungians drew a sharp distinction between Aryan and non-Aryan. They perceived the Vedic Aryans as being activists, optimistic, and life-affirming. In contrast, the non-Aryans were passive, pessimistic, and life-denying. The analysis did not stop at this point. They further divided the non-Aryans into two groups of people—Dravidian and Proto-Australoid. To the Proto-Australoid hunter-gatherers were ascribed the archaic sacrifices and myths. These people, they claimed, provided the deepest strata of human thought.

As Inden writes:

> Thus have the Jungians pushed the Romantic idea of Hinduism as an ambivalent female entity to its extreme. The basement of the Hindu mind would seem to make

India the place where the mentality of primitive man has strangely developed into a civilized form, one that seems opposed to the development of the West.... India is also a place where, given the Jungian's theory of mental and racial stratification, the more primitive unconscious elements of earlier races remain ever present, never being overcome, as in the West, by the later, more progressive and conscious elements of the later races.[8]

This aspect is most significant in the Jungian idea of the 'collective unconsciousness'. This is the deepest layer of the human psyche where are found the basic images of the human mind, termed 'archetypes' by Jung.[9] Two of the most important are the 'anima' and 'animus', the female and male elements respectively, as we saw in Chapter 13. In Indian civilisation 'anima' dominates 'animus', the female predominating over the masculine. Campbell and Eliade have trawled through the religions of ancient societies to find an increasing number of such archetypes.

Jungians believe that while the West has developed scientific rationality, the East has developed the intuitive, mystical, and symbolic aspect of human perception. This does not mean that the Hindu does not think rationally, but uses images and symbols. As this is a form of thinking that Westerners have pushed into the subconscious, its development in the East is of great importance, as it may provide Westerners with access to that part of themselves that they have 'lost'.

The Romantics disagree with the Rationalists, who see human life as being shaped by a reality that is external. Since the human psyche is everywhere and always the same, the Romantics see internal spiritual factors as decisive. Both views perceive India as the 'other'. The Rationalist sees it in negative terms, whereas the Romantic sees it positively.

DISCOVERING A NEW WORLDVIEW

Secular materialism has been successful in enabling humanity to control its environment, and meet its physical needs. No other society in history has been more successful in this objective, but it has, however, failed to meet the inner, spiritual needs of many Westerners. As a reaction to secularism, many have looked towards the exotic and different world-views of India. The richness of Hindu thought and practice allows almost unlimited spiritual creativity and syncretism. But many Western explorers of Indian spirituality have all too often ignored the very contradictions within Hinduism. They have followed the ways of the Romantics and have neglected the ugly among the beautiful, and the poor among the rich.

Reactionism

In practice, only a small proportion of Western people have reacted against their culture and sought to escape into one that is radically different. Such people include those who have joined the class of new religious movements that Roy Wallis called 'world-rejecting'.[10] In reality, what occurs is that they simply transfer from one way of life to another; from one 'world' to another. Some people quickly adapt to the new culture, and find a security under the authority of the new leaders, but others find themselves faced with deep internal conflicts once the initial novelty has gone.

I remember a young Australian woman who had travelled to India in search of a guru to lead her to spiritual enlightenment. She finally settled in an ashram near Madras, where the guru was a very portly old woman. At 4 am each morning, the devotees would rise to offer *puja* to their guru and give her a ceremonial bath. For hours each day, the young woman would listen to the teaching of the guru and sit taking in the *darsan*. Although she would push aside thoughts of parents and home, she could never escape from the contradictions that she saw all about her. Rich people rode in their cars, ignoring the poor and starving by the roadside. Women laboured for hours in the hot sun for the sake of a few rupees while the male overseers exploited them. The day came when she could not handle the contradictions any longer, and she suffered a nervous breakdown. The Australian embassy was grateful to a lady missionary travelling home who offered to accompany the woman on her journey back to her parents.

Although there is much within Indian civilisation to be admired, India itself is in the midst of great economic and social problems. India has turned to Western science and technology to answer many of its economic problems. Satellite television is being used to educate the millions of children in the villages of India. Well-digging equipment is being used to provide clean water to drink and for cultivation. Modern medicine provides the means to cure many illnesses that have plagued the people for centuries.

The idealised picture of India that is often formulated by the Romantics ignores the inadequacies of Hindu society. They neglect to mention the social injustice that results from the *dharma*, and that the stimulus for reform came as a result of contact with the West. As Zaehner writes:

> The impetus for reform came, as might be expected, from the social elite which was most in contact with the new ideas that had been imported from Europe, and it was these ideas that created a desire for reform.[11]

It is because of these issues that most adherents of the Romantic view do not merely aim to replace Western thought by ready-made substitutes from the East, but try to achieve a syncretism of the two.

Syncretism

Joseph Campbell has sought to bring the two modes of thought together as examples of the extremes to which humanity has gone. They are what he calls the separation of East and West. Thus, he writes on the subject of myth:

> Two completely opposite mythologies of the destiny and virtue of man, therefore, have come together in the modern world. And they are contributing in discord to whatever new society may be in the process of forma-tion. For, of the tree that grows in the garden where God walks in the cool of the day, the wise men westward of Iran have partaken of the fruit of knowledge of good and evil, whereas those on the other side of that cultural divide, in India and the Far East, have relished only the fruit of eternal life. However, the two limbs, we are informed [in a study of Jewish legends], come together in the centre of the garden, where they form a single tree at the base, branching out when they reach a certain

height. And if man should taste of both fruits he would become, we have been told, as God himself (Genesis 3:22)—which is the boon that the meeting of East and West today is offering to us all.[12]

Joseph Campbell uses the metaphor of a single tree, arguing that neither the West nor the East represents reality to the exclusion of the other. Devotees of the New Age movement have, however, in their reaction to secular materialism, perceived India as one part of humanity that has managed to preserve the qualities of spirituality and humanness. As Inden writes:

> It is a kind of living museum (and keen marketplace) of religious humanism, of far-out psychic phenomena, yogic health practice, and ultimate experiences.[13]

Many within the New Age movement are attempting to formulate a new worldview based upon the synthesis of East and West. As Amaury de Riencourt writes:

> It might well be that mankind is now on the threshold of a psychological and physiological revolution of a magnitude that will overshadow all the social and political revolutions of our century—made possible by the seemingly incongruous, yet perfectly logical marriage between science and Eastern mysticism's insights.[14]

One illustration of this marriage between science and Eastern mysticism is seen in the principles of Maharishi's 'Vedic science' to produce what is called 'natural law'. This draws an analogy between the unified field theory and the ideas of Maharishi's followers. The unified field theory is an attempt by modern science to draw together quantum physics and Einstein's theory of relativity into a self-consistent whole. The unified field is regarded as a field of consciousness:

> ...a single, unified field of intelligence at the basis of all forms and phenomena in the universe. This universal field of intelligence, the Unified Field, is open to direct

experience through the Maharishi Technology of the Unified Field of Natural Law—Transcendental Meditation and TM Sidhi programme—in the most fundamental state of human awareness, the state of pure consciousness at the basis of the mind.[15]

The guides to this quest are not only Indian gurus, but also the Jungian analysts and historians of religion. Their writings are published both in popular form and authoritative academic texts, and have provided the fuel for the speculative ideas of the New Age movement. They provide a form of logic for the Western world that allows the busy modern executive of a computer-driven world to find expression in the archaic forms of exotic civilisations.

Western writers of the New Age have produced an intriguing explanation of the dichotomy between the thinking of East and West in an attempt to achieve a new syncretism. In the 1960s, several patients suffering from severe epilepsy underwent split-brain surgery. The aim was to try to confine the seizures to one side on the brain. In general, the left hemisphere was found to do the thinking, and the right side to do the feeling. The functions are reversed for left-handed people. The left side restrains the right side from outbursts of inappropriate emotions. The left side is therefore considered as rational and logical, and the right side intuitive.

As Shirley MacLaine explains:

A person who thinks laterally, or with the right hemisphere, is capable of seeing broader connectedness to events that would be little more than a contradictory puzzle to a left-brained Westerner.... Eastern thinkers are more open to intuitive thinking...that addresses higher dimensions and more realities, which enable us to feel connected to the source of what I call God Energy.[16]

A most important function of the human mind is the ability to distinguish between what is real and what is illusion and delusion. If this function does not exist, one is left with total irrationality and therefore meaninglessness.

AN INDIAN INTERPRETATION

To summarise, the debate in the West has for a long time been between Christianity and secular materialism. The discussion has now been joined by those influenced by Hindu thought. Three radically different ways of thought have come into contact: secularism, Hinduism, and Christianity. Although the participants may have changed, the subject of debate remains the same. It is the same question of meaning and reality that has perplexed humanity down through history.

Christianity has often been regarded as a Western religion in India mainly because it arrived at the time of colonial rule. The white man came bringing Christianity dressed in his own cultural forms, that have been clinically rational and lacking in any great mystical dimension. However, Christianity is not a Western religion by origin. It entered Europe from Asia in the first century AD, and from Europe it penetrated many societies throughout the world. Christianity is, in fact, a religion that allows expression of its beliefs in terms that are relevant to the culture of every people while retaining a concept of a universal absolute. Cannot the transcultural principles of Christianity have an Indian interpretation?

Perhaps no better example of Christianity taking on Indian forms can be found than that of Sadhu Sundar Singh.[17] He was born into a family that was commonly considered Sikh, in India, in 1888. His mother was very religious, and she introduced him by her instruction and example to the *Bhagavad Gita* and other Hindu scriptures. She also introduced him to a sadhu (holy man) living near their village, in preparation for him to become a sadhu. Hungering for real peace, he practised yoga, and read the Hindu scriptures till midnight in his quest for satisfaction. His search for spiritual understanding was met by the reply from a Hindu pundit: 'You cannot understand these deep spiritual things now. Why are you in such a hurry to get to it? If this hunger is not satisfied in this life, it will be satisfied in your next rebirths, provided that you keep on trying for it.'

Later in his life, he attended a mission primary school, but at that time he had many prejudices about Christianity, and refused to read the Bible at the daily Bible lessons. In some ways, the young Sundar felt the teaching on the love of God attracted him, but he developed an opposition to the Christian religion and went to the extent of burning the pages of the New Testament he received at school.

He became very miserable, and a few days later he prayed, 'O God, if there be a God, reveal yourself to me tonight.' He planned to put an end to his life if God did not respond to his prayer by morning. Just before dawn, Sundar had a vision of Christ speaking to him in Hindustani: 'Why do you persecute me? See, I have died on the cross for you and for the whole world.' Sundar fell to the ground, his heart was filled with peace, and subsequently his whole life was changed.[18]

Sundar arose a changed man, committed to following Jesus as his guru. Sundar become a sadhu as his mother had wished, but one with the Christian message. He started to travel through the area of the Punjab, Jammu, and Kashmir, preaching the gospel of Jesus Christ. He dressed in a simple robe characteristic of a Hindu guru, and carried with him only a blanket and an Urdu New Testament. The stones on the paths cut his feet, and he became known as the 'Apostle of the Bleeding Feet'.

Sundar was a man of the ordinary people, concerned about the sick and hurting. Service was unthinkable for him without suffering and a simple lifestyle. When a friend brought him a fine rug as a present, Sundar took the rug graciously and then asked his friend to look after it for him.

He followed Jesus in the use of stories to make the gospel meaningful to his listeners. He used illustrations that were relevant to the people of India. 'When you go to a strange country it is good to have friends who will be kind to you. Become friends with Jesus Christ: then in heaven you will have a friend.'

Prayer and meditation were described by Sundar as the opening of the heart to God. He would spend days in prayer and fasting, and receive visions. For him Jesus was not just the Supreme Mystic, 'but the master of mystics, the saviour of mystics'. According to T. Dayanandan Francis, 'his theology is Christ-centred and rooted in the New Testament. It is mystical and evangelical to the core. It is thoroughly Indian and accommodative in outlook.'[19]

His godly life was a challenge to many in both India and

the West. In 1920, he visited Britain and America, where he challenged the churches concerning their materialistic outlook. His mission was to let Westerners see themselves as he saw them. He told an audience:

> I found a stone in a pool among the Himalayas. It was hollow, and when I broke it I found the centre completely dry. So it is here in the West. You have lain for centuries in the water of Christianity, but it has never penetrated to your hearts.[20]

Sundar was always concerned for those places the gospel had not reached. Tibet became his mission field, and during his visits a few small congregations were formed, and he started a little school. In April 1929, Sundar undertook his last journey, walking the long and difficult snow-covered path through the Himalayas to Tibet. He was never seen again. It is generally presumed that he slipped and fell to his death on the dangerous mountain trail.

Perhaps the most perceptive tribute to Sadhu Sundar Singh was that made by Dr Macnicol:

> In him Christianity and Hinduism seem to meet, and the Christian faith stands forth, not as something foreign, but like a flower which blossoms on an Indian stem.[21]

Will the West discover a new reality within Christianity that is both spiritual and rational? Can Indian believers help Western Christians discover new depths of spirituality? Will both East and West find new insights into the message of the Christian gospel?

Notes

[1] Television series of the *Mahabarata*, part 51.

[2] Edward W. Said, *Orientalism* (Penguin: Harmondsworth, 1985).

3 Ronald Inden, 'Oriental Constructions of India', *Modern Asian Studies*, vol 20, no 3 (1986): pp 401–446.

4 V.Y. Mudimbe, *The Invention of Africa* (Indiana University Press: Bloomington, 1988).

5 Ronald Inden, *Imagining India* (Blackwell: Oxford, 1990), pp 89–93.

6 *Ibid*, p 428.

7 Carl G. Jung, *Psychology and the East* (Ark: London, 1986), p 100.

8 Inden (1990), *op cit*, p 123.

9 Jolande Jacobi, *The Psychology of C.G. Jung* (Yale University Press: London, 1973), pp 39–51.

10 Roy Wallis, *The Elementary Forms of the New Religious Life* (Routledge & Kegan Paul: London, 1983), pp 9–39.

11 R.C. Zaehner, *Hinduism* (Oxford University Press: Oxford, 1983), p 149.

12 Joseph Campbell, *The Masks of God: Oriental Mythology* (Souvenir Press: London, 1973), p 9.

13 Inden, *op cit*, pp 435–436.

14 Amaury de Riencourt, *The Eye of Shiva: Eastern Mysticism and Science* (Morrow Quill: New York, 1981), pp 196–197.

15 *Election Communication of the Natural Law Party* (April 1992).

16 Russell Chandler, *Understanding the New Age* (Word: Milton Keynes, 1989), p 38.

17 A.J. Appasamy, *Sundar Singh: A Biography* (Lutterworth Press: London, 1958).

18 Sadhu Sundar Singh, 'My Experience With and Without Christ', *Evangelical Review of Theology*, vol 16, no 2 (1992): pp 196–204.

19 T.D. Francis, 'Sadhu Sundar Singh: The Lover of the Cross', *Asian Journal of Theology*, vol 4, no 1 (1990): p 27.

20 Cyril J. Davey, *The Story of Sadhu Sundar Singh* (Moody Press: Chicago, 1963), p 141.

21 Francis, *op cit*, p 34.

Glossary

There is some variation in the way in which Sanskrit words are Anglicised. The following are taken as the standard forms used in this text.

Advaita	the school of Indian philosophy based upon non-duality and associated with the philosopher Sankara
Agni	the Vedic Aryan god of fire
Agnicayana	the great Vedic fire festival
Agnishtoma	the popular Vedic sacrifice involving the crushing of the *soma* plant
Ahimsa	non-violence
Arthna	one of the four aims of life: making money by honest means
Arya	noble
Aryan	Indo-European-language group of peoples who invaded and conquered India
Ashrama	one of the four stages of life of a man
Astika	the six orthodox schools of Hindu philosophy
Asvamedha	the Vedic horse sacrifice
Atharva Veda	the fourth *Veda*
Atman	the animating energy in any creature, usually referred to as the soul

Aum	the sacred syllable (also spelt Om)—it is believed to contain the sound of all reality. Used during meditation
Avatar	the earthly emanation (incarnation) of the god Vishnu
Avidya	ignorance
Bhagavad Gita	an important and popular religious text
Bhakti	Hindu devotion
Bharat	a name for India. It was probably the name of an Aryan tribe or chief
Bhut	a ghost that causes misfortune
Brahma	the creator aspect of Brahman in the Hindu Trimurti
Brahma Sutras	texts in concise verse containing Hindu philosophy
Brahmacharya	the student stage of life of a twice-born Hindu
Brahman	the ultimate reality
Brahmanas	religious texts composed for the guidance of priests in the performance of Vedic sacrifices
Brahmin	a member of the highest social castes (*varna*). Sometimes written as 'brahman'
Chakra	seven spiritual-energy centres believed by exponents of yoga to exist along the spinal chord
Darsan	the meritorious viewing of a holy image or a person
Dasa	a slave, initially pre-Aryan (literally, 'dark-skinned one')
Deva	Aryan Vedic god, 'shining one'
Devata	a minor deity
Devi	a Sanskrit word for 'mother goddess'
Dharma	the religious and moral duty of a Hindu
Dharma shastra	a text containing the customary law relating to social conduct (*dharma*)
Diksha	the initiation of a *sannyasi* by a guru
Durga	the female goddess Devi in her fierce aspect

Dvaita   the school of Hindu philosophy based upon the theistic teaching of duality

Ganesa   the elephant-headed son of Siva and Parvati. God of prosperity and wisdom

Ganga   Indian name for the River Ganges, often personified as a goddess

Grama   village

Grihastha   the second stage of life—the householder

Gunas   the three 'strands' or qualities of which all matter is composed in various proportions, interwoven like strands of a rope

Guru   teacher, spiritual guide

Hara   one of the names for the god Siva (literally, 'The Remover')

Hari   one of the names for the god Vishnu

Harijan   a named used by Mahatma Gandhi for the untouchable class (literally, 'child of god')

Indra   the Vedic god of war

Indus   a holy river whose Hindu name is Sindhu

Ishtadevata   a personal deity

Ishwara   an individual's chosen personal deity

Jati   the Indian term for a social class usually determined by occupation. There are many *jati* within a *varna*

Jnana   philosophical knowledge of God, man and man's position in the cosmos

Kali   a fearful black goddess

Kalkin   the final *avatar* of Vishnu that will come at the end of the age

Kalpas   cosmic periods of time

Kama   the third aim in life; enjoyment of sensual pleasures

Karma   the total effect of one's action

Karma yoga   the discipline of action as a method of salvation expounded in the *Bhagavad Gita*

Krishna	the most popular *avatar* of Vishnu and hero of the *Mahabharata* (literally, 'Black')
Kshatriya	a member of the second highest caste (*varna*), traditionally warriors
Laksmi	the goddess of good fortune, wife of Vishnu
Lila	divine play, sport
Linga	the sacred phallus of Siva
Mahabharata	the great Hindu epic (literally, 'Great Bharata')
Mahadevi	the supreme reality in feminine form (literally, 'Great Goddess')
Maharaja	great king
Mahatma	'great souled one', an honorific title
Mandala	a religious diagram used for special worship or meditation
Mantra	sacred formula, or sound used in meditation, always in Sanskrit
Maya	illusionary nature of the everyday reality
Meru	the golden mountain at the centre of the world
Moksha	the liberation of the soul from the successive series of births and deaths
Murti	the image of a deity in a temple
Nandi	the mount on which Siva rides
Nataraja	one of Siva's names, the lord of the dance
Nyasa	identification of the worshipper with the deity
Oja	a shaman, or healer, who becomes possessed by a spirit or god
Panchayat	a council of elders ruling a Hindu village
Parvati	a female goddess, wife of Siva
Pinda	a ball of cooked rice offered to the spirits of ancestors
Prakrit	nature, composed of the three *gunas*
Pramana	the knowledge sought by the ascetic (literally, 'reliable knowledge')

Prasad	a blessed offering distributed among the worshippers at the end of a ritual (*puja*)
Puja	a common form of Hindu worship
Puranas	ancient texts containing many Hindu myths and stories about Hindu gods
Purusa	the primeval man
Purusha	'soul' (*atman*) in Samkhya philosophy
Radha	a consort of Krishna
Raja	a ruler, a king
Rama	son of King Dasaratha, regarded as an incarnation of Vishnu
Ramayana	an important Hindu epic telling the story of Rama
Rg Vedas	the first and most ancient of the Vedic texts
Rishi	a Vedic sage
Sadhu	a general term for a holy man that would include *sannyasa*
Sama Veda	the third *Veda*, intended to be chanted
Samadhi	a trance; a state of pure consciousness of oneness with god
Sankhya	a school of Hindu philosophy which divides the universe into inert *purusa* and active *prakrit*, the latter being divided into the three *gunas* (literally, 'the count')
Samsara	the cycle of successive births, deaths, and rebirths
Samskara	pollution caused by a person's actions in a previous life
Sanatana-dharma	the ancient and eternal way of life
Sannyasi	a person who gives up his name, family ties, and possessions, and devotes his life to meditation in order to attain *moksha*
Sat, Satya	the real; hence, the truth
Sati	(literally, 'True Ones'), used for Hindu wives who immolated themselves on their husband's funeral pyres
Satyagraha	non-violence (literally, 'truth force')
Shakti	the female power

Shudra	a member of the fourth *varna* division
Sita	the daughter of Janaka, wife of Rama
Siva	one of the two most popular gods of Hinduism
Soma	the ambrosial offering to the gods by which they sustain their immortality. Personified as a god in the *Vedas*
Tapas	a power, or heat generated by yogic meditation
Trimurti	the 'trinity' of gods: Siva, Vishnu, and Brahma
Upanishad	a set of holy texts of philosophy and religion (literally, 'to sit down in front of')
Vaishya	a member of the third *varna* division
Vanaprastha	the retirement stage of life
Varna	the four major social classes: Brahmin, Kshatriya, Vaishya, and Shudra; originally meant 'colour'
Varuna	one of the most important deities in the *Vedas*
Vedanta	a system of philosophy associated with the scholar Sankara (literally, 'end of the *Vedas*')
Vishnu	one of the two great gods of Hinduism
Yajur Veda	the second *Veda*
Yama	the Vedic god of death
Yamuna	a holy river in the north of India, also spelt Jumna
Yoga	a system of philosophy combining physical exercises and meditation
Yogi	a practitioner of yoga
Yoni	the sacred image of the organ of generation of the goddess

Bibliography

Avalon, A. *Introduction to Tantra Shastra* (Ganeshan & Co: Madras, 1955).

Babb, Lawrence A. *The Divine Hierarchy* (Columbia University Press: New York, 1975).

Barker, Eileen. *New Religious Movements* (HMSO Books: London, 1989).

Basham, A.L. *The Sacred Cow* (Rider: London, 1989).

Basham, A.L. *The Wonder That Was India* (Sidgwick & Jackson: London, 1988).

Bassuk, Daniel E. *Incarnation in Hinduism and Christianity* (MacMillan Press: Basingstoke, 1987).

Bhat, Ramakrishna. *Fundamentals of Astrology* (Motilal Banarsidass: Delhi, 1967).

Bloom, William. *The New Age* (Rider: London, 1991).

Bowen, David G. *Hinduism in England* (Bradford College: Bradford, 1976).

Brent, Peter. *The Godmen of India* (Allen Lane: London, 1972).

Brockington, J.L. *The Sacred Thread* (Edinburgh University Press: Edinburgh, 1989).

Brooke, Tal. *Avatar of Night: The Hidden Side of Sai Baba* (Tarang Paperbacks: Delhi, 1982).

Burnett, David G. *Dawning of the Pagan Moon* (MARC: Eastbourne, 1991).

Campbell, Joseph. *The Masks of God: Oriental Mythology* (Souvenir Press: London, 1973).

Chandler, Russell. *Understanding the New Age* (Word Books: Milton Keynes, 1989).

Chaudhuri, Nirad C. *Hinduism* (Oxford University Press: Oxford, 1979).

Dallapiccola, A.L. *Krishna: The Divine Lover* (Serindia Publications: London, 1982).

Dasgupta, S.N. *Development of Moral Philosophy in India* (Oriental Longmans: Bombay, 1961).

Dasgupta, S.N. *Hindu Mysticism* (Atlantic Paperbacks: New York, 1959).

de Bary, Theodore. *Sources of Indian Tradition* (Columbia University Press: New York, 1970).

de Riencourt, Amaury. *The Eye of Shiva: Eastern Mysticism and Science* (Morrow Quill: New York, 1981).

Dechanet, Jean-Marie. *Christian Yoga* (Search Press: Tunbridge Wells, 1984).

Deshpande, C.R. *Transmission of the Mahabharata Tradition* (Indian Institute of Advanced Study: Simla, 1978).

Dubois, Abbe J. *Hindu Manners, Customs and Ceremonies* (Clarendon Press: London, 1906).

Dumont, L. *Homo Hierarchicus* (Paladin: London, 1972).

Dutt, N. Kumar. *The Aryanization of India* (Firma Mukhopadhya: Calcutta, 1970).

Eck, Dianna. *Darsan: Seeing the Divine Image in India* (Anima Books: Chambersburg, 1985).

Edgerton, Franklin. *The Beginnings of Indian Philosophy* (George Allen & Unwin: London, 1965).

Eliade, Mircea. *Patanjali and Yoga* (Schocken Books: New York, 1975).

Eliade, Mircea. *Yoga: Immortality and Freedom* (Arkana: London, 1989).

Foy, Whitfield. *Man's Religious Quest* (Croom Helm: London, 1978).

Gonda, J. *Visnuism and Sivaism: A Comparison* (Munshiram Manoharlal Publishers: New Delhi, 1976).

Hardy, Friedhelm. *The Religions of Asia* (Routledge: London, 1988).

Hawley, John S. and Wulff, Donna Marie. *The Divine Consort* (Beacon Press: Boston, 1982).

Hiriyanna, M. *The Essentials of Indian Philosophy* (Allen & Unwin: London, 1949).

Hopkins, Thomas J. *The Hindu Religious Tradition* (Wadsworth Pub: Belmont, 1971).

Hume, Robert E. *The Thirteen Principal Upanishads* (Oxford University Press: Delhi, 1990).

Hutton, J.L. *Caste in India* (Cambridge University Press: Cambridge, 1946).

Inden, Ronald. *Imagining India* (Basil Blackwell: Oxford, 1990).

Inden, Ronald. 'Oriental Constructions of India', *Modern Asian Studies* vol 20, no 3 (1986): pp 401–446.

Isherwood, Christopher. *Vedanta for the Western World* (George Allen & Unwin: London, 1948).

Jayakar, Pupul. *The Earth Mother* (Penguin: Harmondsworth, 1989).

Jung, Carl G. *Psychology and the East* (Ark Publications: London, 1986).

Jung, Carl G. *Synchronicity: An Acausal Connecting Principle* (Ark: London, 1987).

Kakar, Sudhir. *Shamans, Mystics and Doctors* (Alfred A. Knopf: New York, 1982).

Kinsley, David. *Hindu Goddesses* (University of California Press: Berkeley, 1986).

Kosambi, D.D. *The Culture and Civilization of Ancient India in Historical Outline* (Vikas Publishing House: Delhi, 1972).

Kumarappa, B. *Hindu Concept of the Deity* (Luzac & Co: London, 1934).

Leslie, Julia I. *The Perfect Wife: The Orthodox Hindu Woman According to the Stridharmapaddharti of Tryambakayajvan* (Oxford University Press: Delhi, 1989).

Ling, Trevor. *A History of Religion East and West* (MacMillan Press: Basingstoke, 1968).

Mangalwadi, Vishal. *The World of the Gurus* (Nivedit Good Books: New Delhi, 1976).

Mascaro, Juan. *The Upanishads* (Penguin: Harmondsworth, 1965).

Maw, Martin. *Visions of India* (Verlag Peter Lang: Frankfurt, 1990).

Michell, George. *The Hindu Temple* (University of Chicago Press: Chicago, 1988).

Miller, Barbara S. *Love Song of the Dark Lord: Jayadeva's Gitagovinda* (New York, 1977).

Minor, Robert. *Modern Indian Interpreters of the Bhagavad Gita* (State University of New York: Albany, 1986).

Mookerjee, Ajit. *Kundalini: The Arousal of the Inner Energy* (Clarion Books: Delhi, 1982).

Mukhopadhyay, P.C. *Journey of the Upanishads to the West* (Firma KLM: Calcutta, 1987).

Nikhilananda, Swami. *The Gospel of Sri Ramakrishna* (Ramakrishna-Vivekananda Centre: New York, 1958).

O'Flaherty, Wendy Doniger. *The Hindu Myths* (Penguin: Harmondsworth, 1975).

O'Flaherty, Wendy Doniger. *Karma and Rebirth in Classical Indian Tradition* (University of California Press: Berkeley, 1980).

O'Flaherty, Wendy Doniger. *The Origins of Evil in Hindu Mythology* (University of California Press: Berkeley, 1976).

O'Flaherty, Wendy Doniger. *The Rig Veda: An Anthology* (Penguin: Harmondsworth, 1981).

O'Flaherty, Wendy Doniger. *Siva: The Erotic Ascetic* (Oxford Univeristy Press: Oxford, 1981).

O'Flaherty, Wendy Doniger. *Women, Androgynes, and Other Mystical Beasts* (University of Chicago Press: Chicago, 1980).

O'Malley, L.S. *Popular Hinduism* (Cambridge University Press: Cambridge, 1936).

Obeyesekere, Gananath. *Medusa's Hair* (University of Chicago Press: Chicago, 1981).

Parrinder, Geoffrey. *Avatars and Incarnations* (Faber & Faber: London, 1970).

Planalp, J. *Religious Life and Values in a North Indian Village* (University Microfilms: Ann Arbour, 1976).

Possehl, G.L. *Harappan Civilization: A Contemporary Perspective* (Aris & Philips: Warminster, 1982).

Potter, K. *The Presuppositions of India Philosophies* (Greenwood: New York, 1973).

Radha, Swami Sivanandra. *Mantras: Words of Power* (Timeless Books: Porthill, 1980).

Rajneesh. *The Book of Secrets* (Thames & Hudson: London, 1976).

Rajneesh. *Neo-Tantra* (Harper & Row: London, 1976).

Raju, P.T. *The Philosophical Traditions of India* (George Allen & Unwin: London, 1971).

Reichenbach, B.R. *The Law of Karma* (MacMillan: Minneapolis, 1990).

Renou, L. *Vedic India* (Susil Gupta Ltd: Calcutta, 1957).

Robinson, Francis. *The Cambridge Encyclopedia of India* (Cambridge University Press: Cambridge, 1989).

Said, Edward W. *Orientalism* (Penguin: Harmondsworth, 1985).

Sankara. *Crest-Jewel of Discrimination* (Mentor Books: New York, 1947).

Sen, K.M. *Hinduism* (Penguin: Harmondsworth, 1975).

Sharma, Arvind. *Women in World Religions* (State University of New York Press: Albany, 1987).

Shaw, Ellis O. *Rural Hinduism: Some Observations and Experiences* (Christian Literature Society: Madras, 1986).

Singer, Milton. *Krishna: myths, rites and attitudes* (East-West Centre: Honolulu, 1966).

Singh, Balbir. *Dharma: Man, Religion and Society* (Arnold-Heinemann: New Delhi, 1981).

Smart, Ninian. *The Making of Early Hinduism* (Open University Press: Milton Keynes, 1987).

Smart, Ninian. *Prophet of a New Hindu Age* (George Allen & Unwin: London, 1985).

Spencer, Sidney. *Mysticism in World Religion* (Penguin: Harmondsworth, 1963).

Srinivasan, Doris. 'Unhinging Siva from the Indus Civilization', *J. Royal Asiatic Society*, vol 1 (1984): pp 77–87.

Stone, Anthony P. *Hindu Astrology: Myths, Symbols and Realities* (Select Books: New Delhi, 1981).

Stutley, Margaret. *Ancient Indian Magic and Folklore* (Routledge & Kegan Paul: London, 1980).

Sukthankar, V.S. *On the Meaning of the Mahabharata* (Asiatic Society: Bombay, 1937).

Sullivan, Herbert P. 'A Re-examination of the Religion of the Indus Civilization', *History of Religions* vol 4, no 1 (1964).

Szandorowska, Barbara. *Escape from the Guru* (MARC: Eastbourne, 1991).

Talbort, Michael. *Mysticism and the New Physics* (Routledge & Kegan Paul: London, 1987).

Tejasananda, Swami. *A Short Life of Sri Ramakrishna* (Advaita Ashrama: Calcutta, 1968).

Vandana. *Gurus, Ashrams and Christians* (Darton, Longman & Todd: London, 1978).

Vaudeville, Charlotte. 'Braj, Lost and Found', *Indo-Iranian Journal*, vol 18 (1976): pp 195–213.

Waghorne, J.P. and Cutler, N. *Gods of Flesh: Gods of Stone* (Anima Books: Chambersburg, 1985).

Wallis, Roy. *The Elementary Forms of the New Religious Life* (Routledge & Kegan Paul: London, 1983).

Weightman, Simon. *Hinduism in the Village Setting* (Open University Press: Milton Keynes, 1979).

Wheeler, Sir Mortimer. *Civilizations of the Indus Valley and Beyond* (Thames & Hudson: London, 1966).

Wolpert, Stanley. *A New History of India* (Oxford University Press: New York, 1982).

Worthington, Vivian. *A History of Yoga* (Arkana: London, 1989).

Zaehner, R.C. *The Bhagavad-Gita* (Oxford University Press: London, 1973).

Zaehner, R.C. *Hindu Scriptures* (Everyman's Library: London, 1968).

Zaehner, R.C. *Hinduism* (Oxford University Press: Oxford, 1966).

Zimmer, H. *Philosophies of India* (Dewer Books: London, 1957).

Zukav, Gary. *The Dancing Wu Li Masters* (Rider/Hutchinson: London, 1979).

INDEX